MILAT

Published in Australia in 2010 by
New Holland Publishers (Australia) Pty Ltd
Sydney • Auckland • London • Cape Town

1/66 Gibbes Street Chatswood NSW 2067 Australia
218 Lake Road Northcote Auckland New Zealand
86 Edgware Road London W2 2EA United Kingdom
80 McKenzie Street Cape Town 8001 South Africa

A record of this book is held at the National Library of Australia

ISBN 9781742571195

Publisher: Diane Jardine
Publishing Manager: Lliane Clarke
Cover Design: Emma Gough
Design: Lisa McKenzie
Production Manager: Olga Dementiev
Printer: McPhersons Printing Group, Maryborough, Victoria.

10 9 8 7 6 5 4 3 2 1

MILAT

Belanglo: the next chapter

Roger Maynard

NEW HOLLAND

Why didst thou promise such a beauteous day
And make me travel forth without my cloak
To let base clouds o'ertake me in my way.

William Shakespeare

This book is dedicated to
Deborah Phyllis Everist
James Harold Gibson
Anja Susanne Habschied
Gabor Kurt Neugebauer
Simone Loretta Schmidl
Caroline Jane Clarke
Joanne Lesley Walters
And the families whose lives were also destroyed

CONTENTS

PREFACE

My first hint of what turned out to be the Australian backpacker murders came in May 1992, four months before the bodies began to be found. I was working as a foreign correspondent for the London *Daily Express* and ITN, the British TV news network, when a paragraph in an afternoon Sydney newspaper caught my attention.

It reported the disappearance of two young British women who had vanished while backpacking around Australia. Their names were Joanne Walters and Caroline Clarke.

It seemed little more than a straightforward missing persons story but I followed it up. I phoned North Sydney Police Station where Mrs Jean Jensen, whose daughter had employed one of the girls as a nanny, had originally reported their disappearance.

The duty sergeant suggested I call Mrs Jensen at her home. When she picked up the phone I could tell by her voice that she was worried.
'I know something terrible has happened,' she said.

Jean's sixth sense about the fate of the two British backpackers suggested this might be the beginning of a much bigger story.

After my initial conversation with Jean I got to know many more of those whose lives had become entangled in one of Australia's worst crimes. I met Joanne's parents Ray and Jill Walters, who'd travelled from their home in Wales to try to find their lost daughter. They followed the backpacker trail around eastern Australia to see if anybody could remember seeing or meeting Joanne or Caroline.

I also remember vividly how Ray telephoned me one Sunday afternoon several weeks later to tell me the tragic news. His voice wavering with emotion he said simply, 'They've found the girls.'

Their bodies had been discovered by some runners in the Belanglo State Forest, a huge national park in the Southern Highlands area south-west of Sydney. They had been brutally put to death.

The Walters and Caroline's mother and father, Ian and Jacqueline Clarke, were inconsolable with grief. But there were still five more young backpackers missing and at this stage the police were not prepared to consider the possibility that a serial murderer was on the loose.

Only as the bodies of Anja Habschied, Gabor Neugebauer, Simone Schmidl, Deborah Everist and James Gibson began to be discovered were they forced to concede the most likely scenario–that this was the work of a crazed killer whose reign of terror began in the early 1970s and may have included the murder of many more.

That monster was Sydney road worker Ivan Milat who was eventually convicted of all seven murders and sentenced to prison for the rest of his natural life.

Milat destroyed many lives, not only those of the backpackers but their parents and families too. There were also the countless family relationships and friendships which were cut short by one man's evil deeds.

This is the story of the backpacker murders and the man who carried them out. It is a sad but compelling testimony to those who died and those who brought the killer to justice. It also provides a cautionary message for all young travellers who tour Australia in search of fun and freedom but ignore the lurking dangers.

In more than four decades in journalism it is one of the saddest cases I have ever covered. It consumed my life for more than four years as I reported on the discovery of the bodies, the hunt for the murderer and his eventual trial.

When more bones were found in the forest in August 2010, the memories came flooding back. It made me think about the other young lives that Milat had almost certainly claimed. And although he couldn't be held responsible for this latest victim, I wondered whether the long-held theory that there were two killers was true. It was only speculation of course but then the backpacker killings had been consumed by rumour from the outset.

The renewed interest in the backpacker murders prompted my return to Belanglo. I realised much had happened in the intervening period since Milat was gaoled on July 27, 1996. The horrendous nature of the killings had entered the Australian psyche and whenever the words backpacker, Belanglo, serial killer or Milat are mentioned memories flood back.

Newspapers, radio and television continue to report every new development in detail. Hunger strikes, self-mutilation, an escape plot and the seemingly endless appeals process involving Milat always attract extensive coverage.

There are constant questions. How does Milat spend his time in his maximum security cell? What is it like there? How much does it cost the taxpayer?

Occasionally the thoughts of inmate Ivan, scribbled on smuggled notes, find their way into the media. It seems our appetite for news of Ivan's life and times is insatiable. The backpacker murders refuse to go away. This odious man and his heinous crime create such a wave of revulsion both in Australia and overseas that the ripple effect continues to be felt.

I thought it was time to update my earlier book on this case. Nearly two decades after I first put pen to paper on the subject the story is still unfolding and there is much more to write.

This new edition of Milat charts the investigation, the trial, and the aftermath. I have taken a fresh look at the evidence and return to some of the key players for their thoughts on what really happened.

While it might raise questions about certain aspects of the case it does not detract from the true horror of the backpacker murders. The culprit might well be incarcerated for life, but for those caught up in the human tragedy the nightmare can never be locked away.

1.

The Discovery of an Eighth Body

Australia's most infamous serial killer is sitting in his 6 x 3 metre cell in the Supermax wing of Goulburn Gaol when he hears the latest news from Belanglo in August 2010.

It is more than 14 years since Ivan Milat was gaoled for the rest of his natural life for the murder of seven young backpackers, a catalogue of savagery which shocked the world.

The trademark grin shoots across his aging face as he listens to the radio about the skeleton found in the forest where it all began. Once again he is the centre of attention as the media try to link him to this latest discovery.

He quietly revels in the notoriety. Now he is in control. He delights in the power of knowing the truth and the satisfaction of keeping it to himself. It is another opportunity to play mind games with the warders, the cops and his fellow inmates.

Soon they will be asking for his opinion. Are the skull and bones found in scrubland near the Red Arm Creek fire trail in the Dalys Waterhole area of the Belanglo State Forest evidence of an eighth victim? Or has another killer, possibly a former accomplice of Milat, struck again?

They are tantalising questions which receive widespread news coverage as police trawl through the suspected crime scene and remove the human remains for forensic examination.

The trail bikers who stumbled across the skeleton about 3.15 p.m. on Sunday August 29, are in shock. Even in bright sunshine the forest has an eerie atmosphere, a malevolence only partly explained by its dark history.

Emmet Hudson makes the initial discovery. He sees what appears to be a human skull tucked away behind a large fallen tree only a few metres off the track. By now his brother Dave and the rest of the group have come to a halt and are staring at the grisly find. They look around for further evidence of a body. Consumed by foreboding they walk further into the bush.

It is not long before their fears are confirmed. More human remains including a rib cage, spine, pelvis and a femur are protruding from the undergrowth. There are remnants of some clothing nearby.

They do not hang around. The riders phone Goulburn Local Area Command who arrive within the hour. Police seal off the area and name the investigation Strike Force Hixson.

Whose body is it? A man or a woman? Young, middle aged or elderly? How long have the remains been lying there? What was the cause of death? More crucially—is it another backpacker?

Some of the questions are answered quickly. The skeleton is definitely a female who was probably aged between 15 and 25. There is no sign that she has been shot.

At first there is speculation that the skull could be the remains of German backpacker Anja Habschied whose decapitated body was found elsewhere in the forest on November 4, 1993. But this would not explain the rest of the skeleton.

There is also evidence to suggest the bones are little more than a decade old, which would remove Milat as a possible suspect.

The police do not want to add to the rumour mill. Acting Superintendent Evan Quamby, Local Area Commander at Goulburn, says they will follow up all lines of inquiry.

'It is early days and far too soon for us to know exactly what's happened,' he tells reporters.

'Obviously there is a lot of speculation surrounding this discovery but we definitely will not be jumping to conclusions,' he adds.

'There are many lines of investigation to explore. We will wait for the results of a post-mortem examination and DNA tests and hopefully they will shed some light on the identity of the deceased and a cause of death.'

While the police are understandably reluctant to say too much, others are going through the missing persons records. More than 8,000 people are reported missing in New South Wales every year. Throughout Australia the total is about 35,000, although the majority are found within a few weeks.

Among the long-term missing are Janine Vaughan, a 31 year-old shop assistant from Bathurst in New South Wales' central west. She was last seen alive as she got into a car after leaving a pub in town on December 7, 2001.

Also still missing, though feared dead, is Kerry Whelan, whose body has never been recovered. Family friend Bruce Burrell, who had lived in the Southern Highlands, was convicted of murdering the 39 year-old mother of three in 1997. But police insist the remains aren't hers.

The Milat connection is played down. Clive Small, the former head of Task Force Air, the special group formed to investigate the backpacker murders in the 1990s, points out that the serial killer buried his victims some distance from fire trails and did not remove their clothing.

In addition the latest discovery is nowhere near the part of the forest where the seven young tourists were killed. In the earlier crime there was also evidence of foul play found nearby, including bullet cartridges and lengths of rope.

Small has been reported as saying that the backpackers were found in a relatively limited area quite close to each other. That part of the forest was subject to a comprehensive police search in the early 1990s, although it did not extend as far as the spot near Red Arm Creek fire trail, where the eighth body was found.

Small also said in newspaper reports that the facts of the latest discovery do not fit Milat's profile, which only serves to deepen the mystery surrounding the newly-discovered remains.

The alternative scenarios may not point the finger at Milat, but are nonetheless disturbing. This is not the body of a woman who died of natural causes given the separation of the head from the rest of the remains. Therefore the only plausible conclusion is that another killer is on the loose.

But why would they choose to dump the body or murder the victim at Belanglo? Could it be some kind of copycat killing? Or an attempt to place the blame for someone else's crime at the feet of Australia's most notorious serial murderer?

Even more chillingly—was this the work of someone who had an intimate knowledge of the forest's bloody past and the man who used it as his own private killing field? Was this Ivan Milat's partner in crime?

The judge who sentenced the backpacker murderer conceded there was a good chance that two people were involved. How could one person overpower two strong adults such as Anja Habschied and her tall, well-built boyfriend Gabor Neugebauer? Surely the physical odds would be against it?

If Milat's alleged accomplice was still out there, could it be another member of his family? His defence lawyer had insisted that one of his brothers was the likely killer, not his client.

As the scientific examination of the latest set of remains continues it is hoped that DNA tests will help to identify the victim and lead detectives to the killer.

A faded, badly decomposed T-shirt found near the body may provide additional clues. Forensic experts think they can establish the original pattern, colour and even a brand name.

The one certainty is that police will get no help from Ivan. In his Supermax cell he tells prison staff that he will not assist anyone who wants to question him.

The Sydney *Daily Telegraph* reports on September 1 that sources at the maximum security gaol say Milat approached staff two days after the body was found and said police would be 'wasting their time' if they planned to interview him.

Denying any involvement he says he has 'no intention of telling investigators anything, even if they came knocking.'

Ivan Robert Marko Milat is a pitiful character. He is no longer the fit and muscular man whose strength was legendary.

Deprived of sunlight and fresh air for much of the day, he exists on a diet of cereal for breakfast, a lunchtime sandwich and meat and vegetables for dinner. Depending on how well-behaved he's been he might be given a sandwich maker, a kettle and even a microwave, to heat his own food and drinks.

Inmates are allowed to buy $60 worth of extra food every week but can have it stopped for any misdemeanour.

Likewise he might have use of a television and radio in his cell, depending on his conduct. He is officially categorised as a 3.3 level prisoner, which according to reporter Chris Masters who visited the High Risk Management Unit on behalf of the *Daily Telegraph*, means he also enjoys 'optimum inmate association as well as visitor and telephone rights'.

The few permanent fixtures are two shelves, a stainless steel lavatory, a shower and a bed with a foam mattress. The bare walls turn the cell into a stark, clinical box. It is hardly five star luxury, yet it costs the taxpayer more than $800 a night to keep him there.

Now approaching 66, his long, shaggy, grey hair, shuffling gait and unkempt appearance is in sharp contrast to the smart, well-dressed Milat who would turn up at family gatherings in a neatly pressed shirt and trousers or chat amiably to neighbours as he proudly polished his four wheel drive and Harley Davidson.

It is a measure of his self-esteem that he has taken to mutilating himself. There have been swallowed razor blades and more recently a severed finger, which he cut off with a plastic knife and tried to post to the High Court in a bid to pressurise the authorities to permit him to appeal against perceived injustices.

There have been hunger strikes and while he was incarcerated at Maitland Gaol in the Hunter Valley, plans to hatch a gaol break.

This is the increasingly frail and desperate old man who once struck terror in the community and inflicted cruel deaths on seven young travellers in the prime of their life.

Remarkably there are still people who believe Milat is innocent, despite the Aladdin's cave of incriminating evidence found in his house and the homes of some members of his family.

They are convinced he was set up to take the rap for the wrongdoing of others; that much of the evidence was planted, that a small gang of serial rapists and killers who roamed the highways and byways hunting for young women and backpackers to satisfy their animal lust were really responsible. Comb the internet and the claims and conspiracy theories relating to the backpacker murders are legion.

Far more probable is that Milat killed many more young people than he was charged with. Some police investigators believe he could have been responsible for at least three additional murders and possibly four.

Others point to many more. There were three young women in the Newcastle area who disappeared in the 1970s when Milat was known to be based in the area as a road worker.

There were two 19 year-old nurses who vanished after leaving the Tollgate Hotel in Parramatta on June 12, 1980, which Milat was later questioned about.

Berowra schoolgirl Michelle Pope disappeared with her boyfriend Stephen Lapthorne in northern Sydney in August 1978.

Milat was also the prime suspect in the murder of Peter Letcher, 18, who went missing while hitchhiking from Liverpool to his family home in Bathurst in November 1987, a couple of years before Milat's reign of terror officially began. The teenager's body was later discovered in Jenolan Forest. He had been tied up, blindfolded and shot in the head in much the same manner as the killer's other victims.

Milat was often brazen in his capacity to kidnap and kill. The case of Paul Onions, the young British tourist who was lucky to escape from him on the Hume Highway, testifies to that. Despite being witnessed by dozens of passing motorists and reported to the police, Milat still managed to evade capture for another four years.

Ivan thought he was invincible and probably still does.

2.

THE FRIENDLY, NEIGHBOURHOOD
SERIAL KILLER

The dawn of a new day was filtering through the windows of 22 Cinnabar Street in the outer Sydney suburb of Eagle Vale when the police took up their positions outside. They announced their presence with an early morning telephone call. 'This is Task Force Air. Will you please look out of your window?'

Inside the house, Ivan Robert Marko Milat stirred but failed to look out of the window. It was Sunday May 22, 1994 and he had been looking forward to a lie in with his girlfriend Chalinder Hughes.

Outside, in scenes reminscent of the closing sequence of *Butch Cassidy and the Sundance Kid*, a small army of gun-toting officers aimed their firearms at the modest suburban bungalow they had encircled.

Detective Sergeant Wayne Gordon, who made the initial call at 6.36 a.m., told Milat the police had a search warrant and asked him to leave the house and walk down the street to meet members of the State Protection Group.

'Now, police are around these premises, they're in possession of a search warrant to search these premises in relation to an armed robbery matter,' the officer advised him.

'No joke,' replied Milat.

When he failed to appear the officer made a second call at 6.41 a.m.

'The situation is there are police who are armed, who have those premises that you are in contained...mate, what I've asked you to do is to leave the premises on your own and then shortly thereafter your girlfriend may leave,' DS Gordon told him again.

'Hang on, hang on. Well, what you're tellin', you know like, I, I, just assumed you were someone from work ringin up,' Milat replied.

'No, mate, I'm from the police. It's no joke. This is real,' the officer made clear.

'Why didn't you knock on the bloody door or somethin'?' Milat enquired, only to be told it was police procedure to ring the occupants of a house before a search.

Milat still gave the impression he was treating the early morning interruption as a joke.

'It's no joke,' insisted DS Gordon.

'I'm asking you to leave the premises and walk to your left from the front of your premises with your arms outstretched where you'll be met by police from the State Protection Group. Do you understand that?'

Milat said he was looking out of the window and could not see anybody.

As the conversation threatened to become even sillier the officer repeated who he was.

'Well, that doesn't mean anything to me,' came the reply.

In all three calls were made that morning as the police urged Milat to come outside.

Milat had been looking forward to a few extra hours in bed after a busy week working on the roads. He and Chalinder had retired early after calling in for a takeaway meal at a Kentucky Fried Chicken outlet.

His night had already been disturbed by a telephone call at 2 a.m. from his brother Bill, who rang to say that the police had been enquiring about a car and an alleged kidnapping, possibly involving Ivan.

'I had no idea what he was on about,' Milat said later.

Increasingly exasperated by his lack of success, DS Gordon again asked Milat to leave the house and walk out of the gate, only to be told, 'We haven't got a gate.'

Ivan was playing for time. He pretended to go back to sleep but in reality he was using those crucial few minutes to hide incriminating evidence which might link him to the backpacker murders, including parts of the Ruger rifle which was used in some of the killings.

Just as it appeared the early morning exchange was going nowhere, Milat agreed to the officer's command.

'I, I can understand what you're saying, I just...like I said, it, it strikes me as slightly weird, but anyway, I'll play your little game,' he said.

DS Gordon repeated his demand that Milat and his girlfriend should leave the house separately.

'I think we'll just walk out. I'm not real keen on this,' Milat responded.

A few minutes later at 6.48 a.m. DS Gordon called a third time. The conversation lasted just 10 seconds.

'Detective Sergeant Gordon speaking again,' the officer announced.

This time Chalinder Hughes came on the line.

'Yeah we're comin' out now; he's just trying to find the keys...he always loses them in the morning,' she explained.

Milat was told to go outside with his hands on his head.

As he appeared at the front door an officer ordered him to hit the deck.

'They yelled out to lay on the ground which I was very reluctant to do as it was very dampish,' he recalled later.

'They were all screaming at me and I wondered "Who are these blokes?" The next minute they were all over us and they whacked these furry things on my hands and that was it.'

Up and down Cinnabar Street the early morning activity had the net curtains twitching and the fly screens discreetly opened.

Kettles were boiling for pots of tea. Morning radio announcers spoke of ideal surf conditions along the coast. Weather forecasters predicted a fine, late autumn day ahead. It was a perfect Sunday for a swim, a drive or a picnic.

And it made the events unfolding just down the road at number 22 all the more incongruous.

The early risers and the simply curious who had glanced out of their windows were understandably surprised by what they saw.

Instead of the ordered suburban scene which they had left the night before, Cinnabar Street resembled a civil emergency waiting to happen.

Milat, dressed in the checked shirt and jeans he had hurriedly thrown on, was spreadeagled on the front lawn, handcuffed and with the barrel of a gun pressed firmly against his skull.

The 49-year-old roadworker was under arrest.

Few of his neighbours would have guessed the horrendous nature of the crimes he was soon to be accused of, but they would certainly have had good reason to suspect that all was not quite right in their street.

For several weeks vehicles unknown to residents had parked in the vicinity. Unmarked vans had come and gone with monotonous regularity. Mysterious figures appeared from them at odd hours of the day and night, only adding to the ominous overtones which had permeated this quiet, law abiding community.

The good folk of Cinnabar Street were understandably concerned. Calls were made to the police about the number of suspicious vehicles, which included a white plumber's van and sinister-looking occupants. Locals feared their houses were being 'cased' by a gang of burglars. Why else would the prying eyes of strangers be trained on their homes?

Low flying helicopters were also frequently spotted in the Eagle Vale air space. Those with over-active imaginations were beside themselves with theories.

A few miles away the response from officers at Campbelltown Police Station did little to explain the mystery. It was all part of a top secret surveillance operation they assured callers.

What had prompted such a thorough, round-the-clock observation could only be guessed at by those not privy to the innermost workings of the New South Wales police.

Why was their attention centred on the recently-built, four bedroom home occupied by Milat and his sister Shirley? The comfortable $190,000 dollar house with its double garage, tiled roof and carefully-manicured front lawn and flower beds looked a haven of respectability.

Parked in the garageway outside, a red, four wheel drive vehicle with its Crimestoppers sticker in the rear window only added to the air of normality. Ostensibly here was a home owned by a middle-aged brother and sister, who had pulled themselves up from their working class roots to become members of the property-owning classes. They were battlers who grew up in a large migrant family in Sydney's sprawling western suburbs and had now made good. Like most of the people in their street they were the living embodiment of the Australian dream, a text book example of success in the nation's great egalitarian tradition.

Neighbours knew Milat as a 'friendly bloke' who would chat over the garden fence or offer a smile and a wave as he mowed the lawn. Most weekends he would spend polishing his prized Harley Davidson, which he had bought six months earlier. He loved motorcycles and had ridden a trail bike as a younger man.

If ever there was a perfect example of domestic bliss, it was seeing Ivan and Shirley relaxing on the verandah on their day off.

Ray Sund, a 30 year-old lorry driver, who lived just across the road remembered the scene well.

'I'd see him on a Sunday morning sitting on the verandah with his sister enjoying a coffee and he'd always give me a wave,' he recalled.

A few days before Milat's arrest Ray had loaned him a garden rake.

'He was such a hard worker but he always took his time to have a chat,' he remembers.

Clifford Esplaing, a black South African migrant from Johannesburg who also lived opposite, reinforced the positive picture painted by his neighbours.

'We all knew him around here. We'd talk to each other all the time. I can't believe this is happening,' he remarked.

Eagle Vale was in a state of shock after the arrest of Ivan Milat. Word spread like wildfire within minutes of that initial police raid, which was by now receiving extensive media coverage on the early morning radio bulletins. Television news crews who had been tipped off in advance were already prowling the area for footage.

It soon began to emerge that the early morning operation had been one of several simultaneous raids involving 300 heavily armed police who had also swooped on addresses in the Sydney suburb of Guildford and the foothills of the New South Wales Southern Highlands.

After a pre-dawn briefing at Campbelltown, members of Task Force Air set off for their separate destinations backed-up by members of the crack State Protection Squad. They drove in convoy accompanied by ambulances, just in case of bloodshed.

At the same time busloads of trainee officers from the NSW Police Academy at Goulburn were driven to remote bushland in the Southern Highlands to help in a new search for clues.

A total of 11 search warrants were executed, including two raids on homes in Queensland, others at Buxton and Hilltop, south west of Sydney, and one on a weatherboard house in Campbell Hill Road, Guildford. The latter was the home of Milat's elderly mother Margaret, who had brought a total of 14 children into the world. Ivan, who was born on December 23, 1944, was her fourth.

Police had allowed Milat back inside his home to escape the intrusive lenses of over-zealous cameramen. If police had hoped to shock him into an early confession, they were not having much luck.

The first officer to have any meaningful verbal contact with him was Detective Sergeant Stephen Leach, a leading investigator in Task Force Air.

He told him he had a search warrant and was making enquiries into the armed robbery of a British tourist on January 25, 1990, on the Hume Highway near the Belanglo State Forest, where the bodies of all seven murdered backpackers were found.

Milat replied: 'I understand what you are saying but I had nothing to do with it.'

Leach intensified his questioning, making it clear he also wanted to interview him about the backpacker killings.

'What do you know about that?' he asked.

'Nothing,' Milat replied.

Sergeant Leach asked, 'Have you ever been to Belanglo?'

Milat replied, 'I know where it is. I have driven up a dirt track that goes past it.'

'When was that?'

'A long time ago...in the mid-eighties,' answered Milat.

When told that the Englishman had identified him as his attacker Milat insisted, 'It wasn't me.'

As the morning wore on, an unnatural calm descended on the proceedings. While interest in the raid had reached fever pitch outside and news of the arrest was already making headlines around the world, the interior of number 22 remained strangely tranquil. Like the eye of a cyclone, the core of the criminal investigation was an oasis of peace amid a maelstrom of rumour and intense police activity.

Sergeant Leach handed Milat a coffee in the family room, but his hands were tied at the back and drinking out of a cup was not going to be easy. The detective re-handcuffed him at the front and the morning coffee break was able to proceed.

Other officers went about their work in a routine and business-like manner, combing the house for clues which might incriminate the man they were holding for questioning.

Although months of detective work had indicated that Milat might have a link with the backpacker murders, they had no evidence to prove it. They had gone to the house with only two charges in mind—the armed robbery and attempted murder of a 24-year-old Briton.

What they allegedly found, however, was beyond the wildest dreams of the most optimistic of investigators. Each room produced new leads.

In a spare bedroom which was used as a storeroom, police discovered a book entitled *Violent Crimes That Rocked A Nation—Unsolved*. In the same room they found a black bag with a German-made, wooden-handled knife inside, as well as several packets of ammunition in a number of shoe boxes.

On a spare bed lay a model aeroplane box—Milat loved constructing and painting toy planes—in which was found a green water bottle.

Detective Senior Constable Andrew Grosse, the official police crime scene officer, noticed some scratch marks on the lid and along the side. Subsequent examination under a polylight, an instrument which produces wavelengths of light and reveals marks invisible to the naked eye, identified the name 'Simi' etched on the surface of the container.

It did not escape the attention of those intimately involved in the backpacker murder inquiry that Simi was the nickname of Simone Loretta Schmidl, 21, who disappeared while hitchhiking from Sydney to Melbourne in January 1991.

As the search progressed other items of interest were drawn to the attention of investigating officers.

They included a bowie-type, Salengen-brand knife, which was made in Germany and was kept in a camouflage-painted sheath, and a radio scanner which was plugged in near the telephone.

There was a mask, a pair of goggles and a paintball pellet holder.

And in another room they found an instruction manual which detailed how to convert a Ruger 10/22 calibre rifle into an automatic weapon. It was hidden inside the pages of a booklet on bitumen surfacing.

Foreign currency from Indonesia, New Zealand and the United Kingdom was also discovered, as well as part of a photocopied map of the Bowral and Mittagong areas and roads leading into the Belanglo State Forest.

A British 20 pence coin was found inside Milat's four-wheel drive. A driving licence bearing the name of Michael Gordon Milat but showing Ivan Milat's photograph was in a bedside drawer, as well as a postcard addressed to a man named Bill.

The detailed search of number 22 was becoming ever more interesting.

Inside a shoe in a hallway cupboard police found a Ruger brand receiver (a part of the gun) wrapped in plastic.

In Milat's bedroom they claimed in court evidence to have opened a cupboard containing two boxes of shotgun cartridges, several bullets, and a telescopic rifle sight.

Next door, in the room occupied by his sister, Shirley, police uncovered two more boxes of ammunition hidden under the mattress. A .22 calibre Winchester rifle was stored under the bed.

In the same bedroom, two sleeping bags, including one made by the German company Salewa and identical to one owned by Miss Schmidl, were found in a walk-in wardrobe. A purple and yellow headband identical to one recovered from her skeletal remains on November 1, 1993 was wrapped around a blue tent.

In the garage they saw a red Air India courtesy bag containing a comb, toothpaste, brush and a sewing kit.

A 7.65mm Browning self-loading pistol was found under the laundry sink. Window sash cord and rolls of black electrical tape did not go unnoticed in various corners of the house, but the most intriguing discovery was yet to be uncovered.

Detectives pulled the house apart and every square centimetre of Milat's home was subjected to the most rigorous of examinations.

Detective Senior Constable Peter O'Connor who climbed into the loft, slid his arm down a ceiling cavity above the front door. Fumbling in the darkness he felt what appeared to be a metallic object in a plastic bag and lifting it out of the confined space immediately recognised its significance.

The hidden package consisted of a bolt assembly, a metal trigger assembly and a single .22 calibre rifle magazine, part of what was later said to be a .22 Ruger 10/22 rifle.

Ivan Milat appeared unconcerned. Asked by Sergeant Leach what the bits and pieces were he replied, 'Looks like something out of a gun.'

'Have you seen it before?' Leach asked, to which Milat replied he hadn't.

Sergeant Leach asked 'This was located in your ceiling. Have you any idea how it got there?'

'None,' said Milat.

'Who's been in your ceiling?' asked Sergeant Leach.

'You blokes and the builders,' said Milat.

Milat insisted he did not own any weapons or ammunition found in the house and later when questioned at Campbelltown Police Station said he had no idea how they got there.

'I presume youse had 'em,' he remarked in a recorded interview.

The search was only a few hours old, but already police had found what they viewed as an Aladdin's cave of potential evidence.

Other locations targeted in the series of dawn raids that Sunday morning were also bearing fruit. At the home of family matriarch Margaret Milat in Guildford, the door was opened by David Milat, Ivan's younger brother who had suffered brain damage in a road accident some years earlier. Inside police found a blue coloured, long sleeve shirt containing a label bearing the brand, The Great Outdoors—Next, identical to one owned by Mr Onions.

They also discovered a 'grandfather' T-shirt, which was later said to be the same as one belonging to Simone Schmidl.

In a spare room they noticed a grey metal box which was locked. It bore the letters RTA and DMR, abbreviations for the Roads and Traffic Authority and the Department of Main Roads, for whom Ivan Milat once worked.

The officer who executed the search warrant, Detective Sergeant Gae Crea and his team, forced open the lid and peered at the contents. Inside they found three firearms, an ammunition belt, a quantity of ammunition, rifle sights, rifle bolts and two Canadian five dollars notes.

One of the rifles had 'Ivan' engraved on it while another appeared to have a screw thread at the end of the barrel which would have been suitable for attaching a silencer.

Detective Sergeant Crea was impressed by the scale of the small arsenal. Particularly as Milat had been living at the same address a few years earlier, at or around the time of the disappearance of some of the backpackers.

Elsewhere further searches were taking place in and around properties owned by two of Milat's brothers.

At Hilltop in the Southern Highlands, numerous firearms and about one tonne of ammunition were found in a room under a house. Inspector Bruce Crouch who led the search, also uncovered three backpacks and bags of clothing.

At this and other locations a huge quantity of potential evidence, including 60 firearms, hundreds of rounds of ammunition, knives, machetes and even a crossbow, was eventually amassed. The guns consisted of pistols, heavy and small calibre rifles and a shotgun.

At Buxton they stumbled across a private firing range, where they collected thousands of spent cartridges after shovelling tonnes of earth through mechanical sifters. Each item was individually and painstakingly placed in plastic exhibit bags and labelled accordingly.

About 100 officers were deployed to search near the Wombeyan Caves in Taralga Reserve. It is a harsh and inhospitable terrain comprising steep rock faces and thick bushland. One officer said it made an earlier search of the Belanglo State Forest seem like a gentle stroll through the countryside.

Police divers with underwater metal detectors plunged into the freezing waters of the Wollondilly River in the search for weapons and ammunition. Others abseiled down sheer escarpments, combing the gullies and dense vegetation.

At another home owned by a member of the Milat family in West Woombye, Queensland, detectives seized a backpack identical to one owned by Simone Schmidl. It had allegedly been given to Joan Milat, Ivan's sister-in-law, by Milat, who said it belonged to a female friend who was returning to New Zealand and no longer required it.

Mrs Milat, wife of Alex, another one of the Milat brothers, was a keen hiker herself and her brother-in-law had offered her the backpack because he knew she loved walking.

By the time the search warrants had all been executed and the police had wound up their intensive hunt for evidence, a staggering two tonnes of material had been seized by police.

Chief Superintendent Clive Small, the head of Task Force Air, was to reveal later that they were genuinely stunned by what they discovered.

'It was never expected we would find the wealth of evidence,' he admitted nearly seven months later on the final day of committal proceedings against Milat.

There was still a long way to go in the sifting, scientific analysis and identification of the vast range of exhibits they had collected. The police would still have to demonstrate there was a case for Ivan Milat to answer and only a trial with a judge and jury could decide his guilt or innocence.

Even so the investigation, which had started so unpromisingly, was now progressing at a rapid pace. The police inquiry into the worst serial killing of its kind in Australia's criminal history was bearing fruit. And it was all thanks to the evidence of one man, whose brush with death nearly five years earlier pointed detectives in a certain direction. That man was Paul Onions, an air conditioning engineer from Willenhall in the English Midlands.

3.

THE LUCKY ESCAPE

It was December 8, 1989 when Paul Onions left England for the holiday of a lifetime. He had already seen some of the world while with the Royal Navy. More recently he had settled down to a job on dry land as a testing engineer for a building services company.

A quietly-spoken, slightly-built individual, he came from the Birmingham area and had a soft Midlands accent. Though he enjoyed life to the full in Britain he still had a wanderlust, an overwhelming desire to see the rest of the world before settling down.

Like thousands of young people he had heard about the joy of travel Down Under. He fancied backpacking around Australia, possibly stopping off in Asia on the way. Still only 24, he also knew he was entitled to get a job for six months while in Australia. Under the terms of the working visa available to British passport holders aged 26 or under at the time, he was allowed to find some casual employment to help fund his journey after he arrived in Sydney. He had been told there were countless opportunities for working for cash, especially fruit picking. If he was in Australia in time for the southern summer, he could probably find a job on a farm.

Paul's mind was made up. He left the United Kingdom just as the British winter was beginning to set in. Ahead of him were six months of warm weather, blue skies and inviting surf. He stopped over in India and Singapore on the way to Australia and flew into Sydney on December 22, 1989.

Soon after his arrival he booked into a youth hostel in the trendy, inner-city suburb of Glebe. He intended to remain in Sydney for some weeks 'to acclimatize himself, get to know a few people and have a few beers,' as he put it. Paul enjoyed Christmas under the harsh Australian sun, a far cry from the cold, dank climate he had left behind. He was also about to learn that his new environment was not without its dangers.

On December 29 he woke to news of an earthquake in Newcastle, 167 kilometres north of Sydney. A total of 13 people died as a result of the severe tremors which brought terror to the large industrial city. It was a tragic reminder of the underlying forces which so often produced natural disasters such as flood, drought or bush fire across this huge continent.

He did not know it then—and neither did the police who would one day form part of Task Force Air—that December 29 would be a significant date for young backpackers Deborah Everist and James Gibson, who arrived in Sydney on that day as well.

By January, Paul was thinking of earning some money. On the backpacker grapevine he had heard there was good cash to be made fruit picking at Mildura, on the border of New South Wales and Victoria.

On January 25, 1990 he set off. At first he had considered catching a bus all the way but conscious of the need to save money he decided to hitchhike instead. He would take a bus from Sydney's Central Station as far as Liverpool on the outskirts of the city and close to the Hume Highway, the main route to Melbourne. There he planned to thumb a ride in a south westerly direction to Mildura.

It was a sizzling hot day and by the time he reached the extremity of Sydney's western suburbs, the temperature was well above thirty-degrees Celcius (86°F). Arriving in Liverpool about 1 p.m., the heat of the mid-day sun on his fair, English skin, burned down with a fierce intensity.

Wearing a T-shirt and shorts, he carried a rucksack containing a pair of jeans, another T-shirt, a camera and his Sony Walkman. He was as free as the air, but his troubles were only just beginning.

As he walked towards the Hume Highway he noticed a road sign to Canberra and assumed he must be heading in the right direction. He had to pass the Australian capital on his way to Mildura, but the journey he had hoped to complete in a day was proving more difficult than he had anticipated.

As cars and lorries roared passed ignoring his efforts to hitch a lift, his morale was low and he became increasingly depressed. He was also extremely thirsty. After walking for an hour a soft drink sign appeared in the distance, like a mirage in the desert.

He quickened his stride and eventually found himself in front of a parade of shops, which included a small newsagency called Lombardo's. Inside he bought an ice cold can of Coke before turning around to continue his journey.

It was at this point that Paul came face to face with a man who later identified himself as Bill. He remembered his features clearly. About 5 feet 10 inches to 6 feet (182 centimetres) tall and with dark hair, 'Bill' sported a Merv Hughes-style of moustache.

Paul remembered the moustache because it reminded him of some of the Australian cricketers he watched on the television in England. 'Bill' was one of the first real Aussies he had met since arriving Down Under.

'Bill', who was wearing a T-shirt and shorts, asked the backpacker where he was heading and if he needed a lift. He was also travelling in the Melbourne direction and would be happy to offer him a ride.

Paul couldn't believe his luck. After almost expiring in the stifling, early afternoon heat, he practically welcomed his new-found acquaintance with open arms.

'Bill' pointed to where his silver four-wheel-drive Nissan was parked and suggested he wait outside while he went into the shop himself.

Clearly relieved that he had at last found transport, Paul stood admiring the two-door vehicle with its large wheels, fat tyres and bull bar at the front. He particularly remembered the latter, as he had never seen one before.

It was a very Australian motoring extra. You didn't see too many cars with bull bars at home in England. Wandering kangaroos and other such beasts were not the sort of wildlife one usually encountered on the highways and byways of Britain.

He also noticed the lambswool seat covers inside which would be comfortable to sit on.

'Bill' appeared from the shop, walked over to his vehicle and motioned to Onions to climb into the passenger seat.

They introduced themselves by their first name to each other and started chatting. 'Bill', who told him he had a few days off work, said he was driving to Canberra to see some friends.

It was one of those matey conversations which foreign travellers are used to enjoying with friendly Aussies on the road. They exchanged personal details about their backgrounds. 'Bill' said his family came from Yugoslavia. He'd been married once but was now divorced. He worked on the roads and was on his way to Canberra.

As they drove together down the Hume Highway, always keeping religiously to the speed limit, Paul began to soak up his first decent view of the Australian bush.

He admired the scenery as they sped past farms, forests and wide open spaces. The parched bushland contrasted sharply with the deep blue of the sky. This was the genuine sunburnt country he had heard about. Not exactly outback, but far enough removed from the city and the surf to be 'the real Australia'.

It was good to be alive and he was tremendously fortunate to have hitched a lift with a good Aussie bloke. Paul began to doze off. It had been an arduous morning and he could do with forty winks.

Something, however, told him to keep awake. That sixth sense which travellers often feel before trouble strikes, had begun to sound alarm bells.

Perhaps it was the tone of the conversation which sparked his misgivings. Paul had just revealed that he had served in the Navy when 'Bill' suddenly became anti-British, mentioning Britain's role in Northern Ireland.

He also became 'a bit anti-Asian' when the conversation turned to the number of Asians living in Australia.

Paul noticed 'Bill's' voice had changed.

'When you're travelling on your own you get a bit paranoid,' he admitted afterwards. 'I thought I would just have to be on my guard.'

He was also determined to make more of a mental note of his travelling companion's features. Though he only had a side view of his face, Paul noticed that he had sideburns and was strong in build. He estimated he was in his late thirties or early forties.

As the pair drove past the pretty country towns of Mittagong and Bowral, the young Englishman could not understand why the driver kept slowing down and looking in his rear view mirror. There was no apparent reason for his behaviour, which was unnerving the backpacker.

'Bill' explained that he was trying to spot a suitable place to pull over and find an audio cassette. They were on the fringe of the Sydney radio transmission area and signals from the metropolitan stations were fading.

It seemed a plausible excuse so when the car eventually pulled into a layby and came to a halt, Paul assumed they would be continuing their journey in a few seconds.

'I thought it was a bit weird at the time because we had some tapes between us. But there was the other side of my brain saying, "Calm down, this guy's given you a lift, you should be happy".'

What he did not know then was the significance of the place 'Bill' had chosen to halt. It was just over a small hill after the Berrima turn-off and only a short distance from the main entrance to the Belanglo State Forest.

The driver climbed out of the vehicle and Paul followed on the pretext of wanting to stretch his legs.

'Bill' seemed to be annoyed by his passenger's decision to get out too.

'He became a bit irritated which I thought was odd. He said, "What are you doing out of the vehicle?"'

After the two men got back in, 'Bill' suddenly appeared to change his mind and climbed back out again, rummaging underneath the seat.

Seconds later he produced a black revolver. 'This is a robbery—do you know what this is?' he barked.

At first Paul could not believe what was happening. 'It didn't seem real to me at the time. I said, "Calm down mate. What's going on?"'

'Bill' reached under the seat a second time and produced a bag containing rope.

'That scared me even more than the gun. I thought this is going to take a bit of time—he's going to do whatever he wants. So I undid my seat belt and just legged it,' he added.

'Bill' shouted after him: 'Stop or I'll shoot,' followed by the crack of gunfire.

'Once I heard the gun go off it was like a massive jolt to my system—you knew it was real,' he went on.

'I just zig-zagged up the road trying to flag someone down, but nobody would stop.'

Drivers merely slowed down to see what was going on and then accelerated away.

At one stage 'Bill' caught up with him and tried to wrestle him to the ground. For a short time they were struggling on the hard shoulder of the Hume Highway as scores of vehicles raced by on either side, their drivers seemingly oblivious to the drama unfolding before their eyes on one of Australia's premier throughfares.

Paul was praying that someone would stop and help him. 'I thought this is my last chance. I've got to get away now. I thought the next vehicle that comes over the hill, I would jump in front of it. It seemed better to stop a car and get killed than go back to that vehicle and meet my end that way.'

The next car over the hill turned out to be a Toyota Tarago driven by a mother with her sister and five children in the back. In a last desperate bid to escape, he threw himself in front of the van, forcing Mrs Joanne Berry to come to a halt a few feet away from him.

Mrs Berry, who was driving back to her home in Canberra, had slowed down after spotting two men standing at the back of a car in the distance by the roadside. Suddenly one of them had raced out into the highway followed by the second who chased him up the road.

She was understandably alarmed by the scene and her instincts told her to have nothing to do with it. But as one of the men ran towards her waving his arms she had no alternative but to come to a halt in the left hand lane.

The younger of the men was clearly distressed. 'He was trembling...very close to tears,' she recalled as Paul ran up to the driver's side window.

'Please stop, he's got a gun!' he spluttered before sliding open one of the doors, diving into the back of the van and locking himself in.

He was worried his assailant might come after them. 'I remember him looking at me. He must have been weighing the situation up himself,' Paul recalled.

But the second man, who was by now some distance away, appeared to have given up the struggle. He ran along the roadside with his right arm hooked around his body before leaping into his vehicle and driving off quickly.

It was 3 p.m. So much had happened since Paul had accepted the lift about an hour earlier that it could have been a scene straight out of an action movie.

Mrs Berry didn't get a detailed view of the older man but recalled he was of medium build, wore shorts and a T-shirt, had brown, receding hair and seemed about 5 feet 5 inches (164 centimetres) tall.

She remembered his four wheel drive more clearly. It was silver with a crimson stripe up the side.

Her new passenger was not keen to hang around. They decided to make for the nearest police station and report the terrifying incident which had just taken place.

They drove back to the pretty, rural community of Berrima but the police station there was closed so they continued on to Bowral, where he gave a detailed statement to the officer on duty.

Police did not realise it then but the horrifying encounter reported by a frightened young British tourist that afternoon was to play a key role in a much bigger criminal investigation four years down the track.

Paul left Bowral Police Station still shaken by his experience on the Hume Highway, but he was determined to put the ordeal behind him and get on with his holiday.

There was, however, one indelible memory about his brush with death and the man who tried to shoot him that Paul could not get out of his mind.

'I just remember his stupid grin,' he said.

4.
HITTING THE BACKPACKER TRAIL.

Tourism is one of Australia's biggest foreign currency earners and the backpacking industry continues to make a significant contribution. More than half a million backpackers visited Australia in 2009, 23 per cent from Britain and 10 per cent from Germany.

Even in the early 1990s, more than 200,000 pack-wielding travellers criss-crossed the nation every year spending $1.5 billion.

The average age of a backpacker was and still is early to mid-twenties and they usually stay for about six months. In those days, around 38 per cent came from the United Kingdom and Ireland, demonstrating the strong family and historical ties that continued to exist between Australia and the British Isles. Twenty eight per cent came from mainland Europe, while 14 per cent visited from the United States and Canada. A modest 10 per cent were Australians, 8 per cent were Japanese and a tiny 1 per cent came from New Zealand.

Most would spend their time following the so-called 'backpack trail' north along Australia's east coast. From Sydney it's a comparatively short hop up the Pacific Highway to Port Macquarie, Coffs Harbour and Byron Bay, a favoured surfing spot at the far end of the New South Wales north coast. It's always been a trendy little town with an easy going lifestyle, 'new age' shops and plenty of backpacker hostels.

In the early nineties it was also popular with the stars. Paul Hogan had a home there and his one-time partner, John Cornell, who produced *Crocodile Dundee*, owned a pub on the seafront. Singer Olivia Newton John also owned property nearby. From there it was only a 90-minute drive to the Queensland border and the Gold Coast, a strip of high-rise apartment blocks overlooking golden sands and the pounding surf of the Pacific Ocean.

Queensland was and still is a mecca for backpackers. It is warmer in the winter than Sydney and has numerous cheap hostels for young travellers dotted along its coast, particularly in the sub-tropical north.

Fraser Island a few hours north of Brisbane is also a popular stopping-off point. It is the world's largest sand island and boasts turquoise blue, freshwater lakes, dense rainforest and vast, empty ocean beaches.

Airlie Beach, the Whitsunday Islands and Cairns are also major draws, not forgetting the Great Barrier Reef. The world's largest coral structure which runs for 2,300 kilometres along the Queensland coast is a must for young divers.

Once they have explored Australia's eastern seaboard many backpackers head west from Cairns travelling inland across the barren outback towards Alice Springs and Uluru. From there they might head north to Darwin or south to Adelaide, 'the city of churches'. They could take the spectacular Great Ocean Road to Melbourne and finally back to Sydney.

Two decades ago most would travel by bus or possibly by a cheap second-hand car purchased from one of the many used-vehicle yards in Sydney. Few would hitchhike, even though some guide books claimed that 'solo guys and couples have a good chance of a lift.'

It was a mode of transport actively discouraged by the police and even lorry drivers were urged by their employers not to pick up hitchhikers.

The centre of Sydney's backpacking industry used to be Kings Cross, with its strip joints, clubs and adult book shops. By night it was frequented by pimps and prostitutes but by day it was and remains an easy-going community noted for its bars, restaurants and cafes. Always a notorious crime hot spot, it was an uneasy hybrid between a bustling red light district and backpacker central.

Dozens of hostels offered budget-priced accommodation to young travellers who were passing through. It was also the hub of their communications network. In the pre-internet age, local knowledge was shared, information about cheap accommodation elsewhere was passed on and transport arranged. Notice boards contained dozens of scribbled messages seeking or offering lifts to far flung corners of Australia.

Anyone who wanted to go to Cairns or Australia's 'red centre' would almost certainly find a lift there and possibly another backpacker who wanted a companion for the long journey.

The close friendships that evolved between youngsters of many different nationalities and social backgrounds thrown together in a foreign country at the bottom of the world, testified to the strength of the international bond that united them.

Not only did they have their youth in common, but they also shared a lust for travel, excitement and new experiences. They were stepping into the unknown and keen to sample the frontier spirit associated with life Down Under.

They also soon learned who to trust and who to avoid. They were carrying most of their worldly possessions on their back and guarded their rucksack with their life. A mislaid or stolen passport, tickets or travellers cheques could be disastrous and lead to a premature return home.

Equally they were as free as the air. Their backpack was a passport to adventure, their address the length and breadth of this vast continent and their youthful energy a pre-requisite for the long-distance travelling, all-night partying and hedonistic lifestyle.

Back home during the cold nights of the northern winter they would have gazed long and hard at the travel brochures with their images of sandy beaches, swaying palms, tropical rainforests and the endless vista of the outback.

Australian movies and exported TV soaps such as *Neighbours* and *Home and Away* would also have added to the popular image of Australia as a youthful paradise where the sun never set and the natives were friendly.

It almost seemed too good to be true. A safe, western society with a near-perfect environment and a reputation for its hospitality. But when news of missing backpackers began to be reported, worried parents on the other side of the world away rued the day they'd waved goodbye to their offspring for their adventure of a lifetime.

In fact, disappearing hitchhikers and tourists were not a new phenomenon in Australia. In Queensland alone police records showed that as many as 15 young travellers had gone missing over the previous two decades, some of them dieing in mysterious circumstances.

In 1974, two trainee nurses from Brisbane disappeared while hitching to Goondiwindi, an inland country town just over the border from New South Wales. The skeletal remains of Lorraine Wilson, aged 20, and her 18 year-old friend Wendy Evans were discovered two years later at the foot of the Toowoomba Range in a spot called Murphy's Creek.

On November 3, 1982, Tony Jones, aged 20, went missing while thumbing a lift to Mount Isa, an isolated mining community several hundred kilometres west of Townsville.

In 1988 Kahl Eckhard set off to hitchhike from Sydney to Brisbane but never arrived.

In May 1987 a young Japanese tourist, Naoka Onda, 22, went missing in Queensland only a few days after checking out of a room in Sydney's Elizabeth Bay. What were believed to be her skeletal remains were later found in the Berraburrum State Forest in Queensland. A Japanese Airlines baggage tag and paper covered with Japanese writing was lying nearby.

In 1991 Edward Ford, aged 20, was hitching from Melbourne to Cairns but never reached his destination.

In the same year 29 year-old Stephen Campbell vanished while visiting Mount Lindesay in the Border Rangers National Park south of Brisbane.

In New South Wales, police files remained open on a number of mystery disappearances, including two nurses Deborah Balkan and Gillian Jamieson who were last seen in the Parramatta area in 1980.

The last reported sighting of Carmen Verheyden, 22, was on March 11, 1991, when she was seen hitchhiking at Casula near the Hume Highway on the outskirts of Sydney. She was sitting outside the Crossroads Hotel at about 12.30 a.m. after going to a party and was attempting to get a lift back to her home in the suburb of Westmead.

The 1970s also produced many unexplained disappearances, including five young people from Sydney's affluent North Shore.

The worst mass murder with the most chilling similarity to the backpacker killings involved seven young women who were brutally slain in South Australia in late 1976 and early 1977. They became known as the Truro murders, after a remote spot in the Barossa Valley, South Australia's famed wine area. In the space of seven weeks most of the women, who were aged between 15 and 26, were snatched off the streets of Adelaide, killed and their bodies dumped in Truro.

The first of the bodies was not found until Anzac Day 1978 and the second nearly 12 months later. A thorough search of the area produced the remains of the rest of the victims in Truro, Port Gawler and Wingfield about 20 kilometres (12 miles) away near the coast.

The murders began shortly after convicted sex offender Christopher Robin Worrell, 23, was released from prison. His reign of terror only ended when he was killed in a car crash in February 1977.

In 1980, James William Miller, 37, a homosexual who fell in love with Worrell in gaol, was convicted of six of the seven murders and sentenced to life imprisonment. Worrell always insisted that he took no part in the killings and had simply helped to dispose of the bodies. Worrell said Miller liked picking up girls for sex.

These and countless other attacks, murders, mystery disappearances and narrow escapes litter the pages of police files. While Australia is probably no more dangerous than most other parts of the world and probably a good deal safer than some, it is foolish not to be alert to the risks.

A total of 35,000 people are reported missing every year but only a tiny proportion of these are never found. The number of long-term disappearances, those who are out of contact for more than six months, is about 1600 nationwide.

In New South Wales more than 8,000 people are reported missing every year and about 7,000 in Victoria, but 95 per cent usually turn up within a week.

Twenty years ago many young backpackers from abroad would vanish for a short time, forgetting to let their families know where they were. There were no emails, Facebook or Twitter pages to encourage them to keep in touch. Intoxicated by their new found freedom after years of living at home, they'd take to the road without a care in the world. They always meant to send a postcard or make a phone call to their anxious parents, but were usually far too busy enjoying themselves to make that crucial contact.

Sydney's Missing Persons Bureau was in the city at Parramatta. A modern office block accommodated its small staff in a large sprawling room containing banks of files, computer screens and photographs. There were pictures everywhere, faces of those who disappeared for months or years at a time.

Some had personal reasons for assuming a new identity. The taxman or the police might be after them. Some went overseas and simply failed to stay in touch with the folks back home. Others might have suffered a violent death, their bodies dumped in remote corners of Australia where their remains would never be found.

There was no shortage of suitable terrain for disposing of a corpse. Unlike the more heavily-populated European nations where there was always a human presence, vast areas of Australia were remote and unpopulated.

A rocky outcrop in the outback miles from the nearest dirt road or an isolated gully in the middle of the bush provided perfect hiding spots.

Though the police, then as now, treat all missing persons cases seriously, they realise that some people just don't want to be found. Youngsters who fall out with their parents are particularly difficult to trace, especially if they become street kids. Those who choose to live in squats or communes can lie low for years before being tracked down. And missing tourists pose a unique problem.

It can be several weeks or months before they are reported missing by their relatives abroad and by then the trail has often gone cold, making it doubly difficult for police to locate them.

But when a son or daughter who rings home regularly goes missing, a parent instinctively suspects that something is wrong. They might wait a few weeks, possibly a month before sounding the alarm, but eventually their concern will lead them to the nearest police station.

****

Deborah Everist and James Gibson were not typical backpackers. They were Australians from Melbourne and enjoyed the benefit of local knowledge.

Unlike foreign tourists they had no language problems, they had friends and relatives to call on and they knew their way around.

They were both 19 and enjoyed similar interests. James loved hanging out with the hippy element and certainly looked the part. His long hair hung down to his neck and he occasionally donned a dark, floppy hat.

Deborah, from Frankston, he met while a student at technical college, had long dark hair and a winning smile. She was outgoing and friendly and didn't have an enemy in the world

James, from nearby Moorooduc, had grown up in a fairly liberal atmosphere, attending Woodleigh School a short drive south east of Melbourne near the Gippsland Highway. Woodleigh encouraged its pupils to find their own level. There were few rules or regulations and teachers tried to be friends rather than figures of authority.

His mother Peggy, a former nurse at London's Middlesex Hospital, had left home in England 30 years previously to move to Australia. Her husband Ray, a softly-spoken, mild mannered man, worked for Hastings Council, as a road grader. Together they had four children who, despite their limited means, were all sent to private school.

Although James loved travelling he was also a home-loving boy and was very close to his family. While waiting to begin a course as a student sculptor he decided to stay at a friend's home at Nimbin, well-known for its communes and the self-sufficient lifestyle of the locals. He was a quiet and reflective lad who was comfortable in the bucolic atmosphere and the easy going society that had been established in this attractive corner of New South Wales near Byron Bay.

He returned to Victoria in October stopping over in Sydney on the way. When he arrived it looked as though he hadn't washed for a month. An acquaintance who put him up for the night remembered he spent at least two hours in the shower.

The next day he was given a lift back to Melbourne by a friend's mother who was driving there to attend her father-in-law's funeral.

Still waiting to begin his course James decided to get a job on Hamilton Island, a well-known tourist resort off the Queensland coast near Airlie Beach. His arrival coincided with a pilots' strike which brought domestic air travel to a near-standstill in Australia and proved financially disastrous for the island which relied on Ansett to fly in the bulk of its guests.

James was soon returning to Victoria again. Back on home territory he met up with Deborah and they began to see a lot of each other. Both committed Green Party supporters, they decided to attend an evironmental gathering called Confest, which was being held at Albury on the New South Wales border in early January.

Mrs Peggy Gibson saw them off on a train from Frankston soon after Christmas and they set off for Sydney intending to stay with friends in Kings Cross. James couldn't be away for too long as he had promised to attend the wedding of his sister Mary Anne early in the new year.

They arrived in Sydney on December 29, 1989 and telephoned home to say they had arrived safely. There was an added reason for ringing. It was the day of the Newcastle earthquake and Deborah knew her mother Pat would be worried.

'Mum, I knew you'd panic,' she admitted.

'Don't panic, we're perfectly all right. We're nowhere near Newcastle,' she explained.

It was their last known contact with home.

When they arrived at Kings Cross their friends were not around but other people who lived in the same property allowed them to doss down on the floor for the night. They enjoyed the slightly bohemian lifestyle of the area but knew they could not stay for long if they were to reach Confest in time.

Two days later on December 31, video company director Steve Mangan was riding his bicycle through Galston Gorge, a hilly, rural area just north of Sydney, when he noticed a camera by the roadside. He picked it up, but he didn't report his discovery to the police for a couple of months until he read a newspaper article about the disappearance of James and Deborah.

Meanwhile the Gibsons and Everists were becoming ever more concerned. Mary Anne's wedding came and went and the entire family was upset. James was very fond of his sister and had promised to attend the ceremony which was to be held in the Gibsons' garden. His absence overshadowed what should have been a gloriously happy occasion.

Afterwards Peggy and Ray Gibson started making enquiries of their own. They established that their son's bank account had not been used and that nobody had seen him or Deborah since December 29. It was all extremely alarming, but they never gave up hope.

On March 13, 1990, switchboard operator Wendy Dellsperger found a red backpack in the Galston area while driving to work. When she picked up the pack and looked inside for a sign of an address she was perplexed by the fact that it contained pine needles. There were certainly no pine trees in Galston Gorge.

The rucksack had been damaged. Its top had been cut or torn off but a closer examination of the interior revealed a name: James Gibson.

After some detective work of her own, Mrs Dellsperger located the address of James's father in Moorooduc and telephoned him. By this time the teenage couple had been missing for nearly three months and the Gibson and Everist families were sick with worry.

The police had already been alerted about their disappearance and the discovery of James's backpack was an important development in the search for them.

When Steve Mangan read newspaper articles about the missing Victorian pair he was reminded of the camera he'd discovered a few months earlier in a Galston Gorge drainage ditch and handed it to police.

After embarking on a more thorough search of the area, police admitted the discovery of the rucksack and the camera was ominous and that they feared for the couple's safety.

Nothing more was heard about the fate of Deborah Everist and James Gibson for nearly four years. They were simply listed as missing.

****

There was an anxious note in Gabor Neugebauer's voice when he last rang home. It was 4 a.m. on Christmas Day 1991 and the 21 year-old German student from Munich told his mother Anke: 'I would like to leave this land as soon as possible and as fast as possible.'

Quite what prompted the remark remains unclear. Perhaps it was the stifling heat of an Australian summer, an uncomfortable and possibly confusing experience for anyone used to spending Christmas in the northern hemisphere. Perhaps he was homesick. Or perhaps he had a sense of foreboding that something terrible was about to happen.

Gabor and his girlfriend Anja Habschied, aged 20, from Karsfield in Germany, had been staying at the Backpackers Inn in Kings Cross but were phoning from nearby Bondi when he made the call to his mother's home in Bonn.

His parents admitted that their son sounded agitated on the phone. Two times he mentioned he wanted to leave as soon as he could. It was almost as if he was in some kind of trouble though he never elaborated and after a brief conversation the line was cut off. It was never established whether he ran out of money or whether the call was forcibly terminated or simply dropped out, as sometimes happens on international calls.

'It wasn't a good line but I could tell he was not good,' Mrs Neugebauer explained afterwards.

Gabor and Anja had pre-paid tickets to fly from Darwin to Bali, the idyllic Indonesian island so beloved of backpackers because of the cheap accommodation and laid-back lifestyle. It was to be the final leg of their two-month tour of Australia and Asia. They were booked on a flight which left Darwin on January 3, 1992, which meant they had just over a week to reach the Northern Territory capital, some 4000 kilometres (2500 miles) from Sydney.

The two Germans, who kept themselves to themselves, were a distinctive looking couple and stood out among other backpackers.

Anja had long, reddish brown hair with scarlet extensions on the right side. Gabor had long, shaggy hair on top and short at the sides. He was also tall, strong and sturdy. A six-footer (183 centimetres), he gave the impression he would be able to look after himself if he ever found himself in trouble.

Anja, a trainee draughtsman, was also in regular contact with her parents. She had written a long letter all about her Australian travels and had promised to post it around Christmas. It never arrived.

The pair was last seen on Boxing Day shortly before they set-off to hitchhike to Darwin. Why they decided to thumb a lift instead of catching public transport is not known. They had $3000 in travellers cheques, more than enough to buy a coach ticket or even fly. Buses have always been relatively cheap in Australia and although air travel was more expensive then, the country's two domestic airlines had several daily flights from Sydney to the 'Top End'. On the other hand seats were always at a premium during holiday periods and it may have been difficult to book public transport over the busy Christmas and New Year.

It was also uncertain which route they planned to travel. There were two possibilities: North to Queensland and then across to Mount Isa, Tennant Creek and the Stuart Highway or west to Adelaide and then north to Alice Springs and Darwin. Either way it would be an arduous journey, not made any easier by the soaring outback temperatures which climbed into the forties celcius at this time of year.

However the spot where their bodies were eventually discovered suggests they probably opted for the westerly route across to Mildura and on to Adelaide before turning north up the Stuart Highway. There was more likelihood of a lift this way, as it was the route favoured by heavy lorries and other tourists who were travelling by car.

The Germans had told friends and relatives to send any letters to Darwin *poste restante*. It was and still is a common practice for travellers with no fixed address to nominate a town they would be passing through in the days or weeks ahead and get their mail sent to the main post office there. Letters mailed to them care of Darwin GPO were never collected.

For a couple who kept in regular contact with home it was odd that the mail and the telephone calls from Gabor and his girlfriend dried up so suddenly. Their families were naturally concerned, but given their limited knowledge of the Australian outback they assumed that communication was difficult.

In fact telephone and postal services in the most isolated corners of Australia were often as sophisticated as those available in more urban areas. Some public phone booths were powered by solar energy and linked by micro-wave dish to the nearest town. Letters might take a bit longer to reach their destination but only by a few days. Such is the level of technological and emergency support available to those who live thousands of kilometres from the nearest sizeable community, that civilization, then as now, was never far away. Even the world-famous Royal Flying Doctor Service has always boasted that it's rarely more than 90 minutes from an emergency. Its doctors and nursing staff have been dropping out of the sky on to make-shift outback airstrips since 1928 to minister to the seriously sick and injured.

Gabor and Anja's parents also wondered if their children had made it to Bali and found it difficult to ring home. The Balinese telephone system was not the most efficient in the world and public call boxes were few and far between, especially in the more isolated mountainous areas.

The two families had many sleepless nights racking their brains in search of a possible answer. They had considered every possible scenario but as the days turned into weeks and the weeks became months, they were faced with the tragic conclusion that their children had met a violent end.

Not that they were prepared to give up hope. Mrs Neugebauer, her husband Manfred and Anja's brother Norbert felt so helpless at home in Germany. They had been in contact with Australia's Federal Police, who had tried to track the couple down, but they now wanted to do something practical themselves. Manfred was not the sort of person to sit idly by while enduring such a traumatic period. He was a retired German Air Force officer and used to getting things done.

In April 1992, the three flew to Australia to investigate Gabor and his girlfriend's last known movements and to retrace their footsteps. Their arrival in Sydney attracted a modest level of media coverage which helped to publicise their mission. If anybody out there had seen the two young Germans, they might at least report it to the police. Photographs of Gabor and Anja were flashed across the nightly television news bulletins and appeared in newspapers, but there were no major leads.

After visiting the couple's known Sydney haunts without success, Mr and Mrs Neugebauer decided to head north in the mistaken belief the two young backpackers had set off for Queensland. They hired a campervan and drove to Brisbane calling in at backpacker hostels on the way in the hope that someone might remember the pair.

They drove to Mount Isa, Darwin and Cairns before finally returning to Brisbane and Sydney having made no significant progress. They had done all they possibly could. As a Federal Police officer who had looked after them at the time was to comment later: 'I think Mr Neugebauer always feared the worst. He worked out very logically they hadn't used any of their traveller's cheques and hadn't cashed in their airline tickets, so it was likely that they had met with foul play.'

The three Germans who had pinned so much hope on their journey Down Under returned to Europe disconsolate and frustrated, not knowing what had happened to Gabor and Anja yet left with the inevitable conclusion that they were no longer alive.

It was to be more than a year before they were to know their fate for certain.

5.

A Maniac On The Loose

Simone Loretta Schmidl was carefree and easy-going. At 21 she had the world at her feet and like so many young people considered herself indestructible. Her friends tried to talk her out of hitchhiking from Sydney to Melbourne but she had done it before and dismissed the dangers.

Apart from anything else she was short of cash and couldn't afford the bus fare to Victoria, where she was due to meet her mother who was about to fly in from Germany.

The date was January 20, 1991, just over three weeks since her two fellow countrymen Gabor Neugebauer and Anja Habschied had disappeared after setting out from a backpackers hostel in Kings Cross.

Simone's friend Christine Murphy had loaned her several dollars so she could catch a train out to Liverpool and the Hume Highway. The two young women had met in August, 1989 while on holiday in Alaska. They got on famously and ended up spending a month touring together.

The two promised to keep in touch after they went their separate ways, Christine back to her home in the Sydney suburb of Guildford and Simone to Regensburg near Munich.

In May 1990 Simone wrote to Christine to say she was planning a backpacking holiday Down Under and would look her up. Naturally her Australian friend offered to accommodate her for a few days when she arrived.

It was an exciting time as Simone pored over maps, worked out her itinerary and assembled her camping equipment. A major expedition like this required a lot of preparation.

Her bus driver father Herbert Schmidl adored his daughter and although he might have had reservations about her travelling alone he was keen to offer all the assistance he could.

Simone was born on June 8, 1969 and lived with her mother Erwinea. Her parents had separated in 1986 but she often saw her father.

Herbert Schmidl recommended a camping shop in which his daughter could find most of the items she required and around June or July 1990 introduced her to one of the staff. Simone's father was a regular customer himself, having bought various sports items from the shop over the previous 10 years.

Retail buyer Georg Wolf, who worked at the Sports Tahedl shop in Regensburg, recognised Mr Schmidl but did not realise the attractive young woman next to him was his daughter until a fortnight later when Simone returned to pick up the tent she had ordered.

He remembered the purchase because the tent had to be specially ordered from the manufacturer.

Simone went on to buy several other camping items including a lilac and pink backpack, a sleeping bag, a cooking set and a Compactomat Band, an elastic cord which is used to tie up sleeping mats. Much of the equipment including the cooking utensils was made in Germany and not available in Australia.

By October 1990, Simone was ready to begin her journey. She had painstakingly planned her schedule and after arriving in Sydney intended to travel to Queensland and New Zealand before returning to Australia to meet her mother in January 1991. Mother and daughter had ideas of buying a campervan and travelling around Australia.

Herbert Schmidl kissed and waved goodbye to his cherished only daughter at Regensburg railway station, from where Simone was to board a train to Frankfurt and catch her flight to Australia. He looked forward to welcoming her back home in the new year, but he never saw her alive again.

Simi, as she was known to friends and family, was a tall, solidly-built girl. She had dark hair with dreadlocks and wore glasses. She had a good command of the English language and her friendly smile and winning manner made her easy to talk to. Though she intended to travel alone there was little doubt that she would strike up many friendships on the way. Indeed she was to seal her first new friendship within a day of leaving Germany.

Jeanette Muller was 20 and like Simone, was leaving Germany for the adventure of a lifetime. The two girls got on famously after they met on their way to Australia and promised to remain in contact when they arrived in Sydney.

Simi took up the offer of some temporary accommodation in Guildford with Christine Murphy, the girl she had met in Alaska. Jeanette booked into a backpackers' hostel but a week or so later Simi and Jeanette decided to explore and opted for a visit to Melbourne. They were two girls together and saw no problem hitching a lift south, which is what they ended up doing.

Like so many other backpackers they'd heard on the grapevine that it was necessary to position themselves on the Hume Highway on the outskirts of Sydney to enjoy a good chance of a lift all the way to Melbourne. So they caught a train to Liverpool and starting thumbing. It was all so easy.

The girls returned to Sydney intending to travel north. They had heard of the Whitsunday Islands near the Great Barrier Reef and wanted to sample the delights of sub-tropical Queensland for themselves. They wanted to do so much in the limited time available before they headed over the Tasman Sea to New Zealand.

There they followed the usual tourist route from Auckland to Rotorua, the well-known Kiwi landmark famous for its bubbling hot springs. While there they also purchased two identical water bottles. Simi wrote her name on hers with a marker.

The two young women shared their food, their tent and their belongings. Travelling on a limited budget it made sense to pool resources where possible.

They also shared the ups and downs of life on the road, no matter what the hardship. When one was feeling ill or tired the other would support her. When one was homesick the other would cheer her up. Simone hurt her ankle on one occasion when she fell off a bicycle. It wasn't a serious injury but it did cause her some discomfort and she had to have it regularly bandaged.

Meanwhile, the New Zealand leg of their holiday was drawing to a close. Simi had to be back in Australia to meet her mother in Melbourne on January 24 so the girls flew back to Sydney on Friday January 19.

The young Germans were welcomed back to Guildford by Christine Murphy and her mother Doris, a school assistant. Simone explained she had to get to Melbourne quickly and was determined to hitchhike.

'It's quite safe,' she insisted.

After all she had done it before and had experienced no problems.

The Murphys were not so sure. They tried to talk Simi out of hitching, especially on a Saturday night when the likelihood of meeting hoons or drunks on the road would be that much greater.

She took their advice and agreed to leave the next morning instead, but she was not prepared to consider public transport. Simi was always trying to save money and was usually short of ready cash. Christine Murphy felt sorry for her and gave her 'between $10 and $20' to catch the train to Liverpool, she revealed afterwards.

It was 8.15 a.m. on Sunday, January 21, 1991 when Simone Schmidl carried her large backback down the garden path and set off in her yellow singlet, khaki shorts and stout walking boots for Guildford railway station where she intended to catch a train to Liverpool.

She gave Doris a big hug and a kiss and promised to ring once she got to Melbourne.

Jeanette also tried to persuade her not to hitchhike.

'I offered her some money to take the bus instead, but she denied it and said: "No I'm just taking the train to Liverpool to hitchhike again."'

The young women had been inseparable on their holiday so far and were unhappy to be parting.

Jeanette walked with Simi to a nearby newsagents' shop and bade her friend farewell. She expected to see her again with her mother in Sydney soon, but as Simone Schmidl set out on that warm Sunday morning in January with 900 kilometres (550 miles) ahead of her, neither girl could have imagined the horror that lay ahead.

Apart from a report of her being spotted later the same day at Albury railway station on the New South Wales-Victoria border she was never seen alive again. Mrs Erwinea Schmidl waited in vain for her daughter to meet her in Melbourne. She reported Simi's disappearance to the police who in turn alerted the media.

Newspaper headlines at the time reported: 'Fears For Missing Hitchhike Girl,' and, 'Mother Pleads For Missing Daughter.' But it was to no avail. A nationwide search for the bespectacled young German woman with the friendly, easy-going manner failed to produce any clues as to her whereabouts.

Mrs Schmidl eventually gave up waiting for news and returned to Germany without her daughter.

Five months after Simone set off down the Hume Highway on that fateful January day, what was believed to have been her sleeping bag and spectacles were found in bushland near the village of Bright, north east of Melbourne and only a relatively short drive off the Hume Highway.

It was to be almost another three years, in November 1993, before Simone's body was found, though her family and friends had good reason to fear the worst long before then. In September of the previous year the badly decomposed remains of two other backpackers were found, forcing the police to admit that this could no longer be treated as a missing persons case.

For the first time since the disappearance of James Gibson and Deborah Everist they had to consider the very real possibility that a maniac was on the loose.

6.

THE FIRST CONCERNS

Caroline Clarke and Joanne Walters could not have come from more socially diverse backgrounds. Caroline was the daughter of a Bank of England regional director, enjoyed a convent school education at Midhurst in West Sussex and grew up in a comfortably-off, upper middle class family at Farnham in Surrey, close to London's stockbroker belt. She left school at 16 to do a two year catering course at Guildford Technical College, which she completed successfully in 1988.

In the autumn of that year her parents moved to the north of England, but the children decided to remain in the south where their friends were. Caroline took a job with Pizza Hut where she had previously worked as a student in the holidays and at weekends.

After some pressure from her mother and father she went on a Pizza Hut management course and was eventually promoted to the position of assistant manageress in one of the company's restaurants.

Caroline had a wide circle of friends who were important to her and she liked nothing better than to socialise with her mates. She was a talented mimic and could entertain a crowd with her impersonations of teachers, family members and television celebrities. She was also a skilled snooker player and often beat the men in her tightly-knit social circle.

From an early age she had a strong and determined character, always holding her own in family arguments with her brother and sister.

Joanne came from more humble stock and lived in a Victorian-style workman's terrace cottage at Maesteg, Mid-Glamorgan, in South Wales. Her father was a boiler house controller in a paper mill factory and her mother a shop assistant. Joanne went to the local comprehensive school where she is remembered as a model pupil.

In the normal course of events neither family would have had much in common, except to say they were respectable, hard working folk determined to give their children the best possible start in life.

Slim, blue-eyed Caroline with her shoulder-length brown hair was dazzlingly attractive. When a home video of her showing-off her 21st birthday present of a pearl necklace was later televised as part of the missing persons search, Caroline looked as though she had come straight out of the pages of *Tatler* magazine.

'She was a happy child with a sunny disposition and I always think of her with a lovely smile and a wonderful laugh,' her mother Jacquie remembered.

Well groomed, dark haired Joanne was equally pretty with her twinkling eyes and wide smile. She was tall, physically strong, self-assured and responsible.

Both had exuberant and outgoing personalities and were drawn together by their sense of fun. They loved life and travelling, yet their paths were still to cross when they set out for Australia in 1991.

Joanne was the first to leave Britain. She flew to Australia on May 26, 1991 with a friend, Pauline Vuletich, whom she had met on holiday in Greece a year earlier. The two young women stayed in Sydney for four days before heading north for some warmer weather in Queensland.

They stopped off at Airlie Beach and later moved on to Cairns. As the southern spring emerged the pair returned to New South Wales arriving back in Sydney about November. Pauline went to New Zealand and Joanne started looking for a job.

Caroline left Britain a few months after Joanne. She had spent a month with her parents at their new home in the village of Slaley, Northumberland, where Ian Clarke and his wife Jacquie were now living. It was her 21st birthday on August 10 and her father and mother wanted to lay on a lavish party. Her sister Emma and brother-in-law came up for the weekend, as well as some of her friends.

She left the day after her birthday for a month-long, inter-rail tour of Europe, before returning to England for a few days in September and setting off for Australia. Caroline had wanted to visit Australia since her early teens and when her brother Simon went backpacking Down Under his travels inspired her to follow suit.

Caroline felt she was at a crossroads in her life and didn't know in which direction to go. When she told her parents she had decided to go to Australia they gave her their full support.

She didn't have the time to say goodbye to her mother and father in person when she returned from mainland Europe four weeks later but called them on the telephone. They never saw her alive again.

Soon after arriving in Sydney Caroline got a job as an au pair. She was happy but she missed the company of other young people so decided to move on. Her next employment was in a T-shirt factory but the chemicals used in the dyeing process affected her sinuses badly and caused severe headaches. The problem was so acute that she was forced to spend a short time in Sydney's St Vincent's Hospital for treatment.

Once again she decided to move on and after spending Christmas with an Australian girl she had met in Greece earlier in the year, Caroline returned to Sydney and met up with Joanne.

They enjoyed each other's company and got on famously. Joanne did not have too much time for a social life because she had found a job as a nanny and was working from 8.30 a.m. to 7 p.m.

Her employer, Sydney hospital executive Debra Jensen, needed her to look after her baby son Nicholas. She had placed a classified advertisement in the newspaper and had been deluged with replies. But out of 120 applicants it was obvious from the interviews that Joanne was the perfect candidate.

Debra remembered her as a very sensible girl—independent, outgoing and never short of friends.

'She was always meeting new people and going somewhere with them. But it seemed to me she was also very trusting. She'd do things I would never do, like catching the train late at night. She wasn't nervous or timid and was definitely the sort of person who could look after herself.'

Debra had complete trust in Joanne. If she took baby Nicholas for a trip out on the bus she knew he would be in safe hands. As a nanny the happy-go-lucky Welsh girl was without equal. Even Debra's mother was impressed. Jean Jensen, who saw Joanne almost every day during the two months she worked for the family, was struck by the empathy between her and Nicholas.

'She was like one of my own daughters around the house and always spoke so kindly and gently to Nicholas. She was a truly delightful girl,' remembers Jean.

Sometimes Joanne would take the baby out in his stroller for a ride on the ferry or a visit to the Botanical Gardens and if she thought she might be delayed she would always telephone Jean to say so.

'I can still hear her now. She'd ring and say, "It's Joanne" in that Welsh lilt of hers. "We're going to be a little bit late."'

Joanne had settled into her new job with ease. She had Christmas off with her friends and spent the day on Bondi Beach in the time-honoured fashion which has become something of a ritual among British backpackers.

Her father Ray who was certainly not a rich man had sent her £300 for Christmas. Although he could ill-afford the gift he was anxious that his only daughter should not go short.

Such generous gestures, coupled with the regular mail and phone contact, would often leave Joanne a little homesick, prompting nostalgic talk about her life and family back in Wales.

'There was clearly such a happy bond in her own family,' Jean recalls. 'She'd often remember her grandma, whom I suppose I might have reminded her of. And she'd speak so kindly of her brother. Such a soft, nice look would come over her face whenever she talked of him.'

Joanne stayed with the Jensens until early February when she decided to continue her travels. She talked about going fruit picking with her friend Caroline, with whom she was now sharing a small flat in Kings Cross. It was a popular way of earning some ready cash among backpackers in the late summer months.

Jean was not so sure. By now Joanne was almost one of the family and although the Jensens would have liked her to stay they also realised that she was essentially on a working holiday and wanted to travel.

She also had a nagging doubt about the wisdom of the venture. As an Australian who had grown up in the countryside Jean had a more realistic view of the outback and people's attitude to outsiders.

She warned her about the dangers of mixing with the 'unusual types' who went fruit picking and who were quite different from normal travellers.

'I also felt townspeople would look down on them and that they wouldn't be welcomed by the locals because of the itinerant nature of their jobs which often made them unpopular in the area.'

Jean offered Joanne the benefit of her local knowledge but never actively discouraged her. Anyway the independent-minded Welsh girl was determined to go and earmarked February 8 as the day she would set off with Caroline and another friend, Nina Tunnicliffe, to spend six weeks grape picking on a farm near Mildura, the well-known vine-growing area on the New South Wales-Victoria border.

Nina, a clerk with Derbyshire County Council, had met Joanne in November 1991 and went on to share a flat with her in Sydney, where she was introduced to Caroline. The trio spent a lot of time together and it was only natural they should join forces for the grape-picking expedition.

The parting look on Joanne's face when she said farewell to the Jensens would remain with Jean for the rest of her life. The family had just developed some colour photographs showing Joanne playing with Nicholas. On impulse Jean handed over the lot because Joanne wanted to send some snaps back home.

'I can still remember the hesitant look on her face as if to say, "Well don't you want to keep some of me?"' It is a very poignant memory,' she admits.

It was as though she somehow knew they would never meet again.

Jean's concern for Joanne's welfare was understandable but she need not have worried. The Mildura fruit farm was geared to backpackers' needs with clean and comfortable accommodation, good food and a convivial atmosphere after a hard day's work in the fields. It attracted travellers of all nationalities who spent many happy evenings together.

Among them was Stephen Wright, an equity specialist from Beckenham in Kent, who had decided to take several months leave from his London job to explore the world. He met Joanne and Caroline in Mildura and together with some other backpackers they became a close circle.

After a few weeks they decided to go their separate ways. Stephen and some friends went on to Melbourne and Joanne and Caroline returned to Sydney, giving Stephen a contact telephone number. When he got back to Sydney about a week later on March 25 they all met up again.

After two days in Sydney they got itchy feet and began to discuss where they might go next. By now they'd developed a wanderlust which required constant gratification and as they'd had such an enjoyable time in Mildura they agreed to try their hand at apple picking in Tasmania.

They left on March 28, 1992 and like the previous journey south decided to go the cheap way—hitchhiking. The friends knew they had to get to the Hume Highway and decided to catch a train to Casula, one station on from Liverpool. By now they were wise to the New South Wales State Railway staffing situation at Casula which did not usually have a ticket collector on duty. They could therefore avoid paying their fare.

Once at the Hume Highway they split into two groups and arranged to meet up in Melbourne to catch the ferry to Tasmania. All went to plan. They arrived in the boatyard and boarded the *Able Tasman* to Devonport, disembarking on March 30.

From there they headed to Launceston, where Joanne and Caroline bought a portable camping cooker and Joanne a new Caribee-brand sleeping bag. The nights were much colder down south. Stephen remembered the purchase because he went into the shop with them.

The group travelled on to Hobart, the picturesque Tasmanian capital with its harbourside hotels, restaurants and pubs. The many historic buildings would have been a reminder of the country they'd left behind.

After a couple of weeks Joanne and Caroline decided to leave Tasmania. They thought of going apple picking in the Snowy Mountains or possibly returning to Sydney. But before they left Stephen suggested they swap tents. After all he had a large, blue, three-man tent, he wasn't planning any more camping and they only had a small two man-version. It was a good quality brand with only one blemish, a small hole caused by Stephen's grape-picking knife when he bent over and accidentally tore the material with the blade. The damage was not serious and had been patched up with the help of an adhesive address label he carried around with him.

Back in Sydney on April 15 Stephen once again ran into the two girls in Kings Cross. They were staying at a backpackers' hostel and were planning yet another trip to Melbourne, only this time they would continue on to Adelaide and possibly north to Alice Springs.

Joanne had several people to say goodbye to, among them Pauline Vuletich who had returned to Sydney from New Zealand on April 14. They had not seen much of each other since the previous November and decided to meet for a drink.

Nina Tunnicliffe was also keen to say farewell to her fellow British friends. She tracked them down to the room they were sharing in Kings Cross. They told her they intended to hitchhike around Australia and planned to travel along the Great Ocean Road from Melbourne to Adelaide, before heading north to Uluru and possibly Kununurra in Western Australia. There was also talk of working with Aborigines in remote outback areas.

Nina met up with the girls again on April 17. She remembered the date because it was not only Good Friday but also a year to the day since she'd left her home in Britain.

They went sightseeing around the city centre and about 2 p.m. decided to go back to Kings Cross. Nina and Caroline remained together for the next hour until they also parted company.

Dennis Sisterson, another British backpacker who was employed as a receptionist at the hostel where Joanne and Caroline were staying, thought he last saw them on April 17. They told him they were catching a late night coach and were aiming for Alice Springs. He last saw Caroline about 10.30 p.m and was struck by the fact she was leaving it so late to begin her journey and apparently didn't have any luggage.

In fact Joanne and Caroline were trying to wangle a free night's accommodation, by pretending to leave but in reality hiding themselves in someone else's room. The ruse worked and they got up at the crack of dawn to escape detection and make an early getaway.

The date was April 18, 1992. Stephen Wright, who spent the night in the same hostel, remembered the day because he entered it in his personal, electronic organiser. He was also leaving the same day to travel north to

Byron Bay. He last saw the two British girls at about 7.30 a.m. Caroline was wearing her Doc Martens boots, blue jeans and a heavy navy blue jumper and Joanne a pair of black leggings and a sweat shirt.

Their movements over the next two days remained unclear. Some reports suggested they stayed with a friend on Sydney's northern beaches. Others claimed they caught a train to Waterfall in Sydney's south and hitchhiked along the Princes Highway towards Wollongong.

Back home in Britain it did not take long for the girls' parents to become agitated. Joanne had last contacted her family on April 15 when she phoned from Sydney to say she had just arrived back from Tasmania. To save her money, Ray and Jill Walters would always take her number and ring back immediately. Joanne told her mother that she was in 'good form' but rather tired. She planned to rest for a few days and then re-commence her travels.

Caroline also telephoned her parents from Sydney just before Easter telling her mother: 'Everything is fine—we're going to go fruit-picking.'

Mrs Clarke said she was 'happy, bright and bubbly.'

Caroline said they were heading for Perth because she thought they had a job lined up picking melons.

'She felt she needed a little more money saved to fund her trip around Australia and the trek home afterwards,' her mother explained later. 'She sounded well and happy and there were no problems. That was the last time we heard from our daughter.'

The Clarkes were away on holiday for the next two weeks and it was only when they returned to their large stone, country house in the Northumberland countryside that they began to wonder what Caroline was up to. Even so they were not unduly alarmed because they always regarded their youngest child as a tough nut.

'From an early age Caroline seemed very accident prone,' Mrs Clarke recalled. 'Any falls or mishaps seemed to be more dramatic when they happened to Caroline but she always seemed to win through in the end and we'd rather come to think of her as a survivor,' she explained.

There were no more calls by either girl and by the beginning of May Mr and Mrs Walters were becoming increasingly concerned. Joanne always telephoned regularly, perhaps a little more so than Caroline. But Australia is a big country and they assumed they were camping somewhere off the beaten track, far from a public phone box.

Ray Walters started making a few enquiries of his own. He tracked down Jean Jensen's telephone number in Sydney to ask if she had heard from Joanne. The last postcard she'd received from her was on April 10 from Tasmania, nearly a month previously.

Even before Ray's call, Jean had been privately concerned for Joanne.

'I was getting a bit worried because I had expected to hear from her over Easter or in early May,' she recalled.

In fact since then the silence had been deafening.

Sensing Ray's innermost fears she offered to help in any way. Both agreed to report Joanne's disappearance to the police both in Wales and Australia.

On May 29, 1992, Jean visited North Sydney Police Station to report 22 year-old Joanne Lesley Walters missing.

Police Constable Gary Booth who was on duty at the time asked: 'Are you just trying to contact her or are you concerned for her welfare?'

Jean had no hesitation with her reply: 'I am concerned for her welfare.'

Back in the United Kingdom Ray Walters began a laborious search of his own, phoning Australian fruit farms, backpacker hostels and country police stations—anywhere his daughter might have been. He would stay up until the early hours of the morning making lengthy international calls and clocking up a massive telephone bill.

He also tracked down the parents of Joanne's travelling companion Caroline. It was the first time the Walters and the Clarkes had spoken. From now on they would become emotionally and spiritually as one, united by their determination to find out what had happened to their lost daughters.

Until Ray's call, Ian Clarke had told himself not to be unduly worried by Caroline's disappearance but on May 8 he began to have serious doubts. It was the birthday of his other daughter Emma and as he later explained, 'Caroline was always fastidious about remembering birthdays.'

When there was no birthday communication from Australia, Ian and Jacqueline Clarke thought long and hard to devise a plan of action. No stone would be left unturned, no avenue would remain unexplored in an effort to discover their daughter's whereabouts.

First they would contact the local Northumberland police, but Ian Clarke had an even better card up his sleeve. He would utlilise the resources available to him through his Bank of England connection.

So he telephoned former Scotland Yard commander Philip Corbett who was head of security at the Bank of England and asked his advice. Mr Corbett had been in charge of the Yard's International and Serious Crimes Branch and consequently had wide knowledge of, and good contacts in, overseas police forces. He knew exactly what to do and went straight to the top, feeding information about the British girls and their last known whereabouts to Federal Police officers stationed at the Australian High Commission in London's Strand.

He also took statements from the two young backpackers' former travelling companions who had by now returned to Britain. Slowly a detailed picture emerged about their movements prior to their sudden and inexplicable disappearance.

The former police commander also realised it was time to alert the media who could offer much useful assistance in the search for Caroline and Joanne. He telephoned the London office of the Sydney *Telegraph Mirror* which ran a story about the missing girls.

Mr Corbett urged the New South Wales police to give the matter top priority because he believed there were a number of aspects of grave concern. His intervention clearly prompted the Australian authorities to give the case their upmost attention. Word had filtered down from the top brass: 'We've got to go big on this.'

The problem was where should they start? After the initial burst of publicity the police had one or two promising leads, notably the report by two women who claimed they had given the British girls a lift to a Caltex service station on the Bulli Pass on April 21. Susan Burns and her friend Myrna Honeyman were not in the habit of picking-up hitchhikers but took pity on the girls when they saw them standing outside Waterfall railway station about 5.30 p.m.

They told how they wanted to get to Yass because they had to meet a friend there and were also intending to go fruit picking. The couple produced a hand-drawn map which was so hopelessly inaccurate that Ms

Burns suggested they might as well re-trace their footsteps.

'I told them they were on the wrong road—that they should be on the Hume Highway,' she revealed later. The pair groaned in disappointment but decided to continue their journey anyway. In fact they were on the Princes Highway and if they turned right just before Kiama they could head across country to Moss Vale and join the Hume Highway.

The two hitchhikers were thankful for the lift and chatted away to the two older women for the next 20 minutes as they made their way towards Bulli Tops. They told of spending Easter with a male friend at Mona Vale, a popular beachside suburb just north of Sydney, after leaving Kings Cross on April 17.

One explained how she had been working as a nanny for a doctor in Sydney while the other had earned her keep doing some computer work.

The woman motorist dropped them off near a Caltex service station at Bulli where she was sure there would be plenty of trucks and a good chance of a lift in the direction the girls were going. Even so Ms Burns, as a mother of two grown-up daughters herself, was a little concerned. 'They were really nice, so nice. I told them to ring me if they couldn't get a lift,' she recalled later.

It was dusk but there was still just enough light to admire the view from Bulli Tops, the spectacular vantage point which offers a staggeringly beautiful aerial vista over Wollongong and its beaches.

The owner of the service station also confirmed he had seen two female backpackers dropped off by a woman in a car near his garage. He was so certain that he rang the police after an appeal for information was broadcast during the rugby league test between Great Britain and Australia on July 3.

The proprietor not only gave a full description of their clothing, which matched what Joanne and Caroline were known to have been wearing when they left Kings Cross, but also claimed they had British accents. He had spoken to them in the service station's cafe and had a detailed mental picture of both. They sat at the counter for nearly an hour before they grabbed their gear and headed outside to wait for a lift under the light from the neon petrol sign.

More ominously the proprietor claimed he saw them hitch a lift with a man in a small, three-tonne truck soon afterwards. The driver of the vehicle was described as 5 feet 10 inches (180 centimetres) tall, with blond hair and wearing black shorts and a shirt. He lifted the roller door at the rear of the vehicle and placed the girls' backpacks inside.

While in the garage the young women had indicated they wanted to get to Yass. If the owner of the truck had taken them in the direction they wanted to go, he would have turned right along the Princes Highway and followed the Appin Way towards Picton, the main access road which links the South Coast to the Hume Highway. Even if he had not been able to take them all the way, the odds are that the girls would have found it comparatively easy to hitch a ride on one of the numerous lorries which used the same route.

'I watched them get into the truck and thought it was a bit foolish,' the service station owner admitted afterwards.

But were these the same two girls? Although there were unmistakable similarities between Joanne and Caroline and the two backpackers picked-up at Waterfall and dropped off at the Caltex service station on the Bulli Pass, there was never any conclusive proof. Detectives investigated the 'sighting' thoroughly but were never totally convinced they were the same backpackers.

Even Jean Jensen wondered whether this really was her ex-nanny when she heard that the hitchhiker thought to have been Joanne ordered a hamburger in the garage cafeteria. Joanne was a vegetarian and never, ever ate meat!

7.
THE SEARCH BEGINS

As the days and weeks went by, reports of Joanne and Caroline being sighted came in from all over Australia. A lorry driver claimed he had given them a lift near the remote Queensland mining town of Mount Isa on May 2. The truckie was shown amateur video and photographs of the two girls and was 100 per cent certain they were the same couple. They were carrying backpacks and were holding a sign which read 'Darwin.'

Other reports suggested they were working as cooks with a roadbuilding gang in Queensland or helping on an isolated cattle station in the outback.

A woman motorist was sure she gave them a lift from Canberra to Cooma at the foot of the Snowy Mountains on April 26. It is a popular base for bushwalkers who want to explore the Australian high country and also for skiers heading for the New South Wales slopes, though April would have been at least two months too early for the snow.

To add to the authenticity of the report the woman, who did not phone the police until early July, said the young hitchhikers, whom she positively identified from photographs of Joanne and Caroline, also had British accents. Police are used to people getting lost in this remote area which covers hundreds of square kilometres.

Detectives also investigated a 'sighting' at Uluru near Alice Springs in the centre of Australia. A woman said she had spoken to two young women matching the descriptions of the missing tourists and thought they were driving a white car with South Australian registration plates.

There were also unconfirmed reports of the couple at Noosa, on

Queensland's Sunshine Coast and a tip from a fellow backpacker who had heard they were planning to travel to Western Australia.

Police also tried to contact a young man who reportedly proposed to one of them before she left Sydney.

Australia's Immigration Department checked its records to see if the two young women had left the country. As they had also talked of travelling on to Indonesia it was possible they might have caught a plane from Darwin across the Timor Sea to Bali. But when officers looked up the list of people who had gone through passport control on their way out of Australia over the previous few months the names of Joanne and Caroline did not appear

There was one significant and arguably authentic 'sighting' which had detectives baffled. It was on April 24 at Bowral, the country town set in the foothills of the New South Wales Southern Highlands and whose most famous son was the legendary Australian cricketer Sir Don Bradman. There is even a Bradman oval and museum on the outskirts in recognition of the town's illustrious link with sporting history.

Bowral is an attractive corner of Australia with its undulating countryside, leafy lanes and English-style architecture. There is even a mock-Tudor pub in the town centre called The Blue Boar Hotel, which is based on the design of a similar country inn where Oliver Cromwell once stayed in Yorkshire.

Staff remember two young women arriving about 10 p.m. and captivating the other customers with their singing. Not any old pop songs but Welsh melodies sung with Welsh lyrics. Later they had a go on the karaoke machine much to the delight of fellow drinkers. It was the night before Anzac Day and the regulars at the Blue Boar were clearly enjoying the free entertainment provided by the two British girls.

The publican, who didn't catch their names, knew they came from Britain because he saw their passports. Like all his young customers his staff had to check IDs to make sure there were no under-age drinkers on the premises.

He recalls how the young women arrived by themselves but were met soon afterwards by three or four men whom they obviously knew. They sipped bourbon and coke and chatted with their friends.

Soon after midnight the girls left by themselves but met up with their male companions again a few minutes later outside. He remembers watching them all climb into the same van. He could not be sure but thought it was a Volkswagen Kombi van or an Econovan.

While their next destination was unknown, another reported 'sighting' two days later on April 26 added a further piece to the jigsaw. A Canberra couple believed they saw them at the Boxvale Tramway Walking Trail picnic site, south of Mittagong, a short distance away. The young women were cooking a meal with a man in his twenties. He was about 5 feet 9 inches (178 centimetres) tall, with a slight, agile appearance and short hair which might have been cropped at the sides.

The Canberra couple also remembered the man had been driving a light coloured or white, early model Volkswagen Kombi in poor condition and with a noisy engine. The trio gave the impression they were using the vehicle to sleep in.

At the front of the van underneath the windscreen was a spare tyre wrapped in a white vinyl cover with a 'smiley face' logo on it. Police and the media were to make great play of the logo in subsequent appeals for information though unfortunately half the Kombi vans in Australia seemed to have the same design on the spare wheel cover. As a result hundreds of people telephoned the police with alleged sightings of the van. Motorists who passed similar vehicles on the road called the police and anybody who had totally unfounded suspicions about their neighbours or workmates would ring detectives, simply on the basis that they owned a VW with a smiley face spare wheel.

Police later revealed that there were two other possible sightings over the same Anzac Day weekend. A woman similar to Joanne was seen speaking to a man at the Blue Boar where she bought a bottle of wine and told him she was touring Australia with a friend and was staying with a resident in the area.

On April 26 both girls were reported to have been seen further up the road in the small township of Berrima, only a 10-minute drive from the Belanglo State Forest.

Detectives were overwhelmed by hundreds of reported sightings such as these and clearly had difficulty sorting the 'possibles' from the 'no ways.' There is little doubt that they were snowed under by the weight of tips from well-meaning individuals whose information sometimes bordered on the bizarre. Every major criminal investigation attracts its share of crackpots with their half-baked theories. National and international publicity only encourages more cranks to come out of the woodwork with all the resultant time-wasting and drain on resources. And as the police had yet to establish that a crime had actually been committed, detectives were still not clear whether they were looking for a killer or a few, fun-loving kids who had gone missing.

Sergeant Peter Marcon of the NSW Missing Persons Bureau was trying to wade through a mountain of data. Every tip and theory, no matter how weak, had to be diligently pursued but they simply didn't have the manpower to work their way quickly through the rapidly expanding pile of information on their desks. It would take time. Meanwhile the lack of a positive sighting which would provide conclusive evidence of the girls' whereabouts did not bode well.

'All I can say is that we haven't given up hope and that we will follow up every report,' Sergeant Marcon assured the media at the time.

Jean Jensen had also been closely following developments and keeping in touch with the Walters back in Wales. She tried to be optimistic but her commonsense told her otherwise. Deep in her heart she knew that if Joanne and Caroline were still alive they would have communicated with their parents.

'There's really no place in Australia where, if you are free, you can't make a phone call. And I also felt that Joanne would have contacted me if she could. She always knew there was a bed for her here at any time,' she explained as the search continued.

Jean had considered the possibility that they might have walked into an isolated area and had an accident. One of them might have fallen down a cliff and the other gone to her rescue,' she surmised.

'The alternative,' she admitted, 'is foul play.'

Joanne and Caroline's families refused to give up hope. They entertained every conceivable theory about their daughters' disappearance and never once publicly acknowledged that they might be dead. Perhaps they really had joined a remote Aboriginal mission, which Joanne had discussed with her friends. Perhaps they were lost in the outback, living-off bush tucker. Perhaps they were being held against their will, unable to write or phone.

It was an anxious and frustrating period for the Clarkes and the Walters who were so desperate to do something positive themselves.

In the end they decided to travel to Australia to carry out their own enquiries and retrace the girls' footsteps. Ray and Jill Walters agreed to fly to Sydney first and Ian and Jacqueline Clarke would follow them. Not only would it provide important therapy for the parents who were by now beside themselves with worry, but it might also act as a spur for the police. Although officers were doing all in their power to establish the fate of the British backpackers they were making little real headway. The presence of the families from the UK might make all the difference.

Mr and Mrs Walters arrived in Australia on August 25, 1992. Within hours of disembarking from a tiring 24-hour flight from London to Sydney they gave a news conference at the New South Wales police headquarters.

Fighting back tears Jill told how 'Jo' was on their thoughts every minute of the day.

'It's not knowing what's happened which upsets us. She was very close and would call every two weeks. Whenever she was going somewhere new she would call us. I just hope that somebody out there has got some information one way or the other,' she implored.

Desperately trying to control his own emotions, Ray explained: 'We know Joanne and Caroline are very reliable and this is out of the ordinary for both of them. That's what worries us most.'

He revealed it was always a dream of Joanne's to come to Australia and possibly work with Aborigines and he would be asking the police to check remote indigenous communities in the hunt for his daughter.

'I guess we can hope they might be on a remote mission somewhere,' he remarked.

In an unguarded moment Ray also hinted that the police might have taken the disappearance of the girls more seriously, a little earlier than they did. It was a comment he later explained was not meant to be in any way critical of the investigating officers.

'I was trying to get across the frustration parents often experience when their child goes missing, unexplained, and is not seen or heard from in five months. In doing so I may have inadvertently given the impression that I was critical of the police. I am not,' he emphasised.

In fact as early as June 18 the NSW police had set up a special toll-free hotline number and widely publicised it in all Australian states inviting callers to ring in with information about the two backpackers.

In view of the pressure the Walters were under and their limited experience of handling the media, the occasional misunderstanding was inevitable. But it was not long before Ray and Jill became seasoned professionals at dealing with the press, radio and television.

For those who have led quiet lives far removed from the glare of publicity, the media spotlight can be a daunting and unnerving experience. But within a few hours of giving their first Sydney news conference the Walters were being driven to Australia's Channel Nine studios in Willoughby for a live appearance on the *Midday Show* with Ray Martin.

The presence of a studio audience did not exactly provide the right ambience for an intimate interview, but Martin, an experienced reporter with an easy-going manner, put the Walters at their ease and, more importantly, allowed them access to his nationwide audience.

It was just what they wanted. The more publicity, the greater the chance of nudging someone's memory.

Jill's message was short and to the point: 'We feel that time is going on and we want to know what has happened one way or the other. I appeal to anyone out there if they know the whereabouts of Joanne would they please contact us.'

The *Midday Show's* predominantly middle-aged, female audience, both at home and in the studio, would have understood what the Walters were going through. Many would have had daughters of their own and the thought of something like this happening would have been the ultimate nightmare.

Ray and Jill's appearance on national television gave Australians the first heart-wrenching glimpse of what this case was all about and the devastating emotional effect it was having on two British families. This was the human side of the disappearance which had received so much publicity both in Australia and abroad.

Once again the public response was overwhelming. Ordinary Australians who recognised Ray and Jill in the street expressed their concern and encouragement. The Walters were moved by the level of help and sympathy offered to them wherever they went. But kindness would not necessarily find their child. They'd only intended to stay in Australia for a month and they had many more miles to travel.

First they called on the backpacker hostels in Kings Cross, where Joanne and Caroline had spent so much time. Then they hired a car and drove south west to Mildura where the girls had gone fruit picking. The journey was so beautiful and the weather so agreeable that there were times they might almost have forgotten about the true nature of their travels.

Wherever they stopped to make enquiries they were welcomed and plied with hospitality. This was the friendly face of Australia, a world away from the horror that would soon engulf them.

8.

WHERE THE BIRDS DON'T SING

Executioner's Drop is deep in the middle of the Belanglo State Forest. Other vaguely macabre reference points identified on maps of the area such as Kelly's Drop, Miner's Despair, Sick Man, Ugly Man and Knapsack Gully, only add to the spookiness, the origin of their names lost in time.

Today as then that part of Belanglo which has escaped the forest workers' axe, is planted with thousands of pine trees. Row upon row, mile after mile of erect trunks wait to be felled as far as the eye can see. Other parts have been cleared, small round stumps the only reminder of the trees that had been planted a few decades previously.

The forest is criss-crossed by dirt roads and fire trails, an intricate network of tracks and paths along which it is easy to get lost. There are no signs to assist visitors who want to explore and no obvious landmarks to confirm their exact position.

A road sign placed alongside the Hume Highway just beyond the Berrima turn-off points to the entrance, which begins as a sealed, tarmac lane but soon becomes a dirt road. On one side there is a picnic site which attracts families at the weekends and further along the occasional worker's cottage dots the landscape.

But this is just the perimeter. It will take some 15 minutes of hard driving to get anywhere near the centre and even then huge areas of this dense bushland will be only accessible on foot or by a four wheel drive vehicle. The steep, hilly tracks and the rocky outcrops make it impossible to take a sedan. Unless you know the forest well the thickness of the vegetation makes a compass and an ordnance survey map essential navigational aids.

There is also a stillness about the area which only adds to the sense of isolation. It is several miles to the Hume Highway and the nearest human habitation. A scream, no matter how loud or how shrill, would never be heard. Even a gunshot is likely to go unnoticed.

Those who visit Belanglo are consumed by a spine-tingling sense of death. It is cloaked in an eerie silence. There is little sign of animal life and even the birds are strangely silent. It is as though nature is in mourning.

It was in this uninviting environment that two members of the Scrub Runners Orienteering Club from Liverpool found themselves on Saturday, September 19, 1992.

Keith Siely and his running partner Keith Caldwell were on the first day of a weekend's orienteering when they entered a wooded glade pitted with large boulders and rocky ledges. They had been jogging through the bush as part of a two day training exercise when they were struck by the smell of decaying flesh.

Mr Siely, an optical mechanic, noticed what appeared to be a pile of rubbish beside a boulder and on closer inspection saw what he thought was a dead wombat. He was about to move on when his fellow runner took an even closer look. For a moment the two men imagined they could see the leg of a kangaroo protruding from beneath some vegetation.

As Mr Caldwell edged closer he saw what appeared to be the joint of an elbow underneath a rocky overhang. Then he became aware of a Doc Martens-type boot about a metre away and to the right of that some matted hair and a piece of clothing.

Mr Caldwell, a marine safety officer, had no hesitation reaching his conclusion: 'It's a body!'

Clearly stunned by their discovery, the two men alerted some fellow orienteers who were in the vicinity. They all agreed to make their way back to a cabin some 10 kilometres away where they were staying the night and where there was a mobile telephone.

The time was 3.45 p.m. and although they didn't know it then, Siely and Caldwell had stumbled across the body of Joanne Walters. Five months after she had disappeared from a Kings Cross backpackers' hostel, the badly-decomposed remains of the girl from Maesteg in Wales had been found in the depths of the Australian bush.

By the time the police were informed and had been taken to the murder scene by the orienteers, night was falling on the forest and the conditions did not allow a detailed search of the surrounding area. They agreed to re-assemble early the next morning.

Constable Susanne Roberts from Bowral was among the first to arrive soon after daybreak. She inspected the spot where the first body was found the previous afternoon and had walked barely 20 metres further on when she saw part of a leg under a fallen tree. Jeans covered the lower part of the leg and on the foot was a brown, leather shoe. From Police Constable Roberts' vantage point it looked as though the body had been pushed under a log and sticks and branches placed on top. This was the bushland grave of Caroline Clarke.

It was a gruesome scene which made even hardened officers sick with revulsion. They had a pretty good idea who the victims were but only an autopsy or evidence of identification could say for sure. A ring was removed from a hand on the first body. Detectives wanted to show it to Mr and Mrs Walters to see if they recognised it.

The Walters had heard about the discovery of the two bodies and naturally feared the worst. They had just got back from a trip south when police broke the news. Suddenly any tiny, lingering hope that their daughter was still alive evaporated and they were faced with the inevitable conclusion that their mission was at an end.

'We are terribly upset,' he admitted that Sunday afternoon.

The following day forensic pathologists took the unusual step of holding a news conference at the Glebe Coroner's Court to reveal the results of post mortem examinations on the two bodies.

Professor John Hilton, the Scottish-born director of the New South Wales Institute of Forensic Medicine, gave a detailed account of the injuries sustained by the victims, the coldness of the clinical assessment only adding to the chilling picture that was slowly emerging.

The terrifying final moments of the British girls became ever more apparent as Professor Hilton detailed the frenzied attacks suffered by both young women. Joanne had died from multiple stab wounds to her upper body while her mouth had been gagged by a cloth tied around her neck. Caroline had been shot several times in the head at close range, her body's advanced state of decay accelerated by a covering of leafy mulch.

Professor Hilton confirmed that the bodies were still fully clothed when found, but he could not rule out the possibility that one or both had been sexually assaulted. 'It's certainly a possibility and in the fullness of time perhaps we will get some sort of answer,' he explained. 'But you must realise that the degree of decomposition is going to make it difficult,' he added.

The condition of the remains suggested that each body had been in the bush since April, when the British backpackers went missing. Any difference in the extent of their deterioration could be explained by the fact that they were left in slightly different locations.

Dental records and X-rays which Ray and Jill Walters had brought with them from Wales had already been compared with the first body, which allowed Professor Hilton to establish 'beyond question' the identity of Joanne.

Caroline's dental records were already on their way from Britain and a positive identification of the second body was expected the next day.

Back in the UK, Ian and Jacqueline Clarke were being kept in daily contact with developments. They heard of the discovery of the bodies as they were driving home from a wedding.

Their local community policeman telephoned them on their car phone and advised Ian to pull over.

'He said the police in Australia had found two bodies. It was such a harrowing experience. You cannot imagine what we've gone though,' Mr Clarke later admitted.

In a way the news had brought a sense of relief. 'Now we have to look back on the happy times she did have,' he added.

Forty-eight hours later the dental records which had been flown to Sydney confirmed what the family had accepted as inevitable. Ian Clarke now only had the memory of his beautiful daughter, the girl who left home some ten months earlier to seek 'a change of direction' in her life.

'It was a good way to go off and think things through and to see the world,' he mused, 'but she discovered the darker side of human nature.'

Caroline's brother Simon added, 'It sounds horrible but in some ways... at least you know what the story is—we can get on and grieve. She was a really, really nice kid. You don't pick your family, but I don't think you could pick any better.'

The Clarkes said they would fly to Australia to bring their beloved daughter's remains home. In the meantime they could only mourn. Mrs Clarke had taken it particularly badly as had Mrs Walters, who was under sedation at a friend's house in the Sydney suburb of Annandale.

Jill Walters could only sob. She was paralysed by grief and incapable of speech. It was left to Ray to convey the feelings she was too heartbroken to utter. 'If she had a gun she would shoot whoever was involved in the killings,' he said. And he clearly meant it.

'We've cried so much since Joanne went missing. Now we're too numb to take it in. It's just unbelievable. The miracle we'd always hoped for just didn't occur. We are utterly devastated and I will not be happy until I find the people who have done it,' he added.

By now the police were under even greater pressure to produce results. It was no longer a missing persons inquiry, but a murder hunt. For the first time since James Gibson and Deborah Everist vanished at the end of 1989, they had to concede that the disappearance of seven backpackers may all be linked. They were not at this stage prepared to entertain the possibility of a serial killer, but they had to admit that more bodies could have been dumped in the Belanglo Forest.

The latest developments had not escaped the families of the missing German and Australian hitchhikers either. Mrs Anke Neugebauer cried uncontrollably when she heard the news from her daughter who had seen a report on the BBC at her home in Holland.

'My wife had a breakdown when she heard the news, she was in tears,' her husband Manfred said from their home in Bonn.

The Habschieds, Schmidls, Everists and Gibsons were similarly affected and were further disheartened by the grim discovery of the bushland graves.

With detectives forced to re-open the files on previous mystery disappearances and facing mounting public demands for the arrest of the frenzied killer or killers responsible for the brutal murder of Joanne and Caroline, the police needed results. They also had hungry Australian and international reporters snapping at their heels, as well as a distraught mother and father on their doorstep.

The Walters were under siege from the media and agreed to hold a news conference at the NSW Police Headquarters in Sydney. It was to be one of the shortest but most electrifying media gatherings assembled there. There were to be no questions, merely two brief statements from Ray and Jill. As it turned out, no supplementary questioning was necessary. The comments stood on their own as testimony to the sheer horror of the couple's past 48 hours.

His rich, Welsh, voice quivering with emotion, Ray stated, 'Whoever has done this thing I wouldn't call them sick, because sick people can be cured to some extent. These are evil-minded people and like dogs with rabies there is only one way—they've got to be put down, because the world has not got the resources to keep these people in gaol. There's got to be some system whereby we destroy these people so they don't put their evil genes anywhere else.'

Jill's message was even more succinct. Her eyes brimming with tears she fought to maintain her composure for a few seconds, before telling the reporters and photographers who were by now hanging on every word: 'All I want to say is that these people who have done this to these girls are just proper animals and they ought to be shot. That's all I can say. They ought to be shot.'

Only the click of camera shutters broke the silence as Ray and Jill Walters stood up and left the room. The media breathed a collective sigh of relief after the drama of the previous few minutes. Some thought it was the end of the story, expressing little optimism for a successful end to the police investigation. The Walters would go back to Britain and the murder of Joanne and Caroline would go down in the files as yet another unsolved crime.

9.

THE STILL SMALL VOICE OF CALM

Sunday, October 4, 1992, dawned with a grey sky and light rain. There was no hint of the sun on this cool spring morning, merely a pallid light which cast a gloomy shadow across most of New South Wales.

In Sydney Mr and Mrs Walters, their 19 year-old son Jonathan and Jill's sister Maureen, knew it was going to be another intensely emotional day. For the past two weeks the family had wanted to hold a service on the site of Joanne and Caroline's makeshift graves. It was not to be a funeral or a memorial ceremony but what they described as a service of serenity.

The Walters also wanted to say thank you to the people of Australia for their sympathy, to recognise the efforts of the police and to mark the role played by locals in the Bowral area who had given so freely of their time. This was to be a service not just for those who were personally involved in the tragedy but for the public as a whole. As Ray said at the time, it would be unfair to exclude the people who had offered them so much help and support.

But there was another reason too. The Walters were imbued with an overwhelming desire to expunge the evil that had taken place in Belanglo some five months earlier. They wanted to exorcise the malevolence which all who visited the forest could feel. Ray and Jill had already been to Executioner's Drop once before, escorted by detectives soon after the bodies were found. Now they felt compelled to face the bush grave site one more time. In a way they hoped it would help to liberate the souls of the young people whose lives were so sickeningly snuffed out there.

The Belanglo State Forest is both geographically and geologically far removed from the British Isles. The harsh terrain has little in common with the green and gently undulating slopes of the United Kingdom. Yet for just over an hour on that overcast day, a service thick with accents, hymns and even the weather of the valleys brought a tiny slice of Wales to the Australian bush.

Given the light drizzle and the predominantly Welsh conversation in the air, it could have been a Sunday afternoon on the way to chapel. The Australian Welsh Friendship Club which had offered so much practical support to the Walters since their arrival, provided the choir and organised the refreshments at the Berrima scout hall afterwards.

There is something about a Welsh choir in full voice that evokes images of love and joy, hope and sorrow. And when the land of your fathers is 12,000 miles away on the other side of the world, the spiritual intensity of the experience becomes overwhelming.

And so it was that day as police and public joined the Walters in song.

For the officers it was also an opportunity to mingle with the crowd, ever-conscious of the well-worn theory that a killer is often tempted to return to the scene of his crime. Detective Inspector Bob Godden, a stout and agreeable bear of a man who was in charge of the investigation at that time, peered at the faces in the crowd but offered no hint of an early arrest.

'We're following up some good leads,' was all he'd say.

Most of those who attended the ceremony had to walk the last several hundred metres to the service, their cars parked alongside the dirt road which is the only access point to Executioner's Drop. Only a four wheel drive is capable of completing the last leg of the journey up and down steep inclines and across jagged boulders. Even after negotiating this hazardous, bumpy track there is a final path which can only be climbed on foot. Though it is not so much a path as a gap between rocks.

Mr and Mrs Walters who were driven there in a police vehicle, were joined by Caroline's second cousin, Nichola Burge and her husband Chris who lived in Adelaide. Jean Jensen was also among the congregation.

'In years to come Ray and Jill will be able to say, "At least we went out to Australia and did something for Joanne,"' she noted.

'At least they were near when the bodies were found.'

The Walters were well aware how harrowing this service would be but they also knew it might help the healing process. Jill, who was still under sedation and had to be supported by her husband as she stood on the site where her daughter had died, sobbed uncontrollably.

In the distance the Red Dragon of Wales was draped across the sandstone rock beneath which Joanne's remains were found. A short distance away the Union Jack was placed across the felled tree which marked the spot where Caroline's body was so crudely hidden.

Candles were burning on the temporary altars which each gravesite had become. As a few hundred eyes wandered across the rocks and spartan vegetation, the 35-strong choir sang:

'Guide me, O Thou Great Jehovah,
Pilgrim through this barren land,
I am weak but Thou art mighty;
Hold me with Thy powerful hand.'

It was while Anglican priest Father Stephen Gray began his opening address that the steady drizzle more in common with the Welsh valleys than an Australian spring began to ease.

'We have come to this wicked place so that it will be peaceful again and its memories put at rest,' he explained.

A few minutes later the Sydney Welsh Choir sang:

'Dear Lord and Father of mankind,
Forgive our foolish ways;
Reclothe us in our rightful mind;
In purer lives Thy service find,
In deeper reverence praise.'

The final line of the third verse referred to the 'still small voice of calm.' Certainly some form of holy presence was palpable that wet Sunday afternoon. As the Walters walked slowly towards the murder scene, the choir sang:

'The Lord's My Shepherd. I'll not want;
He takes me down to lie
In pastures green; he leadeth me
The quiet waters by.'

Jill placed a spray of daffodills on the ground where her only daughter was slain. The family knelt and prayed while the choir broke into the traditional Welsh love song, *Myfanwy*, its haunting melody permeating through the bush.

Then they walked the few steps across to the second altar, which marked the spot where Caroline was found. Once again they knelt and prayed before making their way back to the main party.

It was only when the choir began to sing *You'll Never Walk Alone* that those who had gathered under the forest canopy became aware of a fitting meteorogical phenomenon that was perfect in its timing.

As if by heavenly cue the sun appeared from behind the breaking clouds, penetrating the gum trees with its rays and bathing the two flower -bedecked altars in a yellow light. The scene was breathtaking in its simple beauty.

And the lyrics of the accompanying song were not lost on the congregation:

'When you walk through a storm,
Keep your head up high,
And don't be afraid of the dark;
At the end of the storm is a golden sky
And the sweet silver song of a lark.'

There were no larks that day but many of those assembled wondered whether they were witness to some kind of divine intervention. Whatever the truth, the Walters knew that Joanne and Caroline were at peace in the forest.

The congregation dispersed and began the trek back to their cars. Mr and Mrs Walters shook their hands one by one, relieved that the emotional ordeal was over and convinced the service of serenity had achieved its purpose.

Ray Walters whose inner-strength and composure throughout the tragedy had impressed all those who came into contact with him, explained: 'I just couldn't leave without thanking the Australian people for how they've helped us. To have gone home without this service would have been leaving something out. Now we're putting this area back to how it was and putting the girls to rest.'

10.

THE HUNT GOES COLD

A week after the service of serenity Ian and Jacqueline Clarke flew into Sydney. Like Ray and Jill they wanted to see the site of their daughter's brutal murder.

'I know that Mr and Mrs Walters got a great deal of comfort from that experience and I think we hope to achieve the same,' Mr Clarke explained.

The Walters were still in Sydney and so both sets of parents were able to meet. They had a long evening together in their hotel, consoling each other over the terrible loss which had brought them to Australia.

The next day Ian Clarke and his wife held a news conference in the same NSW police briefing room where the Walters had poured out their hearts nearly a month earlier. Although they were still in shock, the Clarkes were keen to use the opportunity to promote a constructive message and not to dwell too long on the agony they had endured.

'We want to highlight the problems and dangers that are lurking there and bring it home to backpackers that there are things they have to be careful about,' he said.

And he suggested that some kind of register or information service be formed to help young travellers.

'If we can get some sort of trust set up that can act as an adviser to young people, we'd very much like to do something of that sort.' he added.

With the popular use of email and social media still a decade or more away, police and the backpacker industry accepted there was a need to keep tabs on the small army of youthful travellers who were arriving in Australia in ever-increasing numbers.

The problem was that half the joy of backpacking was in the freedom to travel as you wished, unhindered by rules, bureaucracy and the heavy hand of authority. Backpackers did not like to plan too far ahead and reserved the right to change their destination without telling anyone. After all Australia was probably the furthest they would ever get from parental control and they had no intention of buckling down to a strict itinerary.

Nor were they unduly concerned by the backpacker case itself. There had been no noticeable reduction in new arrivals since the two bodies were found and young travellers were convinced they could look after themselves. The only people to be genuinely alarmed by the enormous editorial coverage being given to the murders in the Australian and overseas media were the mums and dads whose offspring they only knew were 'somewhere on the road'.

For the police it was an equally disturbing time. They had two bodies and no suspect. Their only clues were the spent bullet shells found near the bush graves of the dead Britons, which indicated that one or both of the murdered women were killed at the scene.

Police combed a two kilometre-wide area as thoroughly as their limited manpower permitted. Sixty officers including divers and trainees from the police academy at Goulburn searched the surrounding undergrowth for clues but none was forthcoming.

Even more embarrassing for the investigating team in retrospect, was that they initially played down the likelihood of finding any more bodies in the forest and dismissed speculation that a serial killer might be on the loose. Although they did not rule out a link with the disappearance of the five other backpackers.

Whether all these were messages devised for public consumption and part of police tactics remained unclear. What was certain was that the NSW police force needed a lucky break. Somebody out there had some information and maybe a little financial inducement might coax it out of them.

On November 11, 1992, then NSW Police Minister Terry Griffiths posted a $100,000 reward for information about the killing of Joanne Walters and Caroline Clarke. It was an unusual move because it is normally

Government practice to wait until all avenues of police enquiry are exhausted before offering a reward.

'Police are still actively pursuing a number of lines of enquiry but they are of the opinion that posting a reward would assist,' Mr Griffiths explained.

'Certainly this crime is still fresh in the minds of the public and its brutal nature was also a factor in prompting police to ask for a reward,' he added

In addition the NSW Governor would extend a free pardon to any accomplice who did not commit the crime but supplied the information.

The Minister said detectives were particularly keen to hear from associates of the killer or killers. 'To this end I stress the possibility of a pardon for information that leads to an arrest and conviction,' he added.

It was only the fourth time in 12 years that such a large sum had been offered for information on a crime.

Chief Superintendent Peter Wick of the Major Crime Squad pointed out that the ferocity of the savage killings must threaten the safety of anyone harbouring the murderer or a co-offender.

'They could be in a lot of danger too and would be well-advised to come forward,' he warned.

If nothing else the reward succeeded in keeping the case before the public who were continuing to overwhelm the police with information. The media also kept the subject going with overseas press reports in no doubt that a maniac was at large.

The London *Sun*, Britain's highest circulation daily tabloid newspaper, headlined the story, 'Beast of the Bush' and went on to claim that the killer had murdered as many as 20 people over two decades. Such uncompromising assertions did not find favour in Australia where the British coverage was seen as tabloid sensationalism.

Other UK newspapers declared: 'Sadists Execute Hitchhike Girls', 'Cold Blooded Murder of Girl Adventurers', and 'Crocodile Dundee Adventure Girls Found Dead in Wood.'

The allusion to Australia's most successful movie hero did not bode well for the country's tourism industry. For a nation that relied so heavily on the on the likes of laconic Paul Hogan to attract its overseas visitors, any link between violent death and Australia's seductive and carefully-crafted outback image was not welcome. In fact it was an advertising agency's nightmare.

While the extensive local and international media coverage succeeded in keeping up pressure on the police, after a while editors lost interest in the backpacker murders. There was the occasional development which made a few paragraphs in the newspapers including the suggestion that a rogue lorry driver might be responsible for the killings. Detectives in Victoria revealed that police in five Australian states had discussed the possibility of a highway serial killer on the prowl.

But by May 1993, just over a year after the two British girls had disappeared from Kings Cross, police conceded they had made no significant headway in their investigations.

Their only strong lead went back to the sighting at the Boxvale Walking Trail near Mittagong on April 26 of the previous year.

'Two women we now believe were Caroline and Joanne were seen preparing a meal with a man who drove a light-coloured, early model Volkswagen Kombi van,' recalled Bob Godden.

'We have yet to locate this man, despite receiving thousands of calls from people all over Australia with information about Kombi vans and investigating hundreds of reported sightings,' he admitted.

His comments suggested they had made little headway in the 11 months that had elapsed since the search for the two girls was launched in earnest. And this despite one of the most widespread and comprehensive investigations the NSW Police Force had mounted.

Godden told how his team had interviewed more than 500 people about the disappearance and deaths of the backpackers and followed up thousands of other enquiries and calls from the public.

'Our investigations have covered literally millions of square kilometres both here in Australia and overseas. Detectives have travelled extensively throughout New South Wales and made enquiries in areas such as Batlow, Wagga Wagga, Narrandera, Wentworth, Nowra and the Southern Highlands. NSW Police have also travelled to Victoria, Queensland and South Australia as part of their investigations,' he made clear.

They had also liaised closely with senior detectives from the Northumbria Police in the United Kingdom, and received enormous assistance from the authorities in Greece, Italy and The Netherlands.

'I can assure the community that dozens of experienced detectives have poured thousands of hours into this murder investigation and we remain confident of achieving a breakthrough,' he concluded.

But the longer their enquiries continued without success, the more they were forced to consider they might be going down the wrong road. Could the Boxvale sighting be inaccurate? Was the VW Kombi with a Smiley face spare wheel a red herring? More fundamentally was it time for a fresh assessment of the evidence and some lateral thinking?

It was to be another five months before the next major development in the backbacker murders. And it had nothing to do with police detective work.

11.

THE FOREST GIVES UP ITS DEAD

It was a grim discovery and one that clearly shocked bushwalker Bruce Pryor. He knew the Belanglo State Forest well and had spent many happy hours wandering through the trees alone with his thoughts. Even after the bodies of Joanne Walters and Caroline Clarke were found he was not deterred from his regular visits, walking and collecting firewood on his way. For Mr Pryor thought he might find further evidence from the backpacker murders as he strolled through the bush, evidence that could help police with their enquiries.

At 1.30 p.m. on October 5, 1993, he stumbled across something far more grisly than he could have imagined—a finger bone and a human skull. He compared the finger to his own before putting it back. He picked up the skull and carried it back to his waiting vehicle and drove back.

The first person he met was orienteer John Springett who immediately sensed something was wrong. As Mr Pryor drew to a halt, the orienteer asked if had found something.

The answer was chillingly to the point. He said he had a skull wrapped up in a blanket in his car.

Mr Pryor drove on to a ranger station, where he alerted the police by phone. Officers arrived soon afterwards and the bushwalker took them to the spot where the remains were found. It was a rugged and densely covered slope about 100 metres from a fire trail. More significantly it was only about a kilometre north east of the bush gravesites of the two British girls.

Police scoured the surrounding area and at 4 p.m. discovered a second body, the skeletal remains of a man. It was about 50 metres away from the first body and hidden under leaves and bushes.

A piece of cloth thought to have been from a floppy, round-rimmed hat, and a pair of shoes were also recovered from the scene. When Detective Sergeant Steve McLennan who had played a key role in the backpacker murder inquiry heard about two more bodies being found, he admitted he felt 'quite sick in the stomach'.

Detective Inspector Keith Smith of the South West Region Major Crime Squad said the two skeletons, which had been found in 'graves', would now be investigated jointly with the two other backpacker murders.

'It will be a fresh investigation. The backpackers will be looked at in conjunction with this. We will be putting all of our resources into it,' he assured newsmen.

Nobody could be certain who the bodies were but as the bones were taken to the city morgue at Glebe for post-mortem examination all the signs pointed to the two young Australians, Deborah Everist and James Gibson.

Police told Debbie's brother Tim to expect the worst. A hat and jewellery found near the remains suggested the property almost certainly belonged to the two Victorians. After nearly four years of waiting for news the Everists and the Gibsons were now faced with the grim reality that James and Deborah were dead.

'I always hoped I would see her walking down the driveway one day,' admitted Tim. 'You always hold out hope. Until you know something you always hold out hope.'

James's brother Chris said he could not understand why anybody would commit such a senseless act on someone who 'loved life so much'.

'I'm not angry just sad that there could be such a person around,' he told reporters.

Curiously the latest discovery had also coincided with a public meeting which was being held the same week at the Bowral Memorial Hall. The parents of the two British victims wanted to acknowledge the town's support and help one year after their own daughters' bodies were found. They did not know then that the date set for the gathering—just two days after the two Victorians were found—would be so timely. Was random chance that made the public meeting so relevant?

With the death toll now put at four the murder inquiry began to develop at a pace. The police were under mounting pressure for results and a new unit was formed headed by Superintendent Clive Small. It was called Task Force Air.

Amid growing agitation among the local community that a serial killer might be living among them, the people of Bowral wanted action. The memorial hall meeting was often heated as residents demanded progress in catching the killer or killers. Superintendent Small admitted that it had been 'an unfortunate set of circumstances...that we have had this recent occurrence.'

In the eyes of the locals it was more than unfortunate, it was a positive disgrace that four young people had been murdered practically on their doorstep and no one had been apprehended.

Small knew that unless this case was cracked, the state government, his own superiors and the public at large would be on his back. He needed the best team of detectives available and the finest facilities, to follow up leads and cross reference information. It might be a long haul, but if anybody was going to solve this crime it was going to be him.

Small already had an impressive record with the NSW Police Force based on 30 years of dedicated service. His investigative skills had been put to the test on many occasions and on several high profile cases. In 1992 he received a Commissioner's Commendation for his service within Task Force Omega, which investigated the circumstances surrounding the shooting of police officer Michael Drury and uncovered corruption within the force.

He was frequently praised for his organisational talents covering security for royal tours, a papal visit and Australia's bicentennial celebrations. Small also played a key role in dealing with the Bathurst Gaol riot in 1978. Three years later in 1981 he was awarded the National Police Medal for his work.

In 1993 Clive Small was recognised for his professional and command skills during a siege at the CES officers in Liverpool, where 23 people were released safely.

But his greatest triumph until then was his handling of the investigation into the so-called Harry Blackburn affair, which centred around the wrongful arrest and charging of a former officer. Small's inquiry cleared the ex-scientific officer of rape and was highly critical of the way police had dealt with the case. A subsequent Royal Commission also praised Small for his work.

The head of Task Force Air assembled an experienced group of men whom he knew he could trust. He brought in several officers who had successfully investigated Sydney's notorious North Shore 'granny killings', where six elderly women were murdered. The man they caught, John Glover, is now serving a life sentence.

The newly-formed Task Force had hardly begun to get down to business before there was another gruesome find. On November 1, 1993, less than a month after the two Australians were discovered, a fifth body was found following a massive search of the Belanglo State Forest.

Police had been combing Belanglo for over three weeks. By now up to a hundred men had been drafted in to cover every inch of the forest floor, often on their hands and knees. The most thorough of operations was ordered because Small was anxious to ensure that, quite literally, no stone should be left unturned. Cadaver-sniffing dogs were even used at one stage.

Officers made their way through the undergrowth in lines, examining every patch of grass and vegetation in the surrounding area with meticulous attention.

Eventually their diligence paid off. Five kilometres from Executioner's Drop, where Joanne Walters and Caroline Clarke were found, the skeletal remains of Simone Schmidl were discovered hidden in scrub at the junction of the Miner's Despair and Tree Cave fire trails. Her body was lying face down under a small canopy of brushwood and logs about 40 meters into the scrub on a level slope overlooking a gully.

Material which had turned brown from exposure to the elements over the previous few years resembled the yellow singlet top and green shorts which Simone had been wearing at the time of her disappearance. Apart from her clothes, a purple headband around the skull and some small items of jewellery, no other personal property was found at the scene. It was clear that robbery was not a motive for the murder.

Though the cause of death was yet to be established, marks found close to the ribs and vertebrae suggested she had been repeatedly stabbed.

The massive search of the forest which was instigated by Superintendent Small was beginning to pay off. Now it had to be extended even further. So far they had covered an area about 18 kilometres long.

Few knew how close the police came to calling off the search prior to the discovery of Simone Schmidl's skeleton, but there is little doubt that it could not have continued for much longer.

The fact it was the fifth body—as unpleasant as the discovery had been— imbued the police with a new sense of purpose. It was now odds-on that the other two German backpackers were in the same area and the search team was determined to find them.

It was what became known as Sergeant Arthur Seewald's 'magic hoe' that produced the final breakthrough in the search. On Thursday morning, November 4, he was raking backwards and forwards through some bracken about 1 kilometre east of the spot where Simone's remains were discovered a few days earlier when he stumbled across a sixth body. A short time later at 11.30 a.m. the advancing line of officers found a sandal. Further investigation of the surrounding bracken produced a seventh body. Gabor Kurt Neugebauer and Anja Susanne Habschied were now no longer missing persons. Like the other five backpackers who had disappeared over the previous four years they had been brutally murdered.

To make the find even more macabre Anja had been decapitated. Her headless body lay alongside a fallen tree and a pile of sticks and other debris nearby. Like the other bodies, it was lying on its stomach. The deceased was wearing no clothes apart from a halter neck top. A couple of coloured bands were on her wrist.

About 55 metres to the south west of Miss Habschied's skeleton, her boyfriend Gabor Neugebauer's badly decomposed remains were hidden alongside another fallen tree and under a pile of sticks. Again the skeleton was on its stomach with the right side of the skull resting on the ground. A piece of fabric had apparently been tied around the face, indicating a gag had been used. Small holes could be seen in the base of the skull and behind the left ear consistent with bullet entry points.

A wider search of the immediate area produced a clear plastic bag containing an airline ticket and a woman's gold wristwatch. The hands, which had stopped, pointed to 5.35.

From a professional viewpoint, the police were clearly elated by the latest discoveries. Though obviously saddened by the violent nature of the deaths, the full horror of the backbacker murders was now clear and they were assembling a massive quantity of evidence which would hopefully lead them to the serial killer responsible for the crime.

What intrigued detectives and particularly the media was the almost ritualistic style of the killings. Most of the victims had been found lying face down with their hands behind their back in what appeared to be a coffin-like canopy alongside a fallen tree trunk. Whether this was simply to hide the remains in the hope they would never be found or part of some macabre ritual was uncertain.

Campfires ringed by stones were also discovered near each murder site, indicating the killer had either spent some time there or that other bushwalkers had camped in the vicinity.

There was also something odd about the location of each murder spot, which when viewed as a whole, suggested some kind of geographical pattern around the perimeter of the forest. Theories came fast and furious. One suggested that the positioning of the bodies represented a satanic sign. Another that as four of the victims disappeared soon after Christmas, perhaps it was a bizarre gift to the Belanglo Christmas pines. Hundreds of policemen had been ferried over the previous six weeks to comb the search area which spanned 72 square kilometers. At last they could rest. Task Force Air was confident that all the bodies had been found. Now they could get on with the job of finding whoever was responsible.

As search commander Inspector Fred Brame put it during a special service to mark the end of the operation: 'We had a number of objectives put to us—one of which was to gather evidence for the investigative squad, so hopefully the people responsible for this will be arrested.

'And hopefully we have removed the lingering despair of the parents of those seven young people found in this forest,' he added.

'This is one of the largest searches that has been carried out in this country—and you have demonstrated your professionalism and dedication throughout,' he told his men.

It was Police Chaplain Father Barry Dwyer who captured the mood of the occasion as he led the searchers in prayer for the murdered backpackers.

'We are reminded of the fragility of life as we remember those seven young people whose life was brief and who died in such tragic circumstances,' he concluded.

From now on the manhunt would be intense as detectives closed in on the killer. It would be another six months before the dramatic climax to Task Force Air's investigation.

12.
THE BREAKTHROUGH

There was now no doubt that a serial killer was at large in Australia. The problem facing the officers of Task Force Air was how to catch a man whose latest crime was at least 18 months old. His victims' bodies were so badly decomposed that it would be almost impossible to link the remains with any incriminating evidence left behind by the murderer.

Admittedly some strands of hair had been found in Joanne Walter's right hand, indicating she had fought her attacker in a last desperate bid to save her life, but it would require the latest in DNA testing techniques to conclusively match them with others. And without so much as a likely suspect at this stage it was impossible to compare the hairs with those of her killer.

What's more there was no proof that only one person was involved in the brutal murders. The facts of the case suggested that to overpower three couples, two of whom included strong males, would have required more than one man.

Even the Director of the Australian Institute of Criminology, Mr Duncan Chappell, conceded that there could be two attackers. After all how does a single killer lure two people into a deserted forest and murder both of them?

If they put up a struggle, as seems certain, how did a lone operator overcome each of them at the same time? Or did a second offender guard one while the accomplice dealt with the other?

Given that most serial murderers do not kill across genders and rarely kill more than one person at a time, the backpacker deaths were even harder to fathom, though there was no shortage of theories.

With the help of psychiatrists and criminologists, investigating officers built-up a detailed picture of the man they were after. Firstly he was almost certainly the epitome of Mr Average, a man who ostensibly led a very ordinary life with few, if any, distinguishing characteristics.

He would be fit, intelligent and outwardly sociable. He could be your next door neighbour or the bloke you drank with down at the pub. His age was more of a mystery. Police estimates put him somewhere between late twenties and middle-aged, though the methodical and selective way he handled his victims suggested he was more likely to be in his forties.

His normal appearance would be reinforced by the likelihood that he was probably married or in a stable relationship. And although the horrific and ritualistic style of the killings indicated an unbalanced mind, he was unlikely to be suffering from a mental illness as such. As one forensic psychologist put it: 'He's bad rather than mad.'

But behind the mask of Mr Average lurked a grotesque sexual desire which could only be sated by the control and ultimately the death of his victims. Although he might not have had intercourse with them he got his kicks by expressing his bizarre deviations through sadistic aggression, mutilation and finally execution.

This is not an altogether uncommon phenomenon among serial killers. Even the original Jack the Ripper did not have sex with his victims.

There was also another, even more unpalatable theory, which was being canvassed. Could it be that the backpacker killer forced some of his victims to inflict wounds on their partner? It was such a sickening possibility that it was almost unthinkable. But given the fact that in the case of the three couples, one body was always more mutilated than the other, it had to be seriously considered.

As well as formulating countless theories about the physical and mental make-up of the man or men they were after, Task Force Air also had to contend with a continuing avalanche of information from the public. The unit was staffed by 26 full-time detectives, who had been drawn from the four major crime squads around Sydney. In addition nine analysts seconded from the State Intelligence Group assessed all the available data and tried to establish links with other homicides. Even so the Task Force was seriously undermanned. This was almost certainly one of the reasons why they failed to respond immediately to a lead from the man who was to become their key witness.

The young British tourist who was attacked on the Hume Highway in January 1990 after being given a lift by a man named 'Bill', had been following newspaper reports of the backpacker murders with interest from his home in England. Paul Onions wondered whether the same person was responsible. He was eventually prompted to go to the police about his own experience after the discovery of more bodies in the Belanglo State Forest.

First he approached British police who referred him to Australia House in London's Strand. Staff there gave him the telephone number of Task Force Air, which he rang on November 13, 1993. An officer took his name and number but astonishingly nobody returned his call for nearly five months.

'I was surprised at the lack of interest,' he admitted afterwards

Meanwhile, the investigation, which was turning into the biggest criminal investigation in Australian history, was costing the state government millions. Although there were plenty of leads there was still no incontrovertible proof as to the identity of the sadistic killer responsible for the backpacker murders.

Days turned into weeks as the team assembled by Clive Small spent many long hours chasing false leads and following up lines of enquiry presented by the mountain of evidence. They knew the killer used a Ruger .22 calibre rifle to shoot two of his victims and that a defect in the bolt mechanism left unique markings on the cartridge when fired. Though not a common brand of weapon in Australia, police had to establish the whereabouts of every Ruger in the country and endeavour to question the owner. It was a time-consuming exercise and typical of the meticulous attention to detail which had become synonymous with the investigation.

As fast as detectives completed one line of inquiry they were on to the next, transferring all the information they were acquiring on to a massive database. It would have been impossible to check out all the tips had it not been for a sophisticated computer system called Netmap, which enabled detectives to establish if a link existed between thousands of seemingly unconnected names, addresses, times and vehicle sightings.

Amid such intense activity it was easy to forget the emotional aspect of the investigation as police kept the families of the seven victims up to date with developments. Clive Small and his team took every opportunity to remain in contact with the parents who had suffered so much heartbreak.

At a funeral service for Simone Schmidl on December 2, 1993, Superintendent Small and his chief investigator Bob Godden were among the mourners at Sydney's Northern Suburbs Crematorium. Their attendance was not out of professional duty, though that clearly played a role, but reflected a much more personal commitment to those whose lives had been so tragically cut short or torn apart.

They were still hard-nosed coppers but they could not ignore the sadness that had engulfed seven families from Britain, Germany and Australia.

As they sat through the 30 minute Catholic service, Father Wolfgang Sevrin, serving priest to Sydney's German community, reminded the congregation that they were not only gathered in memory of Simone, but for the others who died.

It was a view echoed by Clive Small.

'Today is a day for the families of the victims, for the community and for the police to remember what happened at Belanglo,' he said.

'Let's hope this sort of thing never happens again.'

It was a hope shared by all Australians, but as detectives appeared to be making little or no headway in their search for a suspect, there remained a very real fear among the community that the serial killer could strike again.

The police were also under a degree of political pressure to produce results. The Belanglo Forest where the bodies of all seven hitchhikers were dumped happened to be in the Southern Highlands' constituency of the then New South Wales Liberal Premier John Fahey, whose electorate was also keen to solve the crime.

Mr Fahey's family home was in Bowral, the closest major town to the murder scene, and residents were understandably concerned that there might be a serial killer in their midst.

In his determination to find the killer the Premier had posted a record $500,000 reward for information leading to a conviction. On a visit to the forest he promised: 'All resources necessary will be put into the search and all efforts will be made to bring about a solution to these horrific crimes.'

What Mr Fahey did not know then was that a former legal colleague would later act on behalf of Ivan Milat.

Coincidentally the Premier, a solicitor before he entered politics, had once worked for Mr John Marsden, who had run a successful legal practice in the Camden and Campbelltown areas for over two decades.

Mr Marsden employed him back in the 1970s and the men remained on good terms. When Mr Marsden was falsely accused of being a paedophile in the NSW Parliament in 1994, Mr Fahey stood by him and vigorously defended him.

Twenty years earlier he had appeared for the defence in a case brought by two women against Milat whom they alleged had raped one of them near Goulburn after he gave them a lift on the Hume Highway. It took three years for Milat to come to court because he skipped bail and fled to New Zealand. It was not until he returned to Australia in 1974 that he was re-arrested and stood trial in the New South Wales Supreme Court.

Milat was eventually acquitted after the defence successfully argued that the woman had been a willing partner.

Under the terms of client privilege, Mr Marsden was bound to keep any information relating to that case confidential and could not divulge his previous client's antecedence or any suspicions he might have to Task Force Air. Not that there was any suggestion Mr Marsden had even considered the possibility of a link between his client of two decades earlier and the backpacker murders.

There was less excuse for the police, however. It was surprising that investigating officers themselves appeared not to have taken a fresh look at cases involving sexual assault along the Hume Highway sooner than they did. It was a senior constable who eventually put two and two together and who uncovered the case which was to focus attention on Milat.

Paul Gordon had been checking out the antecedence of several members of the Milat family and Ivan's name had already come up. On November 9, 1993 a woman rang police on behalf of her boyfriend to draw their attention to Ivan's love of firearms.

On February 23, 1994 Gordon drove to the criminal records office at Parramatta with a colleague to establish Ivan's previous form.

It was during that visit when he saw the exact circumstances of the rape case and the unmistakeable parallels with the backpacker murders, that he became convinced that Ivan Milat was Task Force Air's man.

'It was a mistake on my part that I hadn't investigated Ivan earlier,' he admitted later. And he was determined to make up for lost time.

Gordon's decision to check old police files for previous reports of crimes involving hitchhikers who took lifts from the Liverpool area was beginning to pay-off. The case of *Regina v. Ivan Robert Marko Milat* in the NSW Supreme Court on December 12, 1974 was, he believed, the key to the mystery.

Task Force Air continued to pursue many different lines of enquiry. By early 1994 police had amassed so much information that they were able to compile an 'atlas' of homes and suburbs connected with their investigations. Every minor and seemingly insignificant detail associated with the serial killer was cross-referenced with social and geographic data. Rifle registration details could be linked to the most likely ammunition source in any one of a number of given areas.

The police also harnessed satellite technology to provide images of the Belanglo area at certain times of year and during particular weather conditions, in an effort to establish whether a four wheel drive vehicle would have been essential to negotiate the dirt roads when the crimes were committed.

Detectives were increasingly optimistic about the progress of their enquiries. They even co-operated in the production of a special ABC *Four Corners* television report about the investigation, though Clive Small cautioned against an imminent breakthrough.

'The net really is Australia,' he explained, pointing out the enormity of the job in hand.

'We have something like 17 million people—we start from there and work in,' he added.

While there was no hard evidence against Milat, Task Force Air still regarded him as what is euphemistically termed 'a person of interest.' The Observation Squad kept a close watch on the suspect from early March until April, 1993. Frustratingly his movements gave no hint of criminal activity and the 'dogs,' as the squad was known, were called off. At least for the time being.

Paul Gordon went back to the files and along with other officers, painstakingly combed through the mountain of information provided by the public in calls to the Task Force Air hotline.

On April 13, 1994 he stumbled across the lead that had been overlooked the previous November. It was Paul Onions' call alerting the police to his own brush with death in January 1990.

He rang the detective in charge of the case who said he recalled the incident but the file was in the garage. It was never found.

Bowral police faxed Gordon the only remaining information on the incident, a copy of the occurrence pad entry, a few pages of hand-written notes made out by WPC Jennifer Nicholson when an anxious Paul Onions reported his narrow escape.

'All the things we knew about Ivan, his description, his manners, his nicknames, were all consistent with the attacker of Mr Onions,' Gordon said.

In retrospect it is tempting to criticise shortcomings in the police investigation, failures which had they not occurred, might have led to the early apprehension of Ivan Milat and possibly saved lives.

If Paul Onions' report to Bowral Police Station on January 25, 1990, had been properly followed-up five young hitchhikers might still be alive today. The British tourist who was attacked by Milat gave a detailed description of the man who attempted to murder him and the vehicle he was driving. After all 'Bill' had told him his family came from Yugoslavia, he had been married once and he worked for the Roads and Traffic Authority. But no-one was caught and Milat went on to murder three Germans and two Britons.

After cross-referencing Paul Onions' tip with details of the attack, Paul Gordon returned his call. It was April 13, 1994, five months after the backpacker originally took the trouble to phone. It did not take long before Task Force Air realised that the young Englishman could provide the vital breakthrough they had been hoping for.

Within a few days they had booked him on a plane to Australia to view a 'rogues gallery' of likely suspects. On May 4 he was shown a video featuring 13 different men.

He was asked if he recognised any of the people on the tape as the person who had attacked him in 1990. After a few minutes Onions identified one man. 'Bill' was number four. But his name wasn't Bill. It was Ivan Robert Marko Milat.

Encouraged by the latest findings and in no mood to lose the momentum, Task Force Air was eager to strike.

The problem was it had no hard evidence that Milat was its man, let alone a serial killer. If it arrested him now, it could only charge him with the attempted murder of Paul Onions. It needed much more proof before it could link him conclusively to the backpacker killings.

Further enquiries had to be made including a visit on May 21 to one of Milat's brothers, Alex, who was living at West Woombye in Queensland.

It was at his home that police were to find a backpack belonging to Simone Schmidl but this was not the original purpose of the call.

In a curious twist to the backpacker case Alex Milat had earlier reported seeing two young women—possibly the two British victims, Caroline and Joanne—being abducted in a car near the Belango State Forest around the time of their disappearance in April 1992.

Alex's account was remarkable for its detail. In a statement to police in October, 1993 he recalled how he had been driving home from the Bowral Pistol Club with a mate when he saw two cars turn in front of him, into the Belango State Forest.

'I looked down into the cabin of the Falcon and the first thing I saw were the driver's hands,' he said.

'On the fingers of his left hand I noticed shadows which suggested some form of tattoo on his fingers. The driver appeared to be Caucasian, of thin build, 100 kilograms in weight, in his mid-twenties with mutton chop-style side leavers,' he went on.

'In the rear passenger seat I saw a female person in her twenties, of fair complexion. I saw what appeared to me to be a gag of honey coloured material which was wrapped around her head and across her mouth.'

Extraordinarily, Alex was able to provide even more detail about the appearance of other people in the car.

'As my vehicle drew alongside the dual cab I immediately focussed on the female person in the rear seat. She looked at me with her eyes wide open as if she was frightened. I saw that the male passenger in the rear seat was clean shaven and appeared to be well dressed. I noticed his hands were not rough, as if he was an office worker as opposed to a labourer and his hands were clean.'

Perhaps Alex had a photographic memory, but for a man who had only seen the passing car for a couple of seconds he was able to offer an incredible amount of detail.

Police also wondered why he had not passed the information on at the time, given the highly suspicious scene he had encountered.

Now Detective Senior Sergeant Bob Benson who was in charge of intelligence during the backpacker murder inquiry, wanted him to repeat his story.

The sceptical officer was later to claim that the account was 'far fetched' and 'didn't jell.'

'He is either not telling the truth or he is confused about things,' he added.

And what of the other man in the car? The vehicle was driven by a Mr William Ayres who later changed his version of events.

However, Alex Milat always maintained that his sighting was genuine. He even underwent hypnosis to substantiate his story. He also believed that because of his initial report police turned their attention to the Milat family and started investigating their activities.

'I know you might think that because he's my brother I would defend him, but I'll tell you right now—if he was guilty I'd shoot the bastard myself,' he said.

But Alex was convinced his brother was innocent and no amount of evidence to the contrary could persuade him otherwise. His was not a lone voice either. Many of those who came into contact with Ivan Milat over the years were equally certain he was not responsible for the backpacker murders. Those who knew him well, including close women friends, insisted he was incapable of such brutality.

Task Force Air clearly thought otherwise. It is, after all, the hallmark of the serial killer to cloak his Jeckyll and Hyde character in secrecy; to reveal not so much as a chink of latent evil to his closest associates.

So when Clive Small and his colleagues evaluated the character of the man they suspected of perpetrating such a catalogue of terror they were not in the least bit surprised to hear of his benign facade.

This was their man and it was time to strike. Four and a half years after the backpacker serial killer had savagely attacked his first victims and 20 months after the discovery of the initial bodies had sparked the biggest murder hunt in Australia's criminal history, Ivan Robert Marko Milat was under arrest.

The date was May 22, 1994, but it was to be another five months before the prosecution was to reveal the bloody extent of his monstrous double life and 19 months before he was to stand trial.

The full horror of the backpacker murders was only just emerging.

13.
MILAT UNMASKED

Campbelltown is 51 kilometres (31 miles) south west of Sydney with a population of more than 152,000. Generally it was and still is a working class area whose residents aspire to fulfil the Australian dream of owning a house with a quarter acre block. In reality the soaring cost of property has forced many of them into smaller homes with tiny gardens. In today's vernacular they'd be described as 'mortgage-belt battlers'. Even in the early nineties when its population was nearly 140,000, property values were rising but still relatively cheap compared to those suburbs closer to Sydney.

Then as now it had a high migrant population. In 1990 about 26 per cent were not Australian born.

More than 13 per cent were unemployed, significantly higher than the national average. Household incomes were low and crime was rife.

Today it is the central business district of south western Sydney and a major commercial centre. There are modern buildings in the main thoroughfare, a shopping arcade, cinemas and parks.

At the beginning of the nineties it also boasted a new courthouse, which was built to handle an ever-increasing workload.

Campbelltown often featured in the crimes reported in the nightly news broadcast by Sydney's three commercial television stations, but even the locals were stunned by the level of media attention which enveloped them on May 23, 1994.

Suddenly the eyes of the world were focussed on their community and in particular the adjoining suburb of Eagle Vale, where Ivan Milat and his sister Shirley had made their home. This morning the man who had lived in their midst for the previous 15 months was the star attraction in court number six. It seemed every journalist for miles wanted to catch a glimpse of the 'beast of the bush' and seats in the tiny press gallery were at a premium.

Security was tight. Reporters were frisked as they passed through a metal detector at the entrance to the court room.

Once inside they had to wait until late morning before magistrate Kevin Flack turned to the case of Ivan Milat.

A police prosecution against a motorist accused of not wearing a seat belt took prominence over what was to become one of the most sensational cases of the century. For well over an hour the world's press looked on bemused as the circumstances of the alleged misdemeanour were considered.

When Milat entered the dock he could have been just another traffic offender appearing before the bench, such was his untroubled countenance.

He was casually dressed and wore a blue and green chequered, open neck shirt and jeans. He sported a Zapata-style moustache and his ruffled hair was receding slightly. But there was no indication of a man under pressure.

Two police officers positioned either side of him were the only reminders that the man in custody was in serious trouble.

Milat sat silently in the dock throughout the 10 minute hearing, his pale blue, squinty eyes occasionally darting around the court room.

Police prosecutor Sergeant Eddie Billett outlined an alleged robbery and attack on a witness referred to as 'A' in 1990.

He recounted the British tourist's terrifying ordeal in graphic detail, revealing for the first time how the young hitchhiker had zig-zagged across the Hume Highway to escape his assailant's line of fire.

Mr Billett told how after the Englishman had accepted a lift along the main Sydney to Melbourne highway, the driver had stopped his vehicle near the Belanglo State Forest.

When the Briton returned to the vehicle after getting out to stretch his legs, the motorist pointed a black revolver at him and warned: 'This is a robbery!'

Witness A ran for his life with the armed man shouting after him: 'Stop or I'll shoot.'

A single shot rang out as the backpacker weaved across the highway in a desperate bid to save his life. Court staff, press and the few members of the public who had managed to secure a seat, listened as the police prosecutor reached the dramatic climax to the hitchhiker's brush with death.

Witness A, said Mr Billett, luckily managed to stop a passing woman motorist who drove him to Bowral Police Station while his armed attacker made off in the opposite direction.

The defendant, he went on to explain, had been identified as the man who gave the British backpacker a lift. It was further alleged he stole a British passport, an airline ticket, an Olympus camera, a gold chain and other personal belongings from the man worth $500.

Milat allegedly told his passenger at the time that his name was 'Bill' and that he 'worked for the roads at Liverpool.' He was divorced and was of Yugoslav background.

'This information matches the personal particulars of the defendant and can be proven,' Sergeant Billett added.

'The victim described a vehicle used by the offender. At the time the offence was committed this defendant owned an identical vehicle in the name of William Milat. At the time of his apprehension the defendant denied that he used the name of Bill, owned a motor vehicle at the time of the offence, denied owning firearms. But it can be proven that all these denials are false,' the police prosecutor told the court.

Milat was unmoved by the allegations made against him and their implications. Given the serious nature of the charges it seemed pointless to apply for bail, but Milat's lawyer, John Marsden, went through the motions anyway.

He told the court how his client had held down a job for the past 20 years, how he had lived with his ex-wife until 1987 and with his mother for the following six years. For the next 15 months he had shared a house with his sister in Eagle Vale.

This was a man who had enjoyed stability of work and residence for at least two decades but, he admitted, two words made the case against his client an emotive issue—'backpacker' and 'Belanglo.'

Mr Marsden had also referred in open court to a fact which had not been hitherto made public. 'It's been 25 years since this person was last charged with an offence,' he revealed.'

Milat had failed to appear in court in 1971 to answer the charges against him because he was 'a frightened young man,' his defence lawyer claimed.

And anyway he was eventually acquitted of the alleged offences, Mr Marsden pointed out.

As a means to win bail for his client, it was a fruitless effort and Milat was remanded in custody until May 31.

Outside the court members of the public screamed insults at the accused as he was driven away in an armoured police van.

'You maggot—they'll kill you in gaol,' screamed one woman.

A muffled voice from inside the vehicle replied, 'Pump it up your arse madam. I didn't do it. They've got the wrong person.'

As the police paddy wagon made its way out of Campbelltown back to the remand wing at Sydney's Long Bay Gaol, pedestrians turned their heads as shouting continued to be heard from inside the van.

The vehicle stopped for a minute at a set of red traffic lights as the prisoner protested his innocence at the top of his voice.

'I didn't fucking do it,' he roared. 'It was someone else.'

But nothing could stop the legal process grinding inexorably forward as justice took its course. Nothing could prevent the police from advancing to stage two of the prosecution—the charging of Ivan Milat with the backpacker murders.

In the 24 hours since his arrest they had accumulated so much evidence from 22 Cinnabar Street and other homes occupied by members of the Milat family, that they had more than enough proof to substantiate the allegations.

No one was therefore surprised when, at his second court appearance on May 31, Milat was accused of killing the seven young hitchhikers and the attempted murder of Witness A.

Once again he stood expressionless in the dock though he was more smartly dressed on this occasion. The casual clothes had been replaced by a light blue, pinstriped business shirt, freshly-pressed, dark blue trousers with a black belt and shoes. The drooping moustache had also gone. His hair was neat and he was clean shaven. This time, in recognition of the more serious nature of the charges against him, Milat was flanked by no fewer than five guards.

Again demand for seating was intense. Reporters jostled for a position in the lengthy queue that had grown outside the entrance to court number six.

Inside nine members of Task Force Air , some wearing a specially-made tie with a clenched fist and a thumb, took their seats. The police group included Clive Small and his right hand man Bob Godden. None of them wanted to miss this, their hour of glory.

The official Crown Prosecutor Ian Lloyd QC was also making his debut in the case. An amiable man in his early forties, he appeared without his usual wig and gown as he detailed the charges against Milat.

It took nearly 30 minutes to summarise the allegations which even in their abbreviated form, made shocking listening.

He revealed how Joanne Walters had been sexually assaulted before being repeatedly stabbed in the front and back upper body area. A gag had been placed around her mouth and other pieces of cloth covered her face.

Her blindfolded friend Caroline Clarke may also have been sexually assaulted before being knifed and shot no fewer than ten times in the head.

Other backpacker victims, some of whom had also been gagged to stop them screaming, met similar fates.

James Gibson had suffered multiple stab wounds to the upper front and back part of the body.

Only one stab wound could be detected on the remains of his girlfriend Deborah Everist, although several 'slicing-type' injuries and a fracture were located on the skull. Her jaw had also been broken. Knotted pantyhose discovered at the murder scene suggested at least one of them had been bound, he said.

Simone Schmidl had suffered multiple stab wounds to the back.

Fellow German tourist Gabor Neugebauer had been gagged, strangled and shot six times in the back of the head.

His girlfriend Anja Habschied had suffered a single blow with a sharp instrument which decapitated her. The emotion detectable in his voice, Mr Lloyd revealed that her head was still missing.

The Crown Prosecutor told the court that parts of a Ruger rifle, similar to a type used to shoot Caroline Clarke, were found in a wall cavity in Milat's home. Trigger and bolt assemblies were also discovered and a home-made silencer discovered in the garage.

Even more significantly, spent ammunition located near the victims' graves allegedly matched a quantity found in the defendant's bungalow.

There was a momentary silence as the impact of the prosecution's case was absorbed. Milat, whose sister Shirley sat in the court wearing dark glasses and a scarf across her face, appeared unperturbed.

The hushed courtroom's attention now switched to John Marsden, who was not going to be intimated by the mountain of police evidence and the automatic assumption that his client was guilty.

As a civil libertarian and a member of the Anti-Discrimination Board he felt a commitment to the underdog and believed in justice for all. And he feared that Milat, who was still an innocent man in the eyes of the law, was unlikely to get a fair trial.

He made his position plain both inside and outside the court, claiming the charges were based on 'circumstantial innuendo.'

Milat was innocent and deserved a fair trial, he insisted.

'I call upon the press to allow my client to be subject to a fair trial, to abide by the right of every member of our community, that is he is innocent until proven guilty, and to allow the justice system to proceed in all its normal and proper way.

'He denies the serious allegations that have been made against him in court today. I do not intend in any way to minimise the horrific nature of the allegations against him. However, in fairness to my client, who has stated quite categorically that he is not guilty of the allegations and who has not been proved guilty, the media should allow my client a fair trial,' he added.

Mr Marsden made particular reference to what he called the 'outrageous allegations' made in a Sunday newspaper.

The article, in the Sydney *Sun Herald* two days earlier, told of the breakthrough in the police investigation when Senior Constable Paul Gordon linked the backpacker murders with a 20 year-old rape case.

The story did not mention Milat by name or divulge details of the court case and those involved. But in Mr Marsden's view the article was clearly prejudicial to his client.

For the alleged rape, though it could not be publicly stated, was the same case in which John Marsden had defended Ivan Milat those 20 years earlier. Although he was subsequently acquitted, the allegations made in that previous hearing were so chillingly similar to the facts surrounding the backpacker murders that any budding Sherlock Holmes, let alone the full might of Task Force Air, should have been able to link the two.

The key player in both alleged crimes had used ropes and knives as his tools in trade. The only difference between then and now was that Ivan Milat had not graduated to murdering his victims.

The two young women whom Milat picked-up in 1971 were clearly lucky to have escaped with their lives.

'14.
MILAT'S DARK PAST

Margaret and her friend Greta had been undergoing psychiatric treatment at a clinic in the Sydney suburb of Parramatta.

On April 9, 1971 they decided to hitchhike to Melbourne. Like the backpackers who were to follow the same route some 20 years later they caught a train to Liverpool and headed for the Hume Highway.

They were walking towards the main Sydney to Melbourne road when a car drew up alongside them and the driver offered them a lift. They accepted, Margaret climbing into the rear seat and Greta getting in beside the driver.

When they reached the Goulburn area the motorist turned off into a side road and came to halt. Margaret, who was only 18, had been under medication at the time and had been taking sleeping tablets. She was dozing in the back when the motorist stopped.

He turned around to the two young women and told them he was going to make love to them, though it is unclear whether he was addressing one or both of the girls.

Greta remembered her girlfriend saying: 'Oh no you're not,' followed by a reference to her psychiatric treatment.

'I got the feeling he wanted to have sex with Greta and I was just sort of sitting back watching. He made a couple of advances to her,' Margaret explained.

As the conversation continued the driver produced knives and a couple of lengths of rope. He hadn't threatened them with violence at this stage so Margaret suggested he tie them up and leave them by the roadside.

'I was just sort of hoping to get the whole thing over, that he would have sex with one of us and drop us off somewhere and that it would be over,' she said.

'I guess he was pretty sort of sexually excited from sitting near Greta and she was rather tantalising him, I think, with the idea of sex. She was sort of saying, oh, you know, "You can't have it"—but at the same time she was being rather seductive. That was the way I saw it.'

Soon afterwards the women got out of the vehicle and the driver tied them both up with ropes. At one stage another car came along and he seemed worried, forcing them to get back inside.

But the second driver didn't appear to see them and the vehicle went away.

Margaret, whose hands were tied, was anxious to get the whole affair over and done with.

'I just said when the car went away, "If I have sex with you, will you sort of drop us somewhere and we'll let the whole thing go." Greta was making, I think, intermittent threats about the police.'

He agreed to have sex with Margaret. Meanwhile Greta was 'making a pretty big fuss.'

'She had some Valium tablets with her and she was threatening to take an overdose and to be sick all over his car, which also upset him. She'd taken an overdose the night before anyway, so she wasn't too clear either,' Margaret recalled.

The motorist agreed to drop them off at a service station after he had had sex, so Greta climbed into the back and Margaret got into the front passenger seat.

Margaret remembered removing her pants and having sex with the man for about two minutes. He had promised not to ejaculate inside her and he kept his word.

She claimed the driver had never threatened her and she was not particularly frightened by the experience. More significantly she indicated afterwards that she had been a willing partner.

Greta's recollection of their ordeal is slightly different from her girlfriend's and infinitely more dramatic. She claimed he wanted sex with both of them and she pleaded for him not to do it.

She appealed to his better instincts asking him what value he put on human life and how his mother would feel about his actions. She made it clear they were both undergoing psychiatric treatment for depression and he wasn't helping.

'We were just trying to make him...feel sympathetic for us and let us go without trying to do anything.'

The only time he seemed to worry was when Greta threatened to be sick over his car. 'He was very emotional about that,' she recalled.

At one point Greta attempted to escape but he stopped her.

'His reaction was very quick. I don't think I even got my hand on the handle. And I was wearing a leather choker around my neck and he pulled that—they were very fashionable then—and he pulled it tight as though to strangle me and then let it go. He also threatened violence at that stage.'

More ominously he produced two knives and threatened to kill them if they didn't have sex with him.

'I remember one was curved and one was in a sheath. He had it under the directory in the front on the floor,' she recalled.

He also had two lengths of pink nylon cord.

The driver told Greta he made a habit of picking up hitchhikers and was always prepared with the knives.

'When he said he wanted to have sex with us and he had these knives we said, "Oh, you're going to rape us?"'

'He replied, "You could call it that."'

Greta claimed Margaret interjected: 'Well, if we give you sex will you let us go? We won't go to the police.'

She said the man seemed agreeable to that idea and proceeded to tie them up.

Greta's recollection of what allegedly followed was frightening in the extreme.

'I know he was at the boot of his car when he turned around and said very quietly, 'You know what I am going to do. I am going to kill you. You won't scream when I cut your throats, will you?' That is the one thing that I can remember very clearly that he said,' she added.

It was at this point that Margaret agreed to have sex with him.

The man was angry and 'threatened to smack my face,' Greta said. He told her to watch out for other cars while he had sex with her girlfriend.

She could see the top half of both of their bodies. He removed his shorts first, then took down her slacks.

After he climaxed Greta said to her girlfriend's attacker, 'We have done you a favour. Now you could do me a favour. I would really like a drink or else I am going to be sick in your car.'

'He decided that he needed a can of lemonade too. He said he would keep us in the car until morning where we could find a ride on the highway quite easily. He drove us back to a cafe, a restaurant in a garage, where there were a number of people. He allowed Margaret to go in—he kept me in the back seat,' Greta went on.

'She was in for about half a minute and she came out and said, "You can't keep us in the car any longer, you can't do anything about it, we are leaving".'

'About seven people came out and surrounded the car and he had no alternative but to let me out. He drove off at high speed.'

They reported the attack to police and about an hour later he was picked up. When the young women came face to face with their attacker again later that night at a police station, he allegedly said to them: 'You didn't keep your side of the bargain.'

'I remember Margaret saying, "What sort of bargain is that? You used my body".'

The man who had given Greta and Margaret a lift that Friday night was Ivan Robert Marko Milat.

Just over three and a half years later he pleaded not guilty to the following charge: That on April 10, 1971, at Goulburn in the state of New South Wales, he did without her consent ravish and carnally know Margaret.

In layman's terms that meant rape, but Milat was none-too-keen to face the consequences. He skipped bail and fled to New Zealand, not returning to Australia until 1974 when he was re-arrested.

It was not until Thursday December 12 of that year that he appeared in the New South Wales Supreme Court for a jury to decide on his guilt or innocence.

The central issue was whether Margaret had been a willing partner in the sexual act. Judging by her testimony there was good reason to believe that the defendant thought she was.

Under cross-examination Margaret admitted that she wanted Milat to have sex with her.

'Did he in any way threaten you to have sex?' the defence asked.

'No, not really,' she replied.

Q. 'Did he in any way force you to have sex?'

A. 'No, it was my decision, more or less.'

Q. 'It was your decision?'

A. 'Yes.'

Q. 'When you asked him would he withdraw before he climaxed so he would not climax within you, he willingly agreed to that?'

A. 'Yes.'

Q. 'And there were no problems about that?'

A. 'No.'

Q. 'When you said to him, "If I have sex with you, we will drop the whole thing and let us go,"—do you remember that?'

A. 'Yes.'

Q. 'He was not forcing you to have sex? He was not forcing you to stay there until he had sex was he?'

A. 'Not really.'

Q. 'He had not said to you, "I won't let you go until you have sex with me?"'

A. 'No. Probably if I had been clear enough, if I hadn't taken the sleeping tablets, I would have been able to get out of it quite easily.'

Q. 'Would you agree with me that, in reality, now at the present stage, when you think back and think about it, you did want this man to have sex with you?'

A. 'Yes.'

It was a successful cross-examination and the defence lawyer had got the answers he wanted. The victim of the alleged rapist had admitted under oath that she wanted him to have sex with her.

The court had little option but to acquit the accused and his lawyer could chalk up a not insignificant victory against seemingly impossible odds.

No wonder Ivan Milat wanted the same man to represent him 20 years later. Perhaps John Marsden could perform another legal miracle.

For whatever reason Milat and Marsden were not to enjoy such a successful relationship the second time around. Within a few months he dismissed his lawyer.

As he was later to reveal in his 2005 autobiography, Marsden was sacked because Ivan believed he was in cahoots with the police.

'Nothing could have been further from the truth,' the lawyer insisted. 'This was just what some in the police force wanted. If they couldn't get me off the Police Board, they were determined to damage my business,' he wrote.

The 1974 rape case would also have to remain secret for the time being. Any public reference to that hearing could have prejudiced Milat's chances of a fair trial. It was sub-judice and any publicity would have been in contempt of court.

But the fact remained that had the police gone back over their old files sooner and bothered to re-examine the 1974 case of *Regina v. Milat*, Australia's most infamous serial killer might have been apprehended earlier.

As it was the most wanted man Down Under was to remain free for more than two years after committing his last known murder.

15.

IVAN THE FAMILY MAN

What makes Ivan Milat tick? It is a question many people have asked since his arrest in May 1994. Before his imprisonment he was a man of simple pleasures. He didn't smoke or drink and never took expensive holidays. His only luxuries were his four wheel drive and his Harley Davidson. Though he enjoyed sport as an armchair spectator, he was not drawn to any particular game either as a player or spectator.

His recreations included camping, shooting and reading. Among his favourite authors were John Grisham and Patricia Cornwell.

He liked the outdoor life and preferred nothing more than to drive off into the Australian bush.

Few of Milat's friends and workmates had a bad word to say about him. Remarkably for a man who had been painted by the media as a monster, he had few enemies. Indeed those who knew him were unanimous in their praise and were unable to accept he might be guilty.

'There is no way Ivan is a serial killer,' claimed one.

'He is just not capable of the backpacker murders,' insisted another.

Predictably his family were of the same view. While you would expect close relatives to rally behind him, some, like Alex Milat, were convinced he'd been victim to a miscarriage of justice.

'I know you might think that because he's my brother I would defend him, but I'll tell you right now that if I thought he was guilty I'd shoot the bastard,' he admitted.

Alex, six years older, said he never saw his brother lose his temper.

'He was always quiet. He was more of a bookworm than a sportsman and was smarter with a pencil than most of my brothers and sisters—always drawing, reading and writing.'

It was a claim reinforced by Ivan Milat's habit of taking notes in court. Throughout his lengthy committal he was never without a notebook and pen.

Although essentially a blue collar worker performing a manual job, he was not stupid. His former bosses talked of a model employee who was honest, courteous, hardworking, punctual and reliable.

He never caused his employers trouble.

John Whalen, a director of Sweeping Services, where Milat worked for a short spell, said, 'He always treated us, as a company, perfectly. He was a model employee.'

Boral Australian Gypsum, where he worked for nearly a year in the company's plasterboard factory, was similarly impressed. The firm's human resources manager, Lawrence Aked, described him as the best worker they'd ever had.

'If we had a factory full of Bill Milats, we could double our production,' he added.

Milat was known as Bill at work, even though he admitted it was not his real name. He told one employer he preferred the name because of a 'domestic situation'.

He was also known as Mac by members of his family, though the origin of the nickname is not known.

Over the years he had several jobs, most of them on the roads. Sometimes he had as many as 20 men under him as he directed operations.

As a ganger with the New South Wales Roads and Traffic Authority he would often spend weeks away resurfacing the highways by day, and staying in cheap motels by night.

Those who worked alongside him remembered his fascination for guns and hunting. He often talked about his shooting exploits before settling down for the night with a firearms magazine.

'He would read magazines about guns before going to sleep,' recalled workmate Ross Jackson.

'He would always go shooting and spoke about shooting goats and kangaroos,' he explained.

On one occasion Milat told him he had shot a kangaroo near Mittagong after tying the animal to a tree.

Milat was obsessed by firearms. According to his ex-wife, Karen, he was 'gun crazy'. Sometimes he would pretend to be a cowboy, calling himself Tex and carrying a revolver in a holster. Once, on a visit to the Belanglo Forest, he shot two kangaroos.

He slit the second one's throat and kicked the animal to make sure it was dead.

Milat was a strong man and always keen to improve his physical prowess. At home he would exercise with two plastic buckets filled with cement as part of his regular work-out.

However, there was a gentler side to him. Apart from having a close friendship with his stepson—his ex-wife Karen's child, Jason, from a previous relationship—he also enjoyed painting model cars and aeroplanes in his spare time.

But Karen, who was given a new identity, also told friends how her then husband would often beat and sexually assault her with a degree of viciousness that bordered on sadism. He particularly enjoyed coming home in the evening from work, pushing her across the kitchen table and subjecting her to anal sex—a 'trick' which he claimed to have learnt in prison.

Those not privy to life behind the net curtains of Ivan Milat's home had no idea of this darker side to his character. They knew nothing of his swearing and verbal abuse, his physically aggressive behaviour and his threat to shoot Karen if she ever became pregnant.

The warning came as no surprise to a woman whose husband was hooked on shooting and firearms. He was rarely without his pistol and would carry it around with him, wrapped in a sock and often tucked into his boot. The gun was always loaded. Karen was used to her husband's obsession because most of the family lived, ate and breathed firearms. For as long as anyone could remember the Milats had guns.

Most of the kids received an air rifle as a Christmas or birthday present. Alex Milat was 12 when his father gave him a shotgun 'to shoot all the birds who got at the chook feed.' Looking back he couldn't remember any member of his family without access to a firearm.

Ivan's father, Stephen, was born in the former Yugoslavia. A Croatian, he emigrated to Australia after the First World War hoping to find employment as a building worker. As a young country Australia provided plenty of openings for those keen to find work in the construction industry.

In Sydney he met Margaret, a pretty Australian-born girl of 20, whom he eventually married. Though he was twice his wife's age, Stephen went on to father 14 children.

They lived in Junction Road, Moorebank, on the outskirts of the Sydney suburb of Liverpool. The Milats' fourth child, Ivan, was born on December 27, 1944, in Crown Street Women's Hospital and like the rest of the kids went on to attend the nearby St Mary's Infants and later the Patrician Brothers High School.

Ivan played football but did not excel at any particular sport or subject. He disliked the school's rugby playing ethos and objected to the discipline.

One of the Brothers eventually advised Ivan's mother that he might be more suited to Boy's Town at Engadine, which was designed to accommodate rebellious lads from large families.

Ivan loved it. He was even made an altar boy, though his scholastic achievements were few.

In an age when academic qualifications were not considered an essential part of getting a job, it was automatically assumed he would leave school at the earliest opportunity, which would enable him to provide for his 'keep' and contribute to the family budget.

Ivan left school at 14 and followed in his father's footsteps digging holes, building roads and engaged in general construction work. He found employment all over Sydney, taking advantage of the need for unskilled labour created by the post-war property boom of the 1960s.

Milat, in common with his father, had a strict work ethic and was brought up to know right from wrong or face the consequences. Milat senior, a disciplinarian by nature but rarely by deed, only had to whisper his displeasure at his children's behaviour to command their instant obedience.

Ivan and his dad, who died in the early 1980s from bowel cancer, were very close. You had to get on with each other when 16 people occupied one house. Milat's first brush with the law was in 1962 at the age of 17. He was placed on probation for breaking into a house and stealing.

In the same year he was sent to a juvenile correction institution for six months after again breaking and entering a house.

Two years later he got his first real taste of life behind bars when he was sentenced to 18 months imprisonment at Liverpool Petty Sessions. Once again the charge was breaking, entering and stealing.

Another gaol term followed in 1965 when he was found guilty of stealing a motor vehicle and sentenced to two years.

He was only just out of prison when he was back before the courts again charged with being an accessory to theft of a motor vehicle. He was gaoled for three years with 18 months non-parole.

In 1971, the same year he was accused of rape, he was arrested on two counts of armed robbery and possession of a pistol. But he failed to appear to answer the charges at Central Petty Sessions, where a warrant was issued for his arrest.

The month was October. Milat had already jumped bail and fled to New Zealand where he would spend the next three years.

When he returned to Australia in 1974 he was re-arrested on the rape and hold-up charges, only to be found not guilty on all counts.

Ivan's life of crime spanned most of the years he lived at home with his family. The accommodation was modest and rather cramped.

So in the late 1960s Stephen Milat decided to move his family a few miles north to Guildford, another working class suburb and slightly nearer to the city. They bought a large weatherboard bungalow in Campbell Hill Road.

Ivan remained at home until 1984, when he married Karen and moved into his own house at Blackett, near Mt Druitt, in the far western suburbs. They shared the property until they separated three years later.

In the early nineties, Ivan's mother and his youngest brother David continued to live in the Guildford family home which was beginning to show its age. White paint was peeling off the external walls and the red roof tiles were greying. The building was partly obscured by trees, shrubbery, a brick wall and a mesh fence.

A couple of steps led up from the lawn to a small brick veranda and the front door and the window blinds were invariably pulled down. It was a sad, drab property though an ornamental frog wearing a bikini and sunglasses, sat incongruously on top of a small rockery in the front garden.

To the right hand side was a palm tree and an old water heating system was situated between the house and a wooden fence.

An old garage, which had seen better days, stood padlocked at the end of a long driveway.

Ivan Milat returned there after splitting up from his wife in 1987. Locals recalled his friendliness and easy-going manner during the six years he lived there again before moving out to Eagle Vale with his sister Shirley.

Next-door-neighbour Mrs Amira El Hallak remembered how Ivan was the first person to welcome her family to the area when they moved into their home in 1986. He knocked on the door to introduce himself and would often stand and chat over the garden fence.

When their car wouldn't start, Milat was always happy to repair it. When their lawnmower broke down he would loan them his own. And often he would give the El Hallak children rides on his mini-motorbike.

He'd also talk to the family about his love for guns and hunting.

'He once came around to show my husband a box of ammunition which had Arabic writing on it. We come from Beirut so he thought there would be a mutual interest. He wanted to know what the writing said and my husband read it and told him the bullets came from Iraq,' Amira recalled.

The El Hallaks' eldest son Ahmed told how Milat built a go-kart, which he planned to give to him.

'But he was very worried about the brakes and wasn't going to give it to me until he'd sorted them out. Ivan was such a smart man, always fixing things,' he added.

The 'favourite uncle' image which Milat projected in the community was much the same in court. Many of those who sat and watched him day after day during the committal proceedings at Campbelltown were to comment on his passive appearance. Ostensibly here was a man who wouldn't hurt a fly, the least-threatening person you could wish to meet. Was it all an act or an accurate reflection of one side of his Jeckyll and Hyde character?

Milat did not spend many hours at home. He would always complain to the El Hallaks that his job did not give him much free time. They only saw him at the weekend, when he would tinker with his car or Harley Davidson or mow the lawn for his aging mother.

Sometimes neighbours would hear the family arguing and invariably Ivan would intervene and act as peacemaker. Just as quickly emotions would subside and the brothers would be seen outside playing handball in the garden.

The Milats were no angels and had frequent visits from the police in the early years. Their mother, who was always fiercely protective of her children, would often be heard shouting, 'Not my boys, not mine,' as the local constabulary went about its enquiries.

There were also many dramas and occasional tragedies during the Milats' stay in Campbell Hill Road. A younger sister was killed in a car crash and the youngest son, David, was injured twice on the roads, once when he came off his motorbike and injured his arm and on a second occasion when he suffered brain damage in a motoring accident.

Matriarch Margaret was a frail old lady in her mid-seventies when Ivan was arrested. He had promised to build her a granny flat at his new home in Eagle Vale and she had even put her house on the market in preparation for the move. But when her son was charged with the backpacker murders all that changed. The house was taken off the market and Margaret became a prisoner in her own home, as the media laid siege to her front door.

The pressure took its toll on Mrs Milat, who already suffered from diabetes and died in 2001. When she made the occasional visit to the bingo to cheer herself up, acquaintances were shocked by her appearance. Her arched back and snow white hair bore testimony to the emotional and physical stress she had suffered since Ivan's arrest. Margaret Milat, who loved her children so dearly, especially Ivan, was a broken woman.

Neighbours shared her shock. The El Hallaks could not believe that the man whom they had lived alongside for so long, was Australia's most wanted man.

When news of Ivan's arrest became public knowledge the family stood together, as they had done on so many previous occasions when there had been a domestic crisis. As elder brother Alex was to remark afterwards, 'If one of us gets in the shit, the others are there. And that's how it's always been.'

Milat's outwardly friendly nature was not confined to relatives and near neighbours. He liked the company of women and had many girlfriends. He was even involved in a close relationship at the time of his arrest, a woman by the name of Chalinder Hughes who lived near Eagle Vale.

Chalinder, whom he always referred to as Cylinder, was born in India but moved to England with her Hindu family when she was a baby. They settled in the Midlands, ironically, not far from Paul Onions' home near Birmingham.

In the late seventies she emigrated to Australia with her then fiance. They married in 1985 but split up a few years later.

It was in 1992 that Ivan Milat walked into her life. They met through his sister Shirley Soire, who worked for the same Sydney accountancy firm where Chalinder was employed.

One day Shirley invited her to the cinema and Ivan came along too. The film was *Basic Instinct*.

They went back to her place at Kearns, near Campbelltown, for a coffee afterwards. It was the beginning of a relationship that continued for several years

Chalinder, a slim 43 year-old brunette stood faithfully by Ivan after his arrest. While he was in Sydney's Long Bay Prison on remand, she visited him whenever possible.

'She never misses a weekend,' Ivan later revealed in court.

She always maintained that her boyfriend was not capable of striking a woman, let alone raping and murdering one. She maintained he had enormous respect for the opposite sex and would always walk away from arguments.

Their relationship was so close that she had hoped that one day they would marry, but with little hope of Ivan being released, Chalinder eventually decided to make a new life for herself.

Even so it was clear Milat had a way with women. His twinkling eyes and earthy manner seemed to give him a certain animal magnetism.

Ivan's brothers and their wives also saw him as something of a lady's man, a view that was in no way diminished by the appalling allegations made against him.

'My wife reckons all women would like Ivan,' claimed Alex.

'He was always so very polite and kind and never pushed himself on anybody. Some people think he looks a bit like Charles Bronson,' he added.

It was difficult to reconcile this picture with the man accused of being a serial killer, but then nothing was as it seemed in the case of the backpacker murders, as the events of the next few months were to demonstrate.

16.
The Challenge Of A Fair Trial.

During the five months between Ivan Milat's arrest and the beginning of committal proceedings at Campbelltown Local Court, officers from Task Force Air gathered together their case. There were trips to Europe to record statements from people connected with the three German and two British victims. And there was the massive arsenal of weapons and ammunition, which had been found at Milat family properties to wade though. Camping gear and clothing allegedly belonging to the seven young backpackers also had to be examined in detail and witnesses interviewed.

Milat himself was also preparing his defence though relations with John Marsden, who had acted as the family solicitor on previous occasions, did not bode well. Alex Milat suspected that Marsden urged Ivan to plead guilty, a suggestion that was not well received by the defendant. Tension between the two men grew to such a point that Milat sacked his defence lawyer on June 24 and a few days later appointed Brisbane solicitor Andrew Boe to act on his behalf.

It was an interesting move. Boe was not the archetypical legal eagle. He was born in Burma, practised Buddhism and sported a pony tail. Milat had read about one of his previous cases in which he succeeded in quashing a conviction against a woman who had served nearly six years in gaol for murdering her de-facto husband. Boe argued that the woman, Robyn Kina, stabbed her partner after being subjected to continual abuse. She killed him after he threatened to force her niece to submit to anal intercourse. Boe succeeded in having the conviction quashed on the grounds of provocation due to repeated domestic violence.

Milat had heard about the young solicitor from Queensland and liked his style. Several other lawyers had been pitching for the job, but the defendant preferred Boe. A few days after Marsden was sacked, Milat's sister Shirley Soire telephoned Boe and asked him to represent Ivan. She even offered to provide his accommodation in Sydney and give him use of a car if he accepted.

The Brisbane-based lawyer did not need much persuading. In yet another curious sidebar to the backpacker murders, Boe later revealed how he had had a premonition that Milat would contact him. It happened as he sat beside his dying father. Boe was reading a newspaper cutting about the sacking of John Marsden, when he turned to his father and said, 'Look this guy's going to call me.' Seconds later his mobile telephone rang. The caller was Shirley Soire.

Boe later suggested in an interview with *The Australian* newspaper that the fact he was given the Milat case was 'karmic.' He believed there was a certain confluence of events, as his father had decreed that his 29 year-old son should enter the law.

Andrew Boe had moved to Australia with his family a quarter of a century earlier. His American-educated father left Burma, now known as Myanmar, when the military dictatorship proclaimed that English would not be taught there. It was young Andrew's first taste of the unfairness of life and contributed to the character of the man who was to grow into a radical student activist with a strong social conscience.

He formed Lawyers for Social Justice and was later instrumental in obtaining a review of legal aid funding in Queensland. Boe's sense of fair play and support for the underdog—and the fact that he was not representative of the legal establishment—made him an obvious choice for Ivan Milat.

'If Ivan can get a fair trial then we can rest easy that we have a system of justice that works reasonably well,' he said in the interview.

'It is the biggest test to ensure that he gets a fair trial. That's really my greatest duty, to ensure that he gets that.'

He did not have to wait long to make his presence felt. During a 10-minute remand hearing at Campbelltown Local Court, Boe stood up and accused the prosecution of leaking information to the media. And he sought an assurance that his client would not be disadvantaged by any details supplied by the Crown or the police.

'I want it to be known that Mr Milat has not had a criminal conviction since

1968 or for an offence of violence or a sexual nature,' he made clear.

This was a reference to the earlier court appearance when the prosecution revealed that Milat had fled to New Zealand in 1971 while facing the rape charge.

If Boe was prepared to stand up for his client, Crown Prosecutor Ian Lloyd QC was also more than able to look after himself if the going got tough. There were to be several heated exchanges between prosecution and the defence team over the coming months.

Lloyd and Boe were two very different men. Unlike the defence solicitor who delighted in driving a red Porsche, the Crown Prosecutor's preferred form of transport was a grey Toyota Corolla.

Lloyd, who studied law at Sydney University and graduated with honours, was 13 years older that Boe and had a wealth of experience as a lawyer both in Australia and overseas. He was a government prosecutor in Hong Kong, specialising in fraud but was equally at home in murder trials. He took on both government and private work and earned a formidable reputation during eight years of murder briefs and billion dollar fraud and corruption cases.

In 1988 he left the former British colony to return to Sydney after being head-hunted by the then NSW Director of Public Prosecutions Reg Blanch QC.

There were also family reasons for returning to Australia: the education of his son and the failing health of his father. At one stage he considered opting out of the law to pursue a simple country life in the Blue Mountains where he grew up. He even qualified as a wood turner but gave up the idea when the financial implications of leaving the legal profession became apparent. He was made a Queen's Counsel in 1989 and was appointed General Counsel to the NSW Independent Commission Against Corruption (ICAC).

After he was appointed as Senior Crown Prosecutor in 1990 there seemed no doubt that Ian Lloyd would appear for the prosecution in the backpacker murders. Given his wide experience of high profile criminal trials he was the natural choice for the job.

He approached the task with relish, arguing vigorously against attempts for separate hearings of the charges laid against Milat. The defence claimed that the alleged attempted murder of Paul Onions should be heard at the same time as the seven murder charges.

Belanglo State Forest, near Berrima in the Southern Highlands area of New South Wales, where the bodies of seven missing young people were found in the early 1990s. An eighth body was found in 2010.

Ivan Milat in 1983, showing off a World War 1 vintage machine gun at the Buxton home of his brother Alex in the Southern Highlands.

Once a family man: an undated photo of Ivan Milat with his former sister-in-law Maureen Murray.

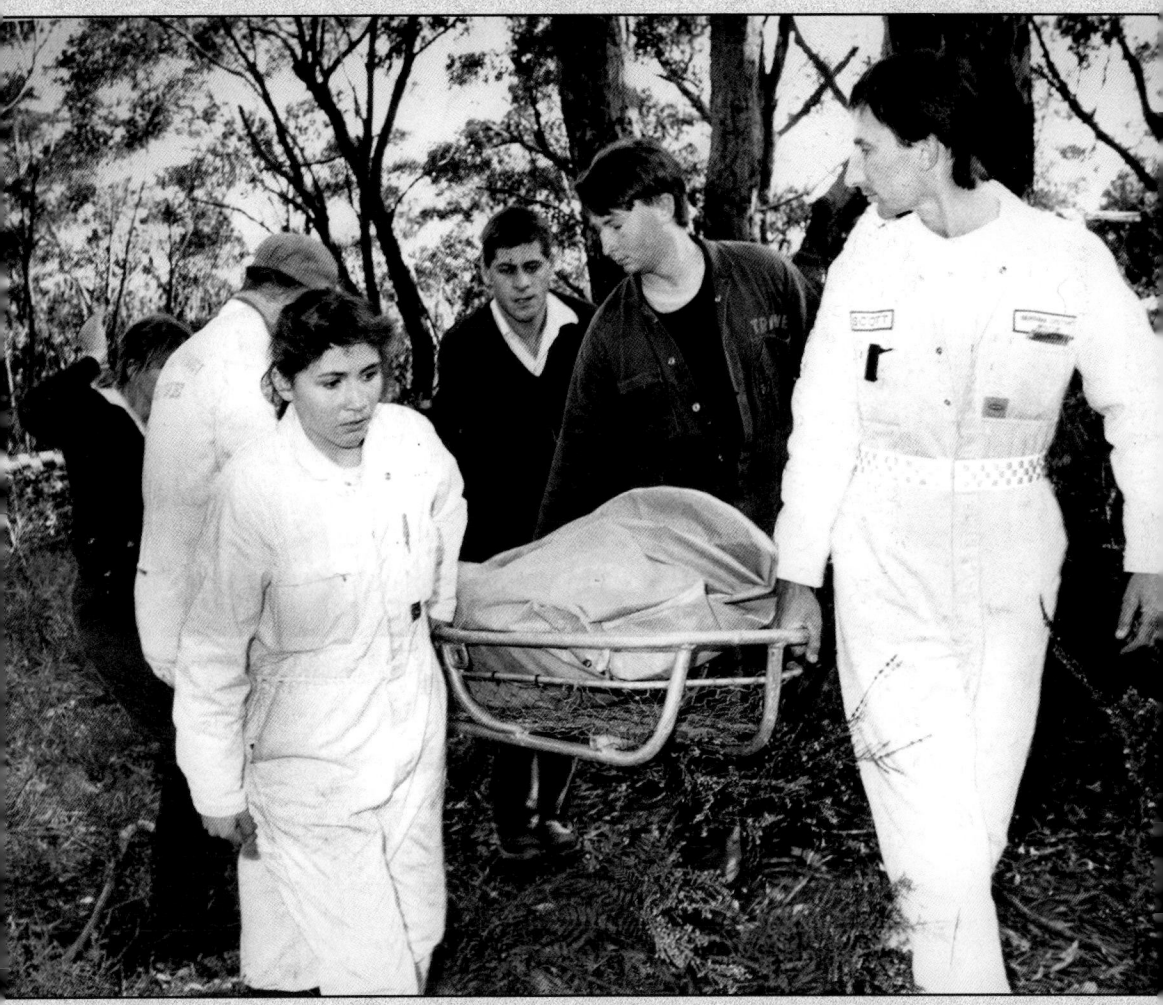

In 1992 the bodies of Caroline Clarke and Joanne Walters were found by orienteers running through the bush in the Belanglo State Forest. It was not until the discovery of five more bodies that one of the biggest manhunts in Australia's history began.

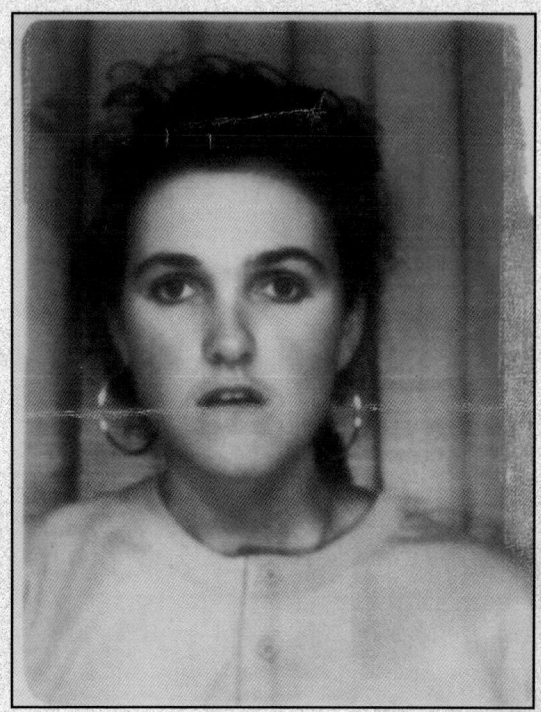

Joanne Walters, a nanny from South Wales in the UK, met up with British girl Caroline Clarke (below) and the two agreed to travel around Australia together. They were listed as missing persons for at least three years.

Caroline (right) and Joanne's last movements are uncertain. They were last seen at 7.30 a.m. in Kings Cross and had talked of hitchhiking to Perth.

German backpacker Simone Schmidl caught a train out to Liverpool and the Hume Highway to begin hitchhiking to Victoria. She was never seen alive again.

German girl Anja Habschied and her boyfriend Gabor Neugebauer were last seen on Boxing Day in 1991, shortly before they set off to hitchhike to Darwin.

Art student James Gibson (right) and his girlfriend Deborah Everist (below) decided to hitchhike to an environmental gathering called Confest in Albury on the New South Wales border in 1989. Nearly four years later their remains were discovered in Belanglo.

Paul Onions, the brave and persistent victim of attempted murder, whose evidence and identification were crucial in Milat's conviction.

Held in Goulbourn's Supermax Gaol, Ivan Milat has attempted to gain attention by severing his finger and lodging several appeals. All have failed. The question of an accomplice remains.

Catherine Holmes, another Queensland lawyer who had been appointed as a member of the defence team, claimed Milat would be denied a fair committal hearing if all the charges were dealt with at the same time.

Lloyd treated the application with barely concealed contempt. He described it as 'futile' and pointed out that many of the witnesses would be coming from overseas. Two separate hearings would mean they would have to be called twice and 'at massive expense.'

Mr Justice Ireland in the New South Wales Supreme Court threw out the defence application. Committal proceedings against Ivan Milat were set for October 24, 1994 at Campbelltown Local Court.

Meanwhile the legal system was desperate for justice to be seen to be done. Conscious of allegations of bias against Milat, who had received massive media attention at home and abroad, the courts were determined that publicity surrounding the case should not prejudice the defendant's right to a fair trial.

After *The Australian* magazine, *Who Weekly* published a photograph of Ivan Milat on its front cover on June 13 and it was fined $100,000 for contempt. The defendant's face was ordered to be covered by black stickers. Even an appeal by publishers Time Inc. that the publication of the photograph did not interfere with the proceedings against Milat because it was simply a 'further reproduction of what happens in court,' was rejected.

The magazine's editor, Thomas Moore, claimed the existing contempt laws were unnecessarily restrictive and outdated. That may have been the case, but such was the Crown's desire to come down on hard on anything that might interfere with Ivan Milat's prosecution, that any infringement of the law had to be dealt with. They could not risk the Crown's case falling down on a legal technicality.

This was to be one of the most important trials in Australian criminal history. The authorities did not want anything going wrong, especially after the lacklustre performance of the police inquiry in the early days of the investigation.

The case against Ivan Milat had to be watertight. The world would be watching when he appeared in court and given the amount of negative publicity the Australian tourism industry had already suffered, the police and the law were desperate for a conviction.

17.
THE PROSECUTION OPENS ITS CASE

They started gathering early at Campbelltown Local Court on the morning of October 24, 1994. A bright, sunny day, the weather was in marked contrast to the gloom that was to overshadow Court Number One for the next seven weeks as some 200 witnesses and a massive volume of evidence bore testimony to the horrific charges laid against Ivan Milat.

Outside an army of newspaper and television cameraman waited for the key players to arrive. Inside journalists and members of the public formed a long queue as they filed through a metal detector at the entrance to the courtroom. Police, who also checked bags and brief cases, were taking no chances with security.

There was insufficient space in the press box for the media throng of over 50 reporters and newspaper artists so journalists spilled over into an upper public gallery.

Beneath them an area for the public had been set aside at the back of the court. A middle-aged man with a pony tail was among the first to claim a seat. His name was Ray Gibson, father of James, who together with his girlfriend Deborah Everist, were the backpacker killer's first victims.

Ray was to spend the next five weeks in the public gallery, using up all of his holiday entitlement in the process. His other son Chris sat next to him and some of Deborah's friends were gathered nearby.

Marita Wallace had travelled from her home at Lismore in northern New South Wales to be there. She had been to school with Deborah and the two had forged a close friendship.

Though it was by now five years since Deborah had been murdered, Marita said she felt compelled to be there. The same applied to Erin Davie and Tanya Rose, two other school friends, who had travelled up from Victoria for the opening day of the committal hearing.

Erin said they'd come to represent Deborah.

'We didn't want her to be a statistic, just one of the victims,' she explained outside the court.

'We want people to know she was a vivacious and lively person—we want people to remember her.'

Sitting in the body of the court were Ian Lloyd for the prosecution, and Catherine Holmes, who together with Andrew Boe, now acted for the defence.

Soon after 10 a.m. the man at the centre of the proceedings climbed the stairs from the prisoners' holding unit underneath Campbelltown Court and emerged in the dock. He gave a cursory glance towards the packed public gallery before turning around to talk to his legal advisers.

Mr Boe smiled and straightened his client's grey and blue check tie. Milat, now clean shaven, wore a navy blue jumper, a light blue shirt and dark trousers.

For a man accused of one of the worst serial killings in the history of modern Australia Milat appeared remarkably relaxed. He rested an elbow on the dock as he passed the time with his defence team and surveyed the full panoply of the law.

The murmer of conversation was only silenced by the arrival of magistrate Michael Price. The court stood as Mr Price took his seat on the bench and invited the prosecution to open its case.

There was no plea from the accused, who apart from two short verbal outbursts, was to say nothing throughout the next seven long weeks.

It took Mr Lloyd 45 minutes to outline the police case against Milat, evidence which he agreed was mainly circumstantial. Nobody had seen the accused stabbing or shooting his victims and there was no incontrovertible proof of his guilt.

Only in the case of Paul Onions, who was so lucky to escape with his life after being given that lift on the Hume Highway in January 1990, was there evidence of identification. The young man had picked out Milat from a set of 13 photographs.

In his opening address Mr Lloyd told the court that the prosecution brief was to enable the magistrate to form an opinion that the evidence was clearly capable of satisfying a jury 'beyond reasonable doubt' that Milat had committed the offences.

There would be evidence from ballistics experts who had examined firearm parts found in the defendant's home.

'Gun parts found at the house were part of the gun which fired the fatal shots at Caroline Clarke,' he alleged.

These included a trigger assembly, a bolt assembly, a spring and guide and a .22 magazine. Winner and Eley brand cartridge boxes and an instruction manual for a Ruger rifle were also discovered there.

A silencer, which had almost certainly been used in the shooting, was found in Milat's garage.

Ballistics experts would say that the dismantled rifle parts could form a .22 calibre Ruger 10/22, with the exception of a barrel, which was never found.

The bolt assembly was later placed into a test rifle, which when fired produced shell markings similar to those on cartridge cases found near Caroline's body.

Winner and Eley brand ammunition boxes lay near the body of Gabor Neugebauer, who had been shot in the head. Ten Winner-type .22 cartridge cases were also found a few metres away from Caroline's body, which had suffered fatal bullet wounds.

Mr Lloyd revealed that some of the witnesses, many from overseas, would identify clothing and camping equipment belonging to the murder victims and which were found in the homes of Milat or his relatives.

Property recovered by the police included a rare Salewa brand backpack and sleeping bag, which allegedly belonged to Simone Schmidl, whose body was discovered in November 1993. A green cover from a water bottle owned by the young German backpacker and found in a bedroom at Milat's home would also be of major importance, the prosecution said.

Much of the camping equipment had been manufactured overseas and evidence would be given that it had never been sold in Australia. Likewise it would be proved that the defendant could not have gone overseas to purchase it.

Milat's employment records also showed that he had not been at work on any of the days when the seven murdered backpackers had last been seen alive.

The court was told that the accused man's ex-wife would confirm how her former husband often drove her to the Belanglo State Forest and that he frequently carried a pistol.

Mr Lloyd said the Crown's case would include evidence from Milat's relatives that Ivan had given them guns and camping equipment found in their possession.

Part of his submission would be based on the sheer isolation of the Belanglo State Forest and the strange manner in which the victims were buried, he added.

Then there was Paul Onions, the prosecution's star witness, whose testimony was so crucial to the Crown's case. The young Briton would allege that Milat had given him a lift in a four wheel drive, which was remarkably similar to the vehicle the accused owned at the time.

He would describe how the two met outside a newsagent's shop at Casula on the Hume Highway, where Milat was a regular customer.

In all Mr Lloyd submitted that the totality of the evidence was capable of satisfying a jury 'beyond reasonable doubt' that the defendant was guilty.

'I will ultimately be submitting to your worship that the evidence clearly shows, whoever killed one of the deceased backpackers, killed them all,' he told the magistrate.

'The discovery of various items in Milat's possession links Milat to the murders of the backpackers and this creates a strong circumstantial case against him,' he added.

The prosecution's case had barely begun when the proceedings were abruptly adjourned because of a bomb threat. Magistrate Price, whose breathless efficiency and no-nonsense approach to his work got the first day of the committal off to a cracking pace, rolled his eyes in frustration and ordered the court to be cleared.

It was yet another drama in a case that would have many unexpected developments over the following months. For this was a crime without parallel, a series of murders so horrific that every twist and turn of the hearing produced more shocks. Those who crowded into Court Number One in the first few days of Ivan Milat's committal were left with a sickening sense of revulsion.

18.

RETURN TO THE KILLING FIELDS

Those following the committal proceedings did not have to wait long for the hearing to produce new evidence of the ritualistic-style of killing which had long been suspected in the backpacker murders.

The next few days of the case revealed a grisly picture of how Caroline Clarke and Joanne Walters met their deaths. The court was told how Caroline's fully-clothed body was found with both arms extending forwards and a maroon coloured cloth draped over her head, which faced south. The cloth was peppered with small holes, a reference to the first day's evidence which disclosed she was shot 10 times in the back of the head.

Joanne's face was also covered with a coloured cloth. Her right arm was stretched above her head, which was resting on the left cheek, and her left arm lay on her hip. In addition there was evidence that her clothing had been disturbed. A T-shirt that she had been wearing was bunched upwards exposing her breasts and abdomen, four buttons on the front of her jeans had been undone and her underwear had been removed.

A second piece of cloth ran through her mouth and around the rear of her head and was tied in a knot like a gag. And a third section of material rested on her neck and chin region.

Human hair discovered in the hands of both sets of badly-decomposed remains indicated that the two young women had put up a desperate struggle to defend themselves. Eleven hairs were found in Joanne's hands. A fewer number of fibres, but slightly larger, were discovered in Caroline's right palm.

But it was a badly-slashed, navy blue shirt which produced the greatest impact. Mounted on a white backboard, the garment drew gasps from the public gallery, the holes in the material bearing grim testimony to the knife which had penetrated Joanne Walter's body no fewer than 20 times. It did not require words to describe the frenzied nature of the attack. The evidence was encapsulated in a few square metres of cloth. There were no fewer than 15 cuts to the back, three in the sleeve and two in the upper front, where she had been stabbed in the left and right breasts. Her lower bra strap had also been cut near the left breast, which corresponded with her wounds.

Caroline's injuries were equally horrific. Three bullets had entered the base of her skull, three more to the right, two to the left, one to the side of the forehead and another to the top of the skull. During the post mortem examination four metal fragments were removed from the brain tissue and a fifth from the left shoulder. The court heard that they were all projectiles which came from a .22 calibre firearm.

The other five bodies, which had been in the forest for a much longer period than those of the two Britons, were by now merely skeletons. It was harder to gather medical or forensic evidence but the fatal injuries they suffered were still detectable.

Pathologists found that James Gibson, who was discovered in a foetal position with the fly zip on his jeans pulled down, had been stabbed nine times in the chest, between the shoulder blades and on his right side. One of his ribs was also broken.

His girlfriend Deborah Everist had suffered a fractured jaw and other wounds to her head. Part of her lower body was missing and loops had been tied around each foot.

Marks on the back and neck of German backpacker Simone Schmidl indicated she had been repeatedly stabbed. The court was told that she was not wearing underclothes and her shirt was bunched up around her shoulders.

Around her skull was a headband which bore the word 'Compactomat.' Significantly an identical band was later found wrapped around a tent in Milat's home at Eagle Vale.

Anja Habschied, who was decapitated by her killer, was naked from the waist down when police stumbled across her body, the prosecution revealed. There were signs that her halter-neck top had been ripped, but because her head was never found, no exact cause of death could be established.

There was no doubt about how her boyfriend Gabor Neugebauer died. He had been gagged with a length of floral cloth before being shot six times in the head. The post mortem found holes at the base and left side of the skull which were consistent with a bullet fired from a .22 calibre weapon.

While the injuries told investigating officers much about the sheer brutality of the killings, other items found near the bodies suggested an even more macabre element to the murders.

As the evidence about the discovery of the two British, two Australian and three German victims continued, police revealed how they had found rope, a leather strap and white cord near some of the bodies. A length of electrical flex was tied in loops, which could have been used as a noose, handcuffs or some other form of restraint.

And there were personal belongings such as jewellery, a money belt, an airline ticket and items of clothing including a pair of black ladies briefs and black pantyhose found near Deborah Everist's body.

The hearing also heard how two Scotch whisky bottles were found near James Gibson's remains and cigarette butts near other bodies. The defence later pointed out that Ivan Milat was not known to smoke or drink alcohol.

Were these items left behind by innocent campers in the forest or did they indicate the involvement of other people in the killings? These were questions which had yet to be answered. Although the weight of the evidence against Milat appeared to be overwhelming, it was still largely circumstantial. Only a jury could decide.

The prosecution's account of the condition of the bodies and the manner of the victims' deaths became daily more sickening, producing increasingly lurid coverage of the proceedings. Newspaper stories and nightly television reports of the unsavoury evidence dominated the print and electronic media and it again raised the question of whether the defendant could ever receive a fair trial.

Unlike the British legal system, where a committal cannot be reported without the consent of the accused, pre-trial hearings in Australia are open slather. Unless the magistrate imposes a suppression order on certain evidence or the identity of witnesses, the prosecution's case can be reported in full. It was therefore inconceivable that a potential juror would not be aware of the detailed allegations made against the accused long before the case went to trial and would not be influenced by the reporting of those claims.

Magistrate Price was clearly aware of prejudicing Milat's chances of a fair trial and the risk of the hearing becoming a media circus when he considered a plan to transfer the court to the Belanglo State Forest.

Both the prosecution and the defence were in favour of the idea, believing that the magistrate would better appreciate the evidence and the geography involved if he toured the scene of the crime.

The danger was that such a move would almost certainly expose the defendant to the cameras, with all the identification issues that would raise. Milat would have a legal right to be there, but because the forest was essentially a public place, nothing could be done to prevent the TV news crews from filming him, even from a distance. In the eyes of the law the visit would also be as much a part of the hearing as the proceedings at Campbelltown Court and therefore the media had a right to be there.

Mr Price's immediate response was that a 'media caravan' accompanying the visit could 'diminish the integrity of the court and its proceedings.'

As he commented on the second day of the hearing: 'An accused person attracting the obvious interest and perhaps even notoriety of Mr Milat, would, in the ultimate, be at the mercy of the court if he were to be placed at the so-called scene of the crime and then captured on film.'

'Any accused person, including Mr Milat, is entitled to look at the court as an impartial adjudicator and to act with fairness,' he explained.

But he ruled: 'Whatever benefit might flow to the court in the appreciation of the evidence, whatever additional comprehension the accused person himself might gain from a roam through the forest, albeit in custody, is not in the view of this court justified in terms of the possible prejudicial effect which might flow. Accordingly this court will not be adjourning to take such a view,' he added.

It looked like the change in court environment was not to happen. But the defence was not to be outdone. After the magistrate's ruling, Milat's lawyer, Catherine Holmes, took advice from her client and shortly afterwards told Mr Price that the defendant would be happy not to join the trip to the forest if it allowed the court's visit to go ahead. Mr Price agreed and the inspection of the crime scene was arranged for the afternoon of Tuesday, November 1, exactly one year to the day that Simone Schmidl's body had been found in the Belanglo State Forest.

Like the service of serenity organised by the Walters family on the site of their daughter's bush grave two years earlier, there were foreboding meteorological overtones to the court's official visit. As the magistrate and the defence and prosecution teams joined a convoy of police vehicles, storm clouds gathered over the Belanglo State Forest.

The bright, sunny morning was replaced by a dark, portentous sky. By mid-afternoon thunder, lightning and torrential rain had turned the visit into a wet and uncomfortable experience.

Detective Sergeant John Goldie led the column of four wheel drive vehicles along the rough, boulder-strewn, bush tracks until they reached Long Acre fire trail, where the bodies of the two British girls were found.

A cross and flowers were lying on the site where Joanne Walters remains were discovered. A poignant note left some time earlier by her broken-hearted parents read simply: 'No birthday card today Joanne. Just the love we have always had. Love always, Mum and Dad.'

Another heart-shaped bouquet a short distance away completed the sombre scene. It marked the spot where Caroline Clarke's body was found a day later.

Dressed in a plastic cape to shield him from the rain, Mr Price toured the murder sites with his usual business-like efficiency. The convoy drove another 600 metres further on to where Australians James Gibson and Deborah Everist had lain for some three-and-a-half years before their discovery.

Finally they came to the area where the three Germans were found, two burnt logs identifying the spot where Gabor Neugebauer and Anja Habschied died. The intersection of two fire trails marked the dense bushland area where Simone Schmidl's skeleton had been hidden.

In all it took the party just 80 minutes to complete the tour before police and officials headed back to Campbelltown. Now the court would have a visual mental record of the murder scene and a better appreciation of the reality of the charges laid against Ivan Milat.

19.
ONIONS FACES HIS ATTACKER AGAIN

The magistrate's inspection of the crime scene was not the only deviation from accepted courtroom procedure that day. Earlier Milat himself had caused a stir when he unexpectedly jumped to his feet to accuse the police of framing him.

It was the first time the accused's voice had been heard since his arrest some six months earlier and it was prompted by the evidence given by Detective Senior Constable Andrew Grosse who had been present during the early morning raid on the defendant's house on May 22.

The officer, who explained he had seen a number of items at Milat's home inscribed with the initials IM, told how a backpack allegedly identical to one owned by Simone Schmidl also bore the letters IM inside the top flap. The backpack was found in the Queensland home of his brother, Alex Milat, on May 21.

The claim drew an instant response from the man in the dock who jumped to his feet and pointed towards the witness box.

'You put it there yourself,' he shouted at Grosse as the scientific investigator stared back, clearly surprised by the sudden outburst.

A member of the defence team turned around and motioned to him to sit down and be quiet. The accused, realising the damage caused by his behaviour, lifted his hand to gain the magistrate's attention and quietly remarked, 'I am very sorry your honour.'

It was not the only time Milat was to lose his temper during the committal proceedings and not the first occasion he was to suggest he had been framed.

Four weeks later, in a further indication of his growing frustration with the legal process, he claimed he was being set-up for the seven backpacker murders.

The second outburst followed a fortnight of adjournments and legal wrangling over who should represent him in court. On Monday, November 14, Milat sacked his second lawyer, Catherine Holmes, who unexpectedly announced to the court that she no longer had instructions to act on his behalf. Quite what had led to her dismissal was not revealed but there had clearly been a fundamental disagreement between the two parties over the weekend and the defendant did not want the female barrister to represent him any longer.

Ms Holmes picked up her handbag and walked out, leaving the press and courtroom officials open mouthed at the sudden turn of events. Andrew Boe, who was still part of the defence team, asked for the case to be adjourned until the next year or for at least three weeks so that another barrister could be appointed.

Such a move did not appeal to the magistrate, who was aware that seven German witnesses had just flown to Australia to give their evidence and could not be expected to wait around for that length of time. The prosecution pointed out that five of the witnesses were expecting to fly home within the next few days and a lengthy adjournment might mean that they would not be around to testify.

'They have come half-way around the world to be here and if they were to be sent home empty handed, they may not return at a later date,' said Ian Lloyd QC.

It was a difficult situation for magistrate Price who had to ensure that Milat received the defence support he was due but also had to weigh such responsibilities with the availability of witnesses. He pointed out that the presence of the Germans had not been without 'very significant' community cost in terms of accommodation and travel. Equally such travel would have a significant impact on the personal and business affairs of those concerned.

He pointed out that the witnesses had travelled long distances so they could be cross-examined by the defence and were it not for that, they would not be there.

Ultimately the magistrate ruled that the Germans' evidence and the testimony of two Dutch witnesses who were due to fly into Australia that day, would be heard that week as planned. As for the appointment of a third barrister, Mr Price was far from happy about the defendant's increasing tendency to sack his lawyers and the inconvenience such action caused.

'This is not the first occasion where Mr Milat, for whatever reason, dispenses with his legal adviser,' he said.

'There can be no guarantee that it will not happen again. Should it occur again, this court would not be quite so accommodating. Indeed another course might well have to be considered,' he warned.

The magistrate eventually agreed to postpone the case for two days that week and two days the following week to allow another defence barrister to be appointed. But on November 29 the backpacker murder case was again thrown into confusion when it looked as though Milat would lose his entire defence team and might have to represent himself.

It happened after his newly-appointed Queensland barrister, Mr Terry Martin, revealed that there had been technical difficulties with his application to practice in New South Wales. Magistrate Price refused to allow him to appear before that application had been duly processed and accepted, much to the annoyance of the Queenslander, a highly-experienced barrister of 17 years standing.

'So I'm not here then?' Martin quipped as he made a short appearance before the bench.

'No,' Mr Price replied.

The courtroom atmosphere was becoming decidedly testy as Mr Boe sought a two day adjournment to appeal against the ruling, but the magistrate was adamant.

As a perplexed Milat looked on, Mr Boe accused the magistrate of prejudicing his client and the course of justice.

'It has got to the intolerable stage where I can't represent Mr Milat at this stage,' he claimed.

The hearing was adjourned for 15 minutes to allow tempers to cool as much as to sort out what should happen next. When the court resumed magistrate Price declared that there had already been too many adjournment applications and he would not sanction another two-day postponement of proceedings.

A furious Mr Boe replied, 'I withdraw from the proceedings,' before storming out of the court.

Ivan Milat looked a vulnerable figure as he watched his entire defence team walk out on him. What followed bordered on high farce as the magistrate invited the defendant out of the dock so that he could take up a position at the bar table next to the prosecution.

The accused was clearly in no position to conduct his own defence and admitted such during the extraordinary exchange that ensued.

He said it was no good going ahead and he might just as well return to the cells.

As the magistrate insisted the case should continue, Milat pointed out that he did not have the professional qualifications or experience to represent himself.

'I'm a roadworker—don't you read the papers? I'm not a solicitor,' he reminded the court.

'I expect you may have no legal training,' the magistrate agreed.

'No, I'm on my own,' he replied.

As the reality of his legal plight sank in, Milat grew agitated.

'I can't defend myself—I'm being framed for seven murders,' he claimed.

Milat accused the magistrate of railroading him.

'You won't let me have my legal team. Haven't I got rights here at all?' he asked with an air of desperation.

The ridiculous nature of the events unfolding in Court One could clearly not continue for long. A 30-minute adjournment was agreed, so as to allow the defendant time to read witness statements and to prepare to cross-examine them.

It was Andrew Boe who ultimately saved the day and came to Milat's rescue. When the court sat again half an hour later, Mr Boe also appeared. Recognising the defendant's predicament the solicitor explained he had changed his mind about representing him. Boe told the court that his withdrawal from the case would obviously leave his client at a disadvantage so he would continue with the case. But he also wanted to make it clear that the defence was at a considerable disadvantage by not having a barrister.

The drama was over for the time being. The defence team was no longer in tatters. But Milat had been given a salutory lesson: You cannot take liberties with the judicial system and keep on sacking your lawyer without the risk of dire consequences.

As it was, Terry Martin's application to practice in New South Wales was accepted shortly afterwards. He proved to be a valuable addition to the defence team, his wit and style providing the occasional entertaining diversion during the long and often depressing days ahead.

On one occasion he asked a witness if he recalled an address in England from many years ago. Much to everyone's surprise the man replied in lengthy and unnecessary detail.

'And the zip code?' Martin queried in his dry manner, much to the amusement of the court.

Such light interludes were rare. The evidence unfolding day by day did not lend itself to humour for the most part and the key players were not there for laughs. The expert witnesses called mid-way through the hearing were intended to shed further light on the value and importance of the police evidence and their link with the deaths of seven backpackers.

Arguably the most important connection was based on DNA testing, which the prosecution alluded to on November 2. The court heard that a length of white sash cord found in a bag in Milat's garage had blood on it and this had been sent for testing by forensic scientists. Fibres from a sleeping bag and a water bottle pouch had also been subjected to DNA testing.

Detective Senior Constable Grosse disclosed that hair and blood samples had also been taken from the defendant for comparison, but the outcome of these tests was still unclear. All the officer would say when asked if there had been a positive match was that the tests 'indicated something.'

For the time being the DNA results remained a mystery.

Clothes also played a key role in the police evidence. A blue-collared, long-sleeved shirt allegedly owned by Paul Onions and a 'grandfather shirt' identical to one owned by Simone Schmidl were found in a police raid on the home of Milat's mother in Guildford.

A white and turquoise Benetton sweat shirt, once the property of Caroline Clarke, was similar to a garment worn by Milat's girlfriend Chalinder Hughes who was seen wearing it in a photograph.

The sweatshirt was among 10 exhibits described as 'similar' to property owned by the backpackers including a sleeping bag, an Olympus camera and a green bedroll.

A photo of Simone Schmidl showed her drinking from an orange cup, which was almost identical to one found in Milat's kitchen. A blue sleeping bag cover and a rainbow coloured strap similar to other property belonging to the young German, was also retrieved from the defendant's home.

The list went on and on, prompting the question: How could such an extensive collection of camping and other personal items, which apparently belonged to other people, come into his possession? Assuming it was nigh impossible for the police to 'plant' such a wide cross section of incriminating evidence, Ivan Robert Marko Milat had a lot of explaining to do.

There were also the firearm parts to take into consideration. A ballistics expert from the NSW police told the court that the rifle bolt found in the ceiling at the defendant's Eagle Vale property almost certainly came from the same gun which fired the fatal shots at Caroline Clarke.

Detective Senior Constable Gerard Dutton established the connection when he fitted the bolt to another Ruger 10/22 calibre rifle and test-fired the weapon. He then compared the markings on the used cartridges with marks on those found near the body of Miss Clarke.

To reinforce his conclusions the court was shown blown-up photographs of the markings which the officer insisted were unique to a specific weapon.

Questioned by the prosecution about the link between the two sets of used cartridges the detective replied, 'There is absolutely no doubt in my mind.'

A spent Winchester cartridge found in Milat's spare room was also consistent with those located near the English girl's body, as well as that of Gabor Neugebauer.

The evidence against Ivan Milat appeared to be overwhelming. Task Force Air had gone to great lengths to prove its case and to ensure that there was no shadow of doubt about the authenticity of the exhibits.

Over and above the physical evidence there was the personal testimony of witnesses associated with the victims. Their presence in court often said more than the words they uttered. One by one witnesses filed into the court to give evidence of identification about an item of clothing or to recall the last time they saw their friend or relative alive.

Each would fix their steely gaze on Milat who did his best to avoid eye contact with them. Parents, fellow backpackers and casual acquaintances of the murdered tourists often fought back tears as they remembered the young hitchhikers whose lives had been cut short.

Some were unable to control their emotions and openly wept as they sat in the witness box. It was a traumatic occasion for all of them, but especially the mothers. Both the prosecution and defence took pity on the relatives and kept their questioning to a minimum.

On the morning of December 2 no fewer than five British witnesses were united in their grief, when the court heard about the known final days of Joanne Walters. As Nina Tunnicliffe, a close friend , recounted their last meeting in Sydney, the mothers of the two murdered Britons sobbed in the public gallery, clutching their husband's hands.

Joanne's mother, Jill, was so upset while giving evidence that her voice was barely audible.

Simone Schmidl's father, Herbert, kept a tighter rein on his emotions but as he left the witness box he could contain his fury no longer. As he strode past the man who allegedly murdered his beautiful daughter he brandished a clenched, right fist and a finger at Milat who could not bring himself to face his accuser.

Mr Schmidl's evidence, like that of so many other witnesses, had been damning. He had identified in court his daughter's camping equipment, which had been found in Milat's home. He told how he had been in the German shop at the time of its purchase. Asked if the initials I.M. had been on a rucksack when it was bought, he replied, 'No, somebody else must have added that onto it. It is not the handwriting of Simone.'

Shown a blown-up, infra-red photograph of the name 'Simi,' which earlier evidence suggested had appeared on Simone Schmidl's water bottle, her father agreed it was her signature.

'It is the handwriting of Simone,' he said.

'Do you have any doubt about that?' asked the prosecution.

'No,' he replied emphatically.

Further evidence of identification came from fellow-German Jeanette Muller, who had befriended Simone in Australia. She was shown a range of camping equipment which had been recovered from the homes of Milat and some of his relatives, including a green tent.

'I am very familiar with this,' she admitted in halting English. 'We had to pitch it every night.'

An English friend of the two British girls also identified a blue, nylon tent which was allegedly found in the home of one of Milat's brothers. Stephen Wright, who had travelled with Joanne and Caroline to Tasmania, recalled giving the young women his own tent because it was bigger than theirs. He said he knew there was a small hole in the material, which he had accidentally torn with his grape picking knife, while staying on a farm at Mildura.

Holding the tent in the witness box Mr Wright pointed to the hole, which he had earlier patched with one of his own adhesive labels. The label was still on the tent when it was found.

Asked if he had any doubt it was the same model that belonged to him, he replied, 'None whatsoever. I slept in it for about six weeks.'

It was clearly going to be difficult for the defence to dispute the veracity of the wealth of evidence piling up against the accused. And even if they could, how could they explain the positive identification of Milat by the British backpacker Paul Onions.

Now on his third visit to Australia in barely five years, Paul Onions had already identified Milat from a selection of photographs shown to him by police when they flew him to Sydney in May 1994. Finally he saw his alleged attacker in the flesh and establish once and for all whether this really was the same person.

The fair-haired, quietly-spoken Englishman, dressed in a green sports jacket, white shirt and tie, sat nervously in the witness box as the Crown Prosecutor asked him to recall his ordeal and to remember the man who took a shot at him as he weaved his way across the Hume Highway.

'Would you be able to identify him again?' asked Mr Lloyd.

'Yes,' came the reply.

'Can you see him in this court?'

'Yes.'

'Where is he?'

'He's the gentleman behind you.'

'In the dock?'

'If that is what you call it,' he responded in his soft Midlands brogue.

Ivan Milat stared back in the same expressionless manner he had adopted throughout the previous few weeks.

Paul, whose name had been suppressed by the court ostensibly for his own safety, had provided the strongest evidence the proceedings had heard so far against Milat. He was the prosecution's star witness and had to be protected at any cost. Without Onions' testimony the police case would be severely diminished. With his evidence of identification the focus of suspicion fell squarely on the shoulders of Milat.

But the committal wasn't over. The court had yet to hear from those who had been much closer to the defendant; friends and relatives of the accused who might be in a position to shed new light on his guilt or innocence.

20.
TWO DIFFERENT STYLES OF KILLING

The Sydney *Telegraph Mirror* on December 7, 1994 thundered 'Backpacker Bombshell—Killer Not Alone.' The headline was based on a comment made by Dr Peter Bradhurst, of the NSW Institute of Forensic Medicine. The forensic scientist who carried out post mortems on all seven victims was giving the court the benefit of his considered opinion about the likelihood of a second person being involved in the backpacker murders.

There had been much speculation about the possibility of more than one killer as investigating officers wondered how a single man could overpower three couples. It was left to Dr Bradhurst to put into words what many people had been thinking.

He told the court that the different pattern of injuries inflicted on the six victims who travelled in pairs suggested that there could have been two backpacker murderers. The evidence indicated that the deaths might have been the work of a number of people because of the different styles of killing.

While Joanne Walters had been stabbed to death, her friend Caroline Clarke was shot in the head.

Australian hitchhiker James Gibson was also stabbed to death but his girlfriend Deborah Everist suffered a fractured skull, a broken jaw and other multiple injuries.

German backpacker Gabor Neugebauer was shot six times in the head but his girlfriend Anja Habschied was stabbed and decapitated.

It is generally accepted that lone serial killers stick to the same method of murder, but three of the backpacker couples had died from markedly different attacks.

If two killers were involved did each keep to his preferred style of execution? Or if there was only one murderer did he simply incapacitate the first victim before dealing with the other? These were questions to which there was no easy answer. Dr Bradhurst could only offer theories based on his wealth of experience in examining those who had died by violent means. And without definite proof he kept his options open.

'I would tend to think it more likely that more than one person was involved,' he told the court.

'But on the other hand it's also my opinion that it would still be possible for one person to have caused the deaths if that person had been able to incapacitate one of the two at the time, before dealing with the other,' he added.

Perhaps it was Dr Bradhurst's comments that prompted the following day's line of questioning, when two brothers of Ivan Milat were called to give evidence. Identified only as Witnesses E and F after the court agreed to suppress their names, the two men got the full treatment from Ian Lloyd QC who went straight for the jugular.

'Have you ever fired a Ruger 10/22 rifle in the Belango State Forest?' the Crown Prosecutor asked.

'No,' replied Witness E.

'Have you ever fired an Anshutz rifle in the Belanglo State Forest?'

'No,' he again insisted.

'Do you know anything about the deaths of backpackers in the Belanglo State Forest?' asked Mr Lloyd.

'No,' Witness E came back.

'Have you ever been with your brother Ivan in the Belanglo State Forest when he's fired a Ruger 10/22 or Anshutz rifle?'

'No.'

There was an equally emphatic response from Witness F.

'Have you ever fired an Anshutz rifle in the Belanglo State Forest?' Mr Lloyd enquired.

'No,' he replied.

'Were you ever present when a Ruger 10/22 or Anshutz rifle was fired in the Belanglo State Forest?'

'No.'

'Did you kill any people in the Belanglo State Forest?'

'No.'

'Do you know anything about the deaths of backpackers in the Belanglo State Forest?' the prosecuting lawyer asked.

'Only what I read in the paper,' said Witness F.

However, the Milat brothers did agree that they had visited Ivan's Eagle Vale home in December 1993 to 'move some guns' from the roof of the property. The defendant had called them to ask for their help in transporting the firearms and ammunition, which he wanted stored at Witness E's property at Hilltop in Sydney's south west. Why he wanted them placed elsewhere was not clear, but Witness E told the court he was under the impression that his sister Shirley who shared the home with Ivan had been complaining about the number of firearms in the house.

Witness F said he was not aware of the reason Ivan wanted the guns taken away, but he remembered the weapons in the roof were wrapped in blankets and rags and that ammunition was stored in wooden and metal boxes. After coffee and a meal the small arsenal was loaded into Witness E's utility truck and taken to his home at Hilltop, where they were stored in a room under the house. This property was among those raided on May 22, 1994, when officers from Task Force Air searched eleven different homes including the defendant's bungalow.

The day before they had also visited the Queensland home of Alex Milat, Ivan's older brother, to clear up the matter of the previous 'sighting' when the two British backpackers were supposedly spotted in a vehicle near the Belanglo State Forest after their abduction. Alex had told the police that he was sure they were the British girls. But in court Detective Senior Sergeant Bob Benson said he was sceptical about the story.

While he never believed that Alex Milat had anything to do with the murders, the officer thought the story was a bit far fetched.

A remark by Alex Milat's wife Joan during the police visit also seemed odd. Without prompting she mentioned to one of the officers that serial killers sometimes kept tokens connected with their deeds.

Detective Senior Constable Stuart Wilkins who was one of three policemen to visit the couple on May 21 recalled Mrs Milat saying 'something about people keeping tokens or backpacks in relation to serial killers.'

'She just brought it up herself,' he told the court. 'It was shortly after that that she produced a backpack,' he added.

Mrs Milat told the committal hearing that the backpack she had handed over to police had been given to her by her brother-in-law Ivan.

He had told her that a friend was returning to New Zealand and no longer required it so she could have it. Mrs Milat also admitted that she had written the initials I.M. under the top flap of the backpack, though she did not explain why.

It was the same backpack which police had earlier suggested belonged to Simone Schmidl.

During the course of their enquiries the police had interviewed most members of the Milat family as well as many of the defendant's friends and acquaintances. While several of them were called to give evidence there was one witness in particular who promised to be of special interest, a woman who probably knew Ivan Milat better than anyone—his ex-wife, Karen.

She had known her husband since 1976 but they did not marry until February 20, 1984. They separated three years later.

Karen, whose current name was suppressed by the court, was identified as Witness C. Then aged 35, she was seeing her ex-husband for the first time in more than seven years when she entered Court Number One at Campbelltown on the afternoon of December 1. She was clearly uncomfortable about the meeting.

Wearing a blue and white floral dress, the woman who had spent a decade of her life with a serial killer found it almost impossible to look Milat in the eye. Slowly she gathered confidence as the prosecution led her through her marriage to the man in the dock. She told of their Sunday outings to the Belanglo State Forest. On one occasion in 1984 her former husband had taken her there intending to shoot kangaroos, but there were too many other people around and they had collected wood instead.

Another time he had shot dead two kangaroos in the forest and slit the throat of one of them. On a third occasion they had simply picnicked by a wooden bridge in a gully. Milat, she added, knew the forest well.

The ex-wife became more upset as the questioning continued. Wiping away a tear she went on to reveal her former husband's love for firearms. He had even given his stepson a rifle for a tenth birthday present.

There were frequent trips to his brother's property where there was a makeshift firing range. Milat was 'gun crazy' and 'used to run around like a cowboy,' she recalled. He also gave himself nicknames such as Bargo Bill, Joe Spanner, Mac and Texas

'I was married to him, I know what he was like,' she reminded the court. She remembered how her former husband engraved his name on his property and she identified the name 'Texas' on a revolver shown to the court bearing a distinctive 'M' with an 'I' through it.

She also indentified a pistol which had been found under a washing machine at Milat's Eagle Vale home.

'In 1981 Ivan showed me this pistol,' she told the court.

Karen went on to explain how the accused often wrapped the firearm in a sock and stuffed it down the side of his boot whenever he went anywhere. 'It was loaded all the time,' she added.

Milat's ex-wife gave little else away about their time together but it was obvious the relationship had ended acrimoniously. She had moved to a secret location in New South Wales to start a new life under a different name. Whether that was out of a desire to put the past behind her or because she was concerned for her personal safety, was not revealed. The truth was probably somewhere between the two.

Evidence of Milat's undoubted passion for guns was reinforced by several other witnesses who spoke about him. Andrew Sara, a former workmate who often travelled with him on jobs, said he knew the defendant had a number of firearms.

Once there was an intriguing aside from Milat who seemed to allude to the backpacker killings. The two men were driving past the Belanglo State Forest when Milat unexpectedly volunteered, 'You'd be surprised what's in there.'

'What, snakes and kangaroos?' enquired Mr Sara.

But Milat did not reply and started to talk about work.

Another acquaintance of the defendant, Mrs Joan Breitkopf, whose late husband had known him well, said she once saw a large knife with an 18-inch blade in Milat's car.

'That's my friendly machete—you never know when you might need it,' he told her.

Milat also revealed to her how he could obtain a wide variety of weapons.

'Anything you want, I can get it for you—crossbow, handgun, anything,' he added.

There was more damning evidence about Milat's movements on the dates that the seven murdered backpackers had disappeared. It came in the form of a statement tendered to the court by the NSW Roads and Traffic Authority, which had gone back over the defendant's time sheets for the period he had been employed as a ganger.

They made fascinating reading. According to the records Milat was not at work between December 23, 1989, and January 1, 1990. The Australians James Gibson and Deborah Everist went missing around December 30.

On January 25, 1990 Milat had an accrued day off. It was the same date that Paul Onions met Milat outside Lombardo's newsagency at Casula and accepted a lift down the Hume Highway, a journey that almost ended in the hitchhiker's violent death.

The RTA records also indicated that Milat was not at work between January 19 and January 21, 1991. German backbacker Simone Schmidl left Sydney to hitch a life to Melbourne on January 20, 1991.

Fellow Germans Gabor Neugebauer and his girlfriend Anja Habschied were last seen alive on December 26, 1991. According to the RTA time sheets Milat was on leave between December 23, 1991 and January 21, 1992.

Finally there was the last reported sighting of the two British girls, Caroline Clarke and Joanne Walters, on April 18, 1992. Milat's records showed that he was not at work between April 17 and April 21, 1992.

It was an extraordinary coincidence that the man accused of the backpacker murders was not working on or around those days when the young tourists went missing. Whether he had an alibi for those dates or could account for the way he spent his time during those periods remained to be seen. After several weeks in the dock, Milat was looking increasingly tired although he never lost his composure and continued to take notes.

His head often bowed, he tried to avoid eye contact with many of the witnesses. But he couldn't ignore the photograph which had been brought into the court by Pauline Vuletich who originally came from the Shetland Islands off the coast of Scotland but now lived in New Zealand. Pauline had flown to Australia with Joanne Walters in 1991 and was among the last to see the British girls alive.

The photograph was a framed portrait of Joanne which she placed by her side in the witness box and directly in front of the defendant. Pauline never explained why she brought the photograph with her and placed it where she did. One could only assume that she felt the image of the young woman who had been such a close friend, would support her through the courtroom questioning and remind those present what this case was all about: The brutal deaths of seven young people who had come to Australia in pursuit of fun and adventure but who tragically fell victim to a monster.

The question magistrate Price had to decide was whether that monstrous act might have been committed by the man sitting before him. His job was not to find the accused guilty but to establish whether there was a prima facie case against him.

Confronted by such a mountain of evidence it was clearly going to be an uphill struggle for the defence to persuade the magistrate that Milat did not have a case to answer. But on what turned out to be the penultimate day of the committal defence barrister Terry Martin tried to achieve just that.

Mr Martin demanded to know why at least 10 witnesses whom he suggested could destroy the police case against his client, had not been called by the prosecution. And he asked Mr Price to adjourn the proceedings until they were called.

Ostensibly it was a reasonable demand. The witnesses included the two women who reportedly gave a lift to Joanne Walters and Caroline Clarke at Waterfall between April 21-23, 1992. One of them, Mrs Susan Burns, had even been hypnotised by the police and had 'specifically identified' Joanne from a photograph.

There was also the reported sighting of Simone Schmidl at Albury railway station on January 21 1991. A railway station employee had told police how he had spoken to a young woman similar to the young German and he particularly remembered a bandage on one of her ankles. Another Albury person who had seen a girl hitchhiking in the main street had given an 'absolute identification of Ms Schmidl,' Mr Martin explained.

'If these sightings are in fact correct, then the police theory about these people going missing on certain days and my client being available to do anything to these people is destroyed,' he claimed.

It was an important point. While Mr Martin accepted that it was up to the Crown to decide which witnesses were material to the case, he argued that the prosecution was mistaken in not calling those he had mentioned.

Not surprisingly the Crown disagreed. Mr Lloyd pointed out there had been hundreds of reported sightings of the backpackers and he viewed the named witnesses as unreliable.

'Just as these people genuinely feel they saw the people in question, there is a mountain of other evidence against that,' he asserted.

The magistrate came down on the side of the prosecution, ruling that he did not have the power to stay the committal. However it wasn't the last time the question of the uncalled witnesses was raised.

21.
TESTING THE ALLEGATIONS

The final witness to take the stand in the case against Ivan Milat was the man who had so vigorously pursued him, Chief Superintendent Clive Small, the head of Task Force Air. It was December 12, 1994, and the climax to a hearing which had begun seven weeks earlier. In that time 171 witnesses had appeared, 1991 pages of transcript had been tendered and 650 exhibits had been shown to the court.

If the magistrate, lawyers and media who had followed the case so religiously were tired no one was showing it. Remarkably for a hearing that had lasted so long, each day produced more surprises, each witness more drama. Sitting in Court Number One at Campbelltown for the duration of the committal proceedings was never boring. And the suspense continued until the court rose for the last time.

In all Chief Superintendent Small had spent eight months on the case and he knew the details inside out. He told how Milat had come to Task Force Air's attention some months before his arrest, but only became a key suspect around March/April after Paul Onions provided what was to prove a crucial lead. He conceded that although detectives had had their suspicions about the defendant before his arrest, it was the evidence of the young British tourist who strengthened their opinion.

Questioned by the defence Mr Small was asked if Milat was the only person who fitted the description provided by Onions.

'He was the only one who fitted the all-round description,' he replied. Apart from the physical similarity, Milat was also a divorcee of Yugoslav family background and had worked for the Roads and Traffic Authority.

Could other members of the Milat family have fitted the same description?

'To a varying degree,' replied the officer, but none of them owned a four wheel drive like the one driven by the accused, a silver coloured Nissan Patrol with sheepskin seat covers and a stripe down the side. It was also known that Milat was 'extremely jealous' about his vehicle and was unlikely to allow anyone else to drive it.

Even so, the police who raided his home in the early morning of Sunday, May 22 did not reckon with the quantity of other potentially incriminating evidence they would find there. They were equally surprised when Mrs Joan Milat produced the backpack, which allegedly belonged to Simone Schmidl, when detectives visited the house she shared in Queensland with Ivan's brother Alex.

'It was never expected we would find the wealth of evidence,' Mr Small admitted.

Thirty minutes after the head of Task Force Air left the witness box, magistrate Michael Price ruled that there was clearly sufficient evidence for Milat to stand trial for the seven backpacker murders. But he also cautioned against anyone concluding that the defendant was guilty.

Normally he would have given reasons for reaching his decision that there was a prima facie case but he was anxious to avoid any suggestion that the court had already made up its mind about the defendant's guilt.

Magistrate Price said he did not want any view which the court 'may be seen to have formed' interpreted as a finding which could be perceived by the public as a judicial determination.

'What this court has heard over recent weeks is but the prosecution's case as tested in cross-examination,' he pointed out.

'The accused person is yet to stand trial and have the factual issues determined by a jury of 12,' Mr Price emphasised.

The magistrate was more than conscious of the danger of the community at large being unduly influenced by what was said in court and drawing their own conclusions. He was anxious that nothing should be said or done which might interfere with the course of justice.

Defence solicitor Andrew Boe conceded there was 'sufficient prima facie evidence' to justify Milat being committed but he was also concerned about his client getting a fair trial. Outside the court he said he was worried about the extensive media coverage given to the case which would make it extremely difficult to appoint an unbiased jury.

'I think if we were honest about it we would all concede that the impact of the publication of untested allegations would affect the fair trial of any person in this country,' he added.

Likening the case to the trial of Lindy Chamberlain who was wrongly convicted of murdering her baby daughter Azaria in 1982, Mr Boe said he believed there was a strong argument for restricting the publication of allegations which might influence potential jurors.

'I think this case will be a test for how this community and the criminal justice system in Australia deals with such a public airing of allegations at committal,' he concluded.

Minutes earlier Ivan Milat, wearing a white shirt and grey tie, stood expressionless in the dock as the magistrate remanded him in custody. He shook his lawyer's hand, smiled and was led back to the cells as Joanne Walters' parents Jill and Ray watched from the public gallery. Mrs Walters sobbed quietly and clutched her husband's hand as the defendant was taken away.

Across the road in Rumpole's Bar, police, lawyers and the media gathered for a lunchtime beer to celebrate the end of the marathon hearing. It had been a long and exhausting dress rehearsal for the big judicial production that would take place 19 months hence in Sydney's Central Criminal Court.

The case was scheduled to last for up to five months. What new surprises the trial of Ivan Milat might hold could only be guessed at. But given the unparalleled daily interest in the committal which had been so widely reported in Australia and overseas, it was reasonable to assume that further revelations about the heinous nature of the crimes and their perpetrator would continue to shock.

22.

The Stage Is Set

There were few people in Australia who had not heard about the backpacker murders on the day Ivan Milat stood trial at the New South Wales Supreme Court in Sydney on March 25, 1996.

Even the judge admitted: 'You would have to be hermits not to have heard anything about this case at all.'

It made the selection of an impartial jury particularly challenging—how to choose 12 men and women who would not have been influenced in some way by the graphic media coverage of the events leading up to this case over the previous four years?

Yet before the selection process got underway, Justice David Hunt made it clear that no juror should be disqualified simply because he or she had seen, heard or read about the killings.

Ivan Milat was still an innocent man in the eyes of the law and had to be regarded as such by those who would later deliberate on his guilt or otherwise.

He warned that the jury would be shown graphic photographs of the victims' injuries. Not fully-clothed bodies, but badly decomposed remains which were little more than skeletons.

Even so they should not allow such photographic evidence to get in the way of their judgment of whoever committed these horrible crimes.

'You will nevertheless inevitably have feelings of sympathy for the victims and their relatives,' he conceded.

'You will have to put that sympathy to the side. Only consider the case on the basis of the evidence put to the jurors in the course of the trial,' Justice Hunt emphasised.

'You will also be directed that the prosecution carries the onus of proving beyond reasonable doubt that Mr Milat is guilty,' he pointed out.

One thousand people had been summonsed for jury service on that day. Only 250 turned up. More than 170 dropped out when told the nature of the trial and how long it was likely to last.

If they suffered from claustrophobia or had a physical disability that prevented them sitting for long periods of time they could be excused, he said.

They could also stand down if they had been telephoned by an organisation conducting a survey into public reaction to media coverage of the case.

None of those remaining took up the judge's offer. Without doubt these were upstanding members of the community who took their responsibilities seriously.

Those who were still in the jury pool had to face a further hurdle before being selected for what was expected to be a marathon trial. Under the Australian judicial system both the defence and prosecution teams are allowed to challenge potential jurors.

What makes a barrister go for one person and dismiss another is a mystery which even the legal profession finds hard to explain. In the search for the perfect juror, appearance, sex and age are sometimes considered, but the reason for the final decision is usually lost on the rest of the court.

That morning, in the 13th floor Queen's Square courtroom where the jury was being chosen, the defence and prosecution were allowed 20 challenges each. It took half an hour to whittle the panel down to eight men and four women. The final selection appeared to be a reasonable cross section of society. There were young men and women, a few middle-aged professional-types and a couple of people who could have been retired.

As it turned out they were a remarkably happy and intelligent bunch according to those court staff who had dealings with them. If they were going to spend the next four months in close proximity they certainly needed to get on with each other.

They also had to be blessed with good health and a strong constitution.

This was going to be one of the most mentally and physically demanding few months of their life. Days off for sickness would have to be avoided if possible.

The court was to sit from 10 a.m. to 4 p.m. There would be a morning tea break at 11.30 a.m., an hour for lunch at 1 p.m. and a two hour sitting in the afternoon.

Friday was to be a half-day so that jurors could attend to their domestic responsibilities in the afternoon.

A beginning-of-school-term feeling pervaded the proceedings with everybody getting to know each other and bracing themselves for the long haul.

Only the 'not guilty' response of Ivan Milat to the eight charges he faced reminded those present of the reason they were there:

That on or about December 30, 1989, in or near the Belanglo State Forest, in New South Wales, he did murder Australians Deborah Everist and James Gibson, both aged 19.

That on January 25, 1990, near the Belanglo State Forest, he did detain Englishman Paul Onions who was then 23, with intent to hold him for advantage.

That on or about January 20-21, 1991 he did murder 21 year-old Simone Schmidl, from Germany.

That between December 26, 1991 and January 1, 1992 he did murder Anja Habschied, 20, and Gabor Neugebauer, her 21 year-old boyfriend, also from Germany.

And that between April 18 and April 21, 1992 he did murder Britons Joanne Walters and Caroline Clarke, who were both 22.

Before the case could get underway there was to be a change of venue. The formalities of jury selection over, the case itself was to transfer that afternoon to the Old Banco Court, a few hundred metres away.

More than a century old at the time, the building, known as St James's Court, just opposite Hyde Park, was and still is a remarkably, well-preserved example of the sort of colonial architecture that symbolised the British judicial system in the last century.

Inside the fittings, furnishings and decor were in tune with its age. There was much mahogany paneling and the cream walls were decorated with gold trim and the occasional crown.

Daylight flooded much of the courtroom from a glass skylight in the high, domed ceiling.

In 1996 there was still no heating or air-conditioning, creating a stifling atmosphere in summer and arctic temperatures in winter.

The only concession to modern technology was a sound system which relayed the proceedings though a number of strategically placed loud speakers dotted around the interior.

The press gallery, at the rear of the court, was just big enough to accommodate 30 journalists. Those who suffered from the long hours of sitting on the hard, wooden benches were encouraged to bring their own cushions.

The public gallery was upstairs and large enough to seat no more than 50 people. A small section was reserved for families of the victims.

A perspex screen had been fitted across part of the public gallery immediately above the spot where Milat was to sit. This would protect the defendant from missiles thrown at him from above but was never put to the test.

Milat did not sit in a conventional dock. Unlike Campbelltown court there were no stairs from underground cells leading directly into the dock.

Instead he sat on a wooden seat to the left hand side of the court surrounded by members of the NSW Corrective Services Department, who escorted him to court every day.

If Milat was nervous or apprehensive he certainly didn't show it. Dressed in a navy blue suit, white shirt and grey, check tie, he sat motionless for much of the time, his right hand draped across his mouth, his thumb planted on his chin and his fore-finger resting on his cheek bone, just below his ear.

Looking smart with his hair neatly combed, he seemed unperturbed by the formality of the proceedings and showed no sign of being intimidated. There was even a hint of a smile as the jury entered.

He listened intently to the judge, dressed in his red robes and horsehair wig. But he rarely turned his head to the packed press bench, just a few feet to his right. And he certainly never lifted his gaze to the upstairs public gallery where mothers, fathers and friends of his victims waited for justice to take its course. The defence team of Terry Martin, Peter Callaghan, Andrew Boe and Alison Ryan had spent many months preparing their case. There had been a lengthy dispute about fees which had delayed the start of the trial. But with the financial differences cleared up and new rates of pay agreed they were determined to concentrate all their efforts on the job in hand.

A few feet away, Crown Prosecutor Mark Tedeschi QC and his team, consisting of Dan Howard and Sarah Hugget, were equally keen to get the case underway.

A wiry looking man with a thin voice to match, Tedeschi's appearance and his speech gave little hint of the tough-talking personality who was to emerge on several occasions during the trial as his tenacious questioning held the courtroom spellbound.

Tedeschi had taken over from Ian Lloyd, who during the long wait from committal to trial had left the Crown Prosecutor's office to take up a legal post in Cambodia.

While in many ways his mild-mannered successor was the antithesis of the extrovert Lloyd, it rapidly became apparent that Tedeschi was more than capable of holding his own in the cut and thrust of the unfolding legal drama.

When the judge adjourned the case on that first day there was an overwhelming sense of occasion. Even when a man is on trial for seven brutal murders it is sometimes easy to forget the stark horror of the act, cloaked as it is in legal jargon.

But today no one could be left in doubt that they were in the company of evil. Over the next 18 weeks the malevolence would manifest itself through the testimony of 140 witnesses and several hundred exhibits which transformed the precincts of the Old Banco Court into a chamber of horrors.

The daily flood of chilling detail would dominate the Australian media for months to come. Rarely had a case captured such public attention. People would discuss the day's evidence in buses, trains and on street corners.

That any man was capable of such savagery was beyond imagination. As the days wore on the evidence became ever more shocking. The questions raised were more difficult to answer, the theories posed seemed more impossible to believe.

Could he have done it by himself? Was there another member of the Milat family involved? Had he been set-up by the police or a brother?

What made a man commit such unspeakable horror? Or was this ordinary looking bloke with a friendly visage genuinely innocent?

The case for the prosecution was about to begin.

Tomorrow the trial of Ivan Robet Marko Milat, a 51 year-old roadworker of Cinnabar Street, Eagle Vale, would reveal his wicked ways in every odious detail.

23.

MILAT THE RINGLEADER?

On the second full day of the trial Mark Tedeschi told the court: 'These killings were for killings sake...ferocious and sustained attacks during which vastly more force was used than was necessary to kill.'

But why? What was Ivan Milat's motive?

The Crown Prosecutor had no doubt that these murders and the kidnapping of Paul Onions were simply carried out in pursuit of the 'accused's psychological gratification.'

And was he acting alone? No one really knew apart from the defendant himself. But there was no doubt that Milat was the ringleader.

'The Crown say either the accused did the acts himself or alternatively the acts were done by him and others in a way in which he would be responsible for the acts of the others,' he explained to the jury.

Mr Tedeschi's opening statement outlining the case for the prosecution was to continue all day. It was a detailed account of the enormous weight of evidence the police had amassed since Milat was arrested just over two years earlier.

Bit by bit the Crown put the many pieces of the jigsaw together. It was an extraordinarily complex case and the jury needed to be metaphorically led by the hand through the maze of information.

Throughout the long, hot morning and well into the afternoon they were treated to the prosecution's interpretation of what happened between December 1989 when the Australian couple disappeared, and Easter 1992 when the two British girls vanished.

There was to be complicated scientific evidence including technical data relating to ballistics and forensic evidence. No stone would be left unturned in the analysis of exhibits and the search for evidence.

The prosecution's view was encapsulated in one short sentence: 'The Crown's case is that the physical evidence inside 22 Cinnabar Street links Ivan Milat with every one of the four groups of bodies found in the Belanglo State Forest.'

Mr Tedeschi spent much of that second day going over evidence already presented at the committal, detailing what the police had found in the defendant's bungalow. It included parts of the 10/22 Ruger rifle including the bolt, which were discovered in the wall cavity and which matched the weapon used to shoot two of the backpackers.

He said the court would be told by ballistics experts that test firing had shown the same bolt had been used to fire 10 cartridges found at the spot where Caroline Clarke had died.

Likewise the same weapon had been used to fire cartridges found near the bodies of Anja Habschied and Gabor Neugebauer.

There would also be evidence that numbers which appeared on a box of .22 calibre Eley brand ammunition in the fourth bedroom matched the numbers on an empty Eley box also found at the Habschied/Neugebauer murder scene, which the prosecution described as a 'shooting gallery.'

Only 600 boxes of that particular kind of ammunition were ever manufactured and they were all made during an eight hour shift at the factory on the same day.

Camping equipment including backpacks, sleeping bags, cooking utensils and clothing were also found in the Eagle Vale house, as well as homes belonging to Milat's mother and some of his brothers.

During that early morning search on the day of Milat's arrest police came across a photograph of Chalinder Hughes who was wearing the green and white Benetton top which was exactly the same as one worn by Caroline Clarke and which was to prove such a vital piece of evidence during the trial.

In a kitchen drawer they discovered an Olympus camera, which had also belonged to Caroline. The Malaysian-made camera had never been sold in

Australia. Black electrical tape similar to that found near the bodies of some of the backpackers was also uncovered in Milat's home.

At his mother's house in Guildford police came across an Indian cavalry sword which the prosecution was later to suggest could have been the weapon used to decapitate Anja Habschied.

A cloth gag which had been tied around Joanne Walters' mouth had been torn from a Gloweave business shirt. Significantly the size of the shirt was 41, an exact fit for the defendant.

In the garage at Cinnabar Street they came across a Compactormat strap, which was used to tie up bulky camping gear such as bed rolls. It was identical to one around Simone Schmidl's head when her remains were found in the forest.

There was also a green-striped pillow case containing five lengths of sash cord. More ominously one of the cords had blood on it. Mr Tedeschi claimed that DNA tests showed the blood was consistent with that of blood from a child of Mr and Mrs Ian and Jacqueline Clarke, Caroline's parents. The chance of this happening was a possibility of one in 118,000.

A sleeping bag belonging to Deborah Everist was found in a wardrobe in Milat's house. A water bottle owned by Simone Schmidl with her nickname 'Simi' scratched out was also discovered nearby.

Police came across all these items after Milat's arrest. The fact that some, like the Ruger bolt, had apparently been hidden in a wall cavity might have explained the minutes that elapsed between Task Force Air's initial contact with the defendant on the telephone and his eventual appearance at the front door.

Police witnesses subsequently indicated they heard noises which suggested movement in the adjoining garage. Was the accused trying to conceal evidence or gain access to the roof so that he could slide the rifle parts down into the wall cavity?

The Crown also told how land owned by one of the Milat brothers who had used it as a rifle range, produced 41 kilograms of spent bullets and no less than 13,640 .22 cartridge cases. In the press gallery someone remarked that it appeared to be not so much a rifle range as a battle ground.

Turning to the nature of the killings, the prosecution lawyer said that all seven murdered backpackers had been found in what appeared to be makeshift graves.

Describing the discovery of Joanne Walters' remains on September 19, 1992 Mr Tedeschi said that such had been the ferocity of the stabbing attack on her that the knife had cut several of her vertebra and her spinal cord, which would have rendered her paralysed.

Caroline Clarke's body had ten bullet wounds to the head and stab wounds to the back and chest area.

Anja Habschied had been decapitated with a sword or a machete which had sliced through her fourth vertebra. The injuries had all the hallmarks of an execution-style killing.

The sickening details were increasingly difficult to stomach. There were some people in the court that day who had to go outside for a breath of fresh air. It made for intensely ghoulish listening.

The prosecution's opening statement continued in much the same grim manner as it had begun. The bodies had been covered with sticks and leaves but not by earth. This would hasten their decomposition under the harsh sunlight that beat down upon the Australian bush but at the same time still conceal the remains.

Interestingly there was no evidence of a struggle as had been suggested at the committal by the presence of hairs in two of the victims' hands.

'Not one of the deceased showed any signs of defensive wounds,' Mr Tedeschi explained.

'All of the bodies were disposed of in a way that ensured their speedy disintegration.'

As for the backpackers' last moments alive, one could only guess at the panic and sheer helplessness they felt, faced with the horror and inevitability of their end.

How long were some of them allowed to remain paralysed before they were finally put out of their misery? What sinister use had the sash cord and electrical tape, found at the murder scene, been used for?

What evil and deviant practises had they been subjected to before or after their death?

While there was strong evidence to suggest that most of the victims had been subjected to sexual assault, such was the decomposed state of the bodies that it was impossible to establish whether anal or vaginal intercourse had taken place.

How could only one person have subdued two people? In the case of the Germans, one was a fit young woman and the other a strong, well-built young man. Was the threat of a gun sufficient to make them do as they were told? Or would it have required at least two assailants.

Was one person killed first, allowing the person or persons responsible to take their time over the second?

The Crown admitted it did not know how many people were involved in the murders at the Belanglo State Forest. It had no proof that Ivan Milat was acting alone or had an accomplice or accomplices.

What was certain in the view of the prosecution was that whoever else might have been connected with the crimes, Ivan Milat played a key role. He was the instigator of the killings. He gave the orders.

He would have been 'responsible for the acts of the others,' Mr Tedeschi told the jury.

How was he so certain of Milat's participation? The jury needed look no further than the witness who was to give evidence the following day: Paul Onions.

The young British tourist who was the only publicly named person to have stared down Ivan Milat's gun barrel and live was to be the star witness in the proceedings that were beginning to unfold in St James's Court.

As the one and only survivor of the backpacker murders he was able to shed much light on how the accused went about his business.

Mark Tedeschi offered a preview of what was to come. In a clear, calm and understated voice he told the jury how Milat had stopped his four wheel drive Nissan Patrol along the Hume Highway just before the entrance to the Belanglo Forest and pulled out a gun and some rope.

His passenger, Paul Onions, whom he had picked up at Casula an hour or so earlier at Lombardo's newsagency, fled in terror but not before Milat had fired a shot after him.

Mr Tedeschi's assessment of the evidence was short and uncompromising. It was the very essence of what this trial was all about.

'The Crown alleges that what actually happened to Mr Onions close to the Belanglo State Forest is some evidence which identifies (Milat) as the person who murdered the seven deceased backpackers and provides some clues as to what happened to them before they were taken into the forest and murdered,' he declared.

'The Crown case is that the accused abducted the seven deceased backpackers in order to take them into the Belanglo State Forest and there to murder them and to rob them of their property, in particular their camping equipment.'

Among the evidence they would hear from Mr Onions was—'most tellingly'—the fact that one of his shirts was later found at Mrs Margaret Milat's home where Ivan had been living at the time.

Without Paul Onions' testimony much of the case against the accused was essentially circumstantial. Certainly a lot of what the police knew pointed the finger of suspicion at Ivan Milat. And there were other 'telling' coincidences such as the defendant's employment records which revealed he was not working on dates when the seven backpackers disappeared and were, most probably, attacked.

But nobody, unless he had a partner, actually saw Milat kill his victims and so far as is known he never admitted it to anybody else. His courtroom demeanour offered no clues. Here was a man who remained seemingly unperturbed throughout the first few days of the trial and beyond, although there were to be some occasions over the next 18 weeks when the mask would drop.

If there was an inner turmoil seething beneath that composed exterior he was not showing it. Sitting a few feet away from Ivan Milat for hours on end it was possible to monitor his every movement. Yet his eyes, his mouth, the way he held his body, gave nothing away.

One wondered whether Ivan Milat himself ever accepted he was a serial killer. How could the man who raped, shot and stabbed his victims with such manic ferocity remain so tranquil in the face of such overwhelming evidence?

Or was there another Milat beneath that quiet facade? A personality so evil that the other side of his character refused to acknowledge it.

Did Ivan Milat genuinely believe he was not guilty?

24.
'HE'S GOT A GUN. HELP ME!'

If anything is guaranteed to concentrate the mind it is the fear of imminent death. Paul Onions had reached that stage in the space of a few short terrifying seconds. Now he was staring straight down the barrel of a black revolver which Ivan Milat was pointing at him.

In the kaleidoscope of raw emotion that raced around his body there was little time for reasoning. His survival instincts took over and his eyes concentrated on the epicentre of the threat: The bullets in the gun.

Unlike most ammunition these bullets had copper tips, which were now aimed precisely at his head.

'You could see the copper bullets in the chambers. The copper tips of the bullets were the biggest image to me,' he told the Supreme Court of New South Wales shortly after entering the witness box on March 27, 1996.

For the fourth time in just over six years, Onions had flown half way around the world. The first for a working holiday in late 1989. The second to identify the man who attacked him. The third trip to give evidence at the committal proceedings in Campbelltown. And now to convince a jury that there was no doubt about the identity of the man who kidnapped him, albeit for only a few minutes but nevertheless against his will.

Onions was clearly apprehensive about coming face to face with his attacker on that morning. He would pass within a few feet of Ivan Milat but their eyes didn't meet.

His voice quiet, yet compelling, Onions stood in the witness box dressed in a navy blazer, beige trousers, white shirt and tie. His neatly combed hair was parted in the middle. The backpacker's recollection of the day Ivan Milat walked into his life was so riveting that the court sat spellbound for much of the morning.

Onions began by recalling his state of mind as he approached Lombardo's Newsagency on that fateful morning of January 25, 1990.

He was feeling tired, disappointed and disillusioned by his lack of success in getting a lift. He was also thirsty.

Onions' verbatim account in the New South Wales Supreme Court on March 27 of the few hours that almost ended his life is as compelling now as it was then.

'In the distance all I could see was a red sign which I thought was a Coca Cola sign. I needed a drink so I headed for it. I bought a Coke in the shop and then proceeded to walk out.

'This gentleman approached me and asked me if I needed a lift. I thought, "Great - yes." He just asked me where I was heading and I said to Canberra. I said, "I'd like to go to Mildurra."'

'He said, 'That's my vehicle over there I'm going to Canberra.' I thought "Great. That's half way."'

'He walked into the shop himself and I walked over to the vehicle and waited for him to come out. I was waiting round the back of the vehicle with my rucksack and he said, "Come round to the front and throw it into the back seat."'

'He opened the passenger door and I waited there. He went over to the driver's door and gave me a hand to put the rucksack in the back seat. I just got into the vehicle and away we went.'

As Milat and Onions drove off they passed the time making friendly chat.

'Initially it was getting-to-know you conversation. I explained what I was doing in Australia and he asked me if I had family and where I came from in England.

'I said my family lived in England and that I'd just left my job to travel around Australia on a working holiday. I introduced myself as Paul and he said his name was Bill. I said I came from Birmingham. I don't think he knew where that was and so I said in the middle of the country. I explained that I had been working as a testing engineer and had served in the navy previously.

He asked me if I'd served in the special forces or Northern Ireland and I said 'no.'

'I said I had no family in Australia and that I was in no rush and just here for the experience.

'I asked him what he did for a job and he said that he lived in Liverpool and worked on the roads. He was on holiday and going to see some friends in Canberra.'

As the journey proceeded they exchanged more personal detail about their lives.

'During this time there was quite a lot of conversation between us about what we did for a living and things like that. I think he said he was divorced at the time. He said that his family wasn't Australian but that they were from Yugoslavia.

'It was great, you know. Once we got on the freeway it was my first impression of the Australian bush. Then his attitude changed a little bit and he was not quite so friendly. He started to talk about people who lived in Australia, about non-Australian people. He talked about all the ethnic people in Sydney and Australia and how they shouldn't be there.

'Then he talked about the British in Northern Ireland and thought that they shouldn't be there. I found it a bit odd really. I thought he was a bit of an anti-person. He disliked Asians, Japanese and Vietnamese.'

As the conversation progressed Onions started feeling a little uneasy.

'I was getting a little bit nervous about his change in attitude. I was also feeling tired, though when you are travelling you like to stay awake. I started looking at the side of his face. We must have travelled for thirty minutes and he started slowing down a little and that also made me nervy. I couldn't see any other vehicles on the road and couldn't see what the problem was. I just couldn't see the reason why he was slowing down.

'Then he told me that you lose the radio around there and he wanted to pull over and put some tapes on. I thought it was odd at the time because there were cassettes between the two seats. As soon as he started to slow down he decided he was going to get out for some cassettes. He pulled over to the left hand side and I was obviously a bit uneasy. I thought I would get out of the vehicle and stretch my legs. I was a bit paranoid really.

'He said, "Why are you getting out of the vehicle?" And then started messing about under the driver's seat.

'I thought, "Well I'll give him the benefit of the doubt." I thought, "Calm down." So I got back into the passenger seat and put the belt back on. He also got back into the driver's seat and I thought we were okay.'

'Then he said, "I'll look under the seat one more time for a cassette." I thought "What's going on?" He looked under the seat and produced a revolver. It was a dark coloured gun and you could see the copper tips of the bullets in the chamber. The barrel was four to six inches long. The one thing I remember was the copper tips of the bullets. They were the biggest image to me so I knew it was for real, like.

'He was leaning on the driver's side of the vehicle and the gun was pointing straight at me. I could feel my voice shaking. I couldn't believe it. I said, "Calm down, what's the problem?"'

'He said, "Do you know what this is?" I said, "Yes."

'He said, "This is a robbery."

'I started to take my seat belt off and he said, "Put it back on again."

'He leant under the driver's seat again and I saw some rope sticking out from under the seat. He was holding his gun with his right hand and he leaned underneath with the other hand and picked it (the rope) up. It was all so fast.

'It was just a bag with dirty coloured rope. When I saw the rope that scared me more than the gun. I jumped out of the vehicle and ran back towards Sydney.

'He shouted, "Stop or I'll shoot." I heard the gun go off and I started dodging and weaving as best I could. There were vehicles coming over the hill and people were slowing down to see what was happening. Then they drove off again. There were two vehicles which I stood in front of which slowed down and then accelerated away.

'I was just about to give up and I looked around and the man was right by me again. He was holding onto my shirt and I tried to free myself. I looked round and thought, "This is my last chance, I've got to get away now." '

Onions realised his only hope would be to force a passing motorist to stop by throwing himself into the path of an oncoming vehicle.

'Once I broke free I thought the next vehicle that comes over the hill, I'm going to stand in front of it and if it runs over me, so be it.'

It was time for Mrs Joanne Berry to join the dramatic sequence of events being played out on the hard shoulder of the Hume Highway.

Her Toyota Tarago contained five children and her sister. The Canberra mother was understandably frightened by what was happening in front of her.

'They seemed to wrestle a little bit and then the first man (Onions) got up again, came back on the road...he stood right in front of my car and I stopped. I would have hit him if I hadn't stopped,' she told the court later.

Paul Onions raced up to the vehicle and begged to be allowed in.

'He came to the driver's side window and he said, "Please help, stop, he's got a gun, help me."'

'He was absolutely petrified and very close to tears,' Mrs Berry added.

Onions agreed he was terrified, but he was desperate.

'The people inside were all panicky saying, "Get out, get out" and I said, "This man has got a gun; I'm not going anywhere."'

Appreciating the urgency of the situation Mrs Berry turned the vehicle around, drove across the central reservation and headed back the way she'd come.

As Onions looked back towards the man who had tried to abduct him, he saw him standing by the side of the road with a 'stupid grin' on his face.

Ivan Milat climbed back into his Nissan four wheel drive and roared off with the British tourist's backpack, passport and other personal belongings on the rear seat

Mark Tedeschi, who had led the young witness through his evidence that day, turned to Onions and asked, 'If you saw that person in the courtroom now would you be able to identify the man who was the driver of that car?'

'Yes,' Onions replied.

'Can you look around the courtroom and say if you see that man?'

'It's that guy there,' said Onions, pointing at Milat with his right hand.

The defendant didn't flinch.

Onions was also asked to identify a blue Next brand shirt which was found in Margaret Milat's house in Guildford.

He pointed out to the court that it was not only the same size but also the same colour as one he had owned. He had placed it in his backpack the morning he left Sydney intending to hitchhike to Mildura.

It was the same backpack he left behind in Ivan Milat's car.

25.
'THAT'S A KNIFE'

If Ivan Milat had friends he certainly needed them now. Lucky to have escaped police attention in January, 1990 after the Onions attack, his good fortune was beginning to run out.

More than anything he needed an alibi in relation to those days when the backpackers disappeared. It was provided by his sister-in-law, Mrs Carolynne Milat, who is married to William, also known as Bill. She told the court that she remembered Ivan being at a family gathering on Boxing Day 1991 when the German couple, Gabor Neugebauer and Anja Habschied, were last seen.

She was certain Ivan was there in his mother's house on that day because she recalled him horsing around with one of the children when they arrived

'We were blasted by a water pistol by one of them who was being egged on by Mac,' she explained, referring to Ivan's family nickname. She had known Milat for 26 years and they got on well. He called her 'Caza.'

Carolynne said she arrived about 1-1.30 p.m. with her husband and didn't leave until about 6.30-7 p.m., after they had dinner.

'Was Mr Milat there all afternoon?' she was asked in court.

'Oh yes, I spent most of the day speaking with him,' she replied.

'Was Ivan Milat there when you left?' defence barrister Mr Terry Martin enquired.

'Yes he could not move because my vehicle was in the driveway,' she pointed out.

The questioning continued. Carolynne Milat appeared to be irritated by prosecution suggestions that she had not co-operated fully with the police.

'I am under oath and I intend telling the truth,' she said, her voice rising.

'Have you discussed anything with your family about what happened on Boxing Day?' Mr Tedeschi pressed her.

'No.'

'Have you discussed it with your husband?'

'With my husband of course,' she admitted.

'But not other family members,' she added.

'I suppose you recall very vividly when Ivan Milat was arrested?' Mr Tedeschi went on.

'Oh, yes,' she said.

'Did you notice one of the charges was an allegation in relation to two backpackers who disappeared in Easter 1992?'

'I didn't notice this until a few months ago,' she insisted.

The prosecution's line of questioning had a purpose. Mark Tedeschi wanted to introduce a piece of evidence which was to raise doubts about the accuracy of Carolynne Milat's memory.

He produced a photograph album which contained pictures of Ivan camping with her family at Wombeyan Caves, supposedly during Easter, 1992 when the British victims went missing. At least that is what the date said, but the writing appeared to have been amended from March 1991 to March 1992.

'Did you do it to provide an alibi for Ivan?' the Crown enquired.

'Definitely not,' came Mrs Milat's abrupt reply, though she did admit changing the dates herself.

'Is it possible the original date of Easter 1991 was correct?' he asked.

'It is possible,' she admitted.

'Is it possible you are wrong in your recollections about Boxing Day 1991?' he came back.

'Anything is possible. I just don't know,' she conceded.

As the rest of the court hung on her every word, Mr Tedeschi asked Mrs Milat to remove the photographs from the cellophane cover in the album and read what was on the back.

The handwriting was Ivan Milat's. The dates were clear and without question: '29-3-91' and '31-3-91.'

Carolynne denied altering the dates to help her brother-in-law.

'Are you deliberately seeking to give evidence in an attempt to protect Ivan Milat?' the Crown prosecutor demanded.

'No, no,' she replied.

'I suggest to you that you changed the 1991 to 1992 after you had found out that Ivan Milat was charged with an offence that is alleged to have occurred in Easter of 1992,' he went on.

'No,' she added.

Later in the trial it emerged that another person once connected with the Milat family, Ms Elizabeth Smith, a former girlfriend of Richard Milat, had given a statement to police suggesting that Ivan was not at his mother's house in Guildford on the morning of Boxing Day.

'If you ask me if I saw Mac, I would say no, not at all during the day,' she said in the statement.

Cross-examined by Terry Martin about whether she had a precise memory of the family get-together she replied,'Yes..yes and no.'

However, Elizabeth's recollection was clouded by her mental and physical state in those days. She admitted to being an alcoholic at the time and 'scatterbrained.' She might have made a mistake in the police statement.

She remembered spending the night with Richard at his mother Margaret's home in Guildford on the night before Boxing Day.

Elizabeth, who is the mother of Richard's six year-old son, said she had got up at 6 a.m. and went to another room where she kept a bottle of brandy. She drank about a middy-glass full.

She remembered looking out of the window and seeing the garage door open, which usually indicated Ivan was out.

In an effort to explain the confusion Elizabeth pointed out that her statement had been given to police in May 1994 while she was being treated for alcoholism in hospital.

On the day in question—Boxing Day, 1991—she admitted drinking beer and brandy and smoking marijuana. As a result she would usually sleep for part of the day.

Past and present members of the Milat family provided engrossing listening in the witness box, if only for the insight they provided into the lives of those close to Ivan.

They were under enormous pressure and their every utterance faced the full glare of publicity. Occasionally it got too much for some of them.

When Mr William Milat escorted his wife Carolynne out of the St James's Court on March 27 he was in no mood to pose for photoraphs.

When a photographer from the *Sydney Morning Herald* attempted to snap him William blew his top. Television footage of the confrontation showed cameraman Warren Clarke being punched by Mr Milat who tried to grab his photographic equipment.

'He came at me like a train,' Mr Clarke said afterwards.

'I was just trying to protect my gear but he kicked one of the cameras.'

Mr Clarke suffered from minor concussion and bruising. What was of greater importance to him was his camera which was was valued at $3,500.

It was destroyed during the incident.

The strain was also showing on Ivan's ex-wife Karen when she entered the witness box. A shy and obviously nervous woman with shoulder length auburn hair, she wore a dark striped suit and a troubled expression as she recounted her life with the backpacker killer.

She told the jury how he was known by several nicknames including Joe Spanner, Texas, Bargo Bill, Tex and Mac. They met in 1975 and married in 1983. She left him in 1987 and they divorced two years later.

She recalled days out with Ivan, including trips to the Belanglo State Forest. They would often drop into Lombardo's on the way, where Ivan would buy some chewing gum and a can of drink.

Karen remembered going to Belanglo on four occasions including her first trip to the forest in 1983. She said her exhusband was obviously familiar with the area because of the way he entered the forest and appeared to know his way around.

As always he had a firearm with him. He'd hoped to take a few pot shots at a kangaroo but in the end gave up the idea because there were too many people around collecting firewood.

He had better luck on the second visit when he managed to bag two kangaroos. The third time they just drove around the fire trails and on the fourth occasion they enjoyed a picnic by a little wooden bridge alongside a bush track.

Karen had no doubt he knew the area because 'Ivan didn't say anything.'

She also revealed that her then husband liked to engrave his property, especially his guns.

Shown a black-barrelled revolver, she identified it as his. She said it was kept under the bed in a wooden box which was hand painted in camouflage. The gun was engraved three times with the name Texas.

'Ivan just liked guns,' she explained.

'Ivan knew how to handle them and was confident about handling them,' she added.

In addition to the revolver he owned a pistol, a rifle and a slug gun. Some times he would wrap the pistol in a brown and white sock and take it out with him. If they went to the cinema he would stuff it down the side of his zipper boot. In the car he would hide it under the driver's seat.

For a woman who lived in fear of her ex-husband her spell in the witness box must have been particularly gruelling. Fighting back tears, her voice trembled with emotion. Eventually the ordeal became too much. Visibly upset she was asked if she would like to leave the courtroom to compose herself.

There was a brief adjournment and Karen Milat returned a few minutes later holding a tissue.

Ivan's love of firearms was reinforced by some of his workmates.

Mr Marco Koskinen, a former plant operator with the Roads and Traffic Authority, said he talked of little else. Guns were his main topic of conversation and he was always speaking of his weekend shooting trips at his brother's property.

He once spotted a rifle in Milat's car and on another occasion saw the defendant showing his revolver to another workmate. He had also seen a bowie knife in his glovebox.

'He said he likes to keep a gun under his seat sometimes in case he runs into trouble,' Mr Koskinen recalled.

Another former workmate, Mr Anthony Sara, said on two occasions he had visited a gun shop with Milat. The accused had told him he had a couple of guns and that he once bought $400 worth of ammunition.

Milat also liked reading about firearms and enjoyed gun magazines. Once Milat showed him a picture of a gun silencer which he intended to buy.

'You can order them in South Australia—you can't get them in New South Wales,' he told Mr Sara.

He said Milat told him he had a .38, which the Department of Main Roads used for security when delivering payrolls.

Mr Sara also identified a bowie knife which he had seen in Milat's possession. It was the same knife which was found where Milat had been living and which the Crown suggested might have caused some of the stabbing wounds inflicted on his victims.

In a dramatic courtroom gesture the judge held up the knife. Removing the eight-inch blade from its sheath, Justice David Hunt raised the knife aloft so that the jury could view it properly.

It was a scene that would have done comic actor Paul Hogan proud, prompting mental flashbacks to Mick Dundee's confrontation with a New York hoodlum who brandishes a switchblade in *Crocodile Dundee*.

'That's not a knife,' Dundee sniggers at his assailant. 'That's a knife!' he declares, withdrawing a massive blade from underneath his jacket.

The judge, perhaps sensing the parallel, quickly put the knife down and continued with the case.

There was further evidence of the accused's love of weapons when the man who bought his Nissan four wheel drive car in November 1992 told the court how he found an unused bullet beneath the driver's seat.

Mr David Gill came across the bullet while vacuuming the vehicle. When he brought it to the attention of police two years later they examined the car and found a bullet hole in the side.

It was consistent with a hole made by a .22 bullet. What's more it seemed to have been fired by someone in the driver's seat at someone on the passenger's side of the vehicle.

'The Crown case is that Ivan Milat must have used a firearm in subduing and controlling them (the backpackers),' Mr Tedeschi pointed out.

Had he fired at one of them before tying up the second? Had there been a struggle as Milat drove them into the forest in which the gun had accidentally gone off? Or had a second killer shot one of the hitchhikers while his accomplice drove?

It was all speculation of course. But the discovery of the bullet hole almost certainly pointed to a sinister cause.

26.

TRUE OR FALSE SIGHTINGS

As the days turned into weeks at the backpacker murder trial, evidence came thick and fast. At the beginning of April the first of the parents to enter the witness box, Mrs Patricia Everist, gave Milat an icy stare as she walked past him.

Recalling the last time she spoke to her daughter Deborah in December 1989 she said she phoned home to say she had arrived safely in Sydney and that she and her friend James Gibson were both fine. She promised to send her mum a postcard and would ring again the next day.

Mrs Everist identified a green sleeping bag found in a wardrobe at Milat's Eagle Vale home. It was the same as the one her daughter used. Deborah's brother Timothy also identified the sleeping bag. It belonged to him and Deborah had borrowed it before leaving Melbourne.

When Mrs Everist heard nothing more she became so concerned she telephoned James's mother Mrs Peggy Gibson. It was the first time the two mothers had spoken.

Mrs Gibson told the court how she called her son's friends to see if they knew where he was. Then on March 14, 1990 a woman telephoned her saying she had found James's backpack in Galston Gorge. His address and telephone number were written on the bottom. The address had also been written on the top of the backpack but this had been cut out for some reason.

In December, 1989 Ivan Milat had been working on the roads only a few miles away at Dural in Sydney's rural north-west.

Three weeks after the trial began, the two sets of British parents flew to Australia to give evidence at the Supreme Court of New South Wales. It was the second time they had come to face to face with their daughters' killer, but the experience was no less bearable.

In what turned out to be the saddest and most emotionally charged day of the entire hearing, Ian and Jacqueline Clarke and Ray and Jill Walters filed into the New South Wales Supreme Court to recall the last contact they had with their daughters Caroline and Joanne.

Mr Clarke told how his daughter had made friends with Joanne in Sydney before they went fruit picking in Victoria and Tasmania. She kept in fairly regular contact and had last telephoned home about April 8 or 9, 1992.

Mrs Clarke identified a green and white Benetton top which Caroline bought before she left Britain. It looked the same as the one Chalinder Hughes was wearing in the photograph Milat had taken of her.

Joanne's father Ray recalled how his daughter always kept in regular contact during her working holiday.

'She wouldn't go anywhere that we didn't know her address,' he told the court.

She last telephoned home on April 15, 1992 saying she intended to travel to Melbourne. When she had not made contact for five weeks he called her bank to see if there had been any transactions. But she had not withdrawn anything for more than a month.

The last of the British parents to give evidence was Mrs Walters. Of all the mothers whose lives had been destroyed by Ivan Milat's reign of terror, this woman's emotional scars were etched most vividly.

Her eyes blackened by the grief that overwhelmed her four years earlier, she was led sobbing and shaking to the witness box on April 16.

Clutching a screwed-up tissue and trying desperately to control herself, Mrs Walters' voice was little more than a shivering murmer.

Justice David Hunt asked her, 'Are you alright to go on?'

'Yes,' she whispered before bursting into tears.

When the judge suggested she might like to stand down for a while, she nodded and walked out.

Mrs Walters was never recalled.

She was not the only person closely associated with Joanne to show her emotions that day. On one occasion a witness verbally abused the defendant through gritted teeth.

Pauline Vuletich who had travelled to Australia with Joanne in 1991 muttered, 'Scum,' as she passed him in the dock. Milat appeared to raise his eyebrows in response.

Scottish-born Ms Vuletich, whose maiden name was Reed, came from the Shetland Islands but now lived in New Zealand.

She told the court how Joanne wasn't afraid to hitchhike.

'We hitched most places,' she said.

She'd last seen her friend on April 18, 1992 outside a nightclub in Sydney's Kings Cross, a few hours before Joanne and Caroline were due to leave Sydney to seek work fruit picking.

'That was the last time I heard from Joanne,' she said.

Friends and relatives of the dead from all over the world descended on St James's Court to give their few short minutes of evidence. Anja Habschied's mother Olga had to speak through an interpreter as she identified the necklace she had given to her daughter on her eighteenth birthday. She wept when shown a photograph of Anja and her boyfriend Gabor Neugebauer.

She told how she last had contact with her daughter at Christmas 1991 when Anja phoned with seasons greetings. The young woman said they were off to Darwin where they were booked on a flight to Indonesia.

There was a similarly sad story from Gabor's mother Anke Neugebauer who also remembered a Christmas telephone message. She recalled how she'd sent her son a parcel containing a box of Christmas cookies and other tasty morsels. The parcel was returned to her marked unclaimed in May 1992, six months after the pair disappeared.

Simone Schmidl's father Herbert was asked to identify the word 'Simi,' which had been written on his daughter's water bottle and which had been found in Milat's garage. He agreed it was his daughter's writing.

Christine Murphy, Simone's Australian friend who put her up in Sydney, told of the morning she left to make her way south. The date was January 20, 1991.

She said her friend intended to catch a train to Liverpool and from there walk to the Hume Highway in the hope of hitching a lift to Melbourne where Simone planned to meet up with her mother.

The pretty young German had no qualms about the risks she might be taking. Like so many backpackers she assumed Australia held no danger for hitchhikers.

'She was very easy going towards it. She believed she was quite safe doing it,' Christine told the court.

'She had hitchhiked before and hadn't had a problem. She had always found people to be friendly and helpful.'

Despite Simone's confidence, Christine asked her to ring as soon as she got to Melbourne. But four days later there had still been no call.

Several people claimed to have seen Simone after she left Christine's home in Sydney. A woman by the name of Janette Wallis recalled seeing her walking near Liverpool station soon after 9 a.m. on the Sunday morning.

And curiously there was another sighting the following day at Albury railway station which is 585 kilometres south west of Sydney on the New South Wales-Victoria border.

If this was a genuine sighting then Milat must have altered his routine. It was a railway employee who claimed to have spotted Simone. Mr Ronald Bennett, a former assistant stationmaster at Albury insisted the young woman bore a 'remarkable similarity' to the German.

'What sticks in my mind more than anything else is the hairstyle...I have a definite memory of the dreadlocks,' he told the court.

Simone's hairstyle was not easily forgotten. Dreadlocks were relatively uncommon among Australian youth in the early nineties.

But was it really Simone or somebody with a similar appearance? The Crown claimed it was a false sighting and to illustrate the point called Albury nurse Linda Chalmers, who also had dark, curly hair.

She admitted walking past Albury railway station on or about January 20 or 21, 1991 with a backpack. But when Mr Bennett was asked to look at Ms Chalmers in court to see if it was her he might have spotted that day his reply was an emphatic 'no.'

The Albury nurse was not the only person to be classified by the Crown as being a 'false sighting.'

The two women who thought they gave Joanne Walters and Caroline Clarke a lift from Waterfall to the Bulli Pass in April 1992 were also placed in the same category. Susan Burns and her friend Myrna Honeyman were so convinced these were the two British hitchhikers that they even underwent hypnosis at the suggestion of police.

One even recalled the young woman she believed to be Joanne talking about working as a nanny for a Sydney doctor. Joanne was employed by hospital executive Debra Jensen while living in Sydney.

The women also maintained that the date of the lift was April 21, 1992, the Tuesday after Easter. The Crown case was that two Britons disappeared three days earlier.

So could Susan Burns and Myrna Honeyman have been mistaken? The prosecution pointed out that people were often influenced by media reporting and could have got confused after seeing photographs of Caroline and Joanne in the newspapers or on television.

If these were not the two British girls why didn't the hitchhikers who really were picked up on April 21 ever come forward? Or had they continued their backpacking travels overseas oblivious to the 'false sighting' and the manhunt going on in Australia?

The answer will never be known.

27.
CONFUSION OVER DNA

While some of the parents and those close to the victims chose not to sit through the more gruesome evidence including the appalling injuries suffered by the seven young backpackers, many felt compelled to be there.

A few saw it as a form of therapy, believing they could only come to terms with the horror of their children's end by hearing every clinical detail, thereby gaining a sense of what they went through in their final minutes.

The jury had no choice in the matter. They had to sit through it all regardless, including graphic photographs of the wounds suffered by all seven victims.

The judge reminded them that despite the repulsive nature of the pictures they should remain dispassionate and objective. Certainly they would feel sympathy for those who died and their families. After all the skeletons they were about to view were once the healthy young people they had seen very much alive in earlier photographs, he said.

Even so this should not influence their views about the defendant, Justice David Hunt emphasised.

The man whose task it was to carry out the post mortems on the victims, pathologist Dr Peter Bradhurst of the New South Wales Institute of Forensic Medicine, said the circumstances of Deborah Everist's death suggested a deviant sexual motive.

Black pantihose found near her body appeared to have been used as some form of restraint.

'The....pantihose indicated to me a bondage aspect to the death,' he told the court.

Her head, which had been found by bushwalker Bruce Pryor, had several stab wounds and fractures including a broken jaw which looked as though it had been smashed by a blunt instrument such a piece of wood or a boot. Her feet and hands had probably been tied together prior to her murder.

James Gibson also had a number of stab wounds including one through his spinal cord which would almost certainly have paralysed him. He would also have suffered considerable internal bleeding because two of the stab wounds went through his lungs. As a result he would have had great difficulty breathing.

Dr Bradhurst said Gibson's body had been lying in a foetal position with the fly on his jeans undone.

'This indicates a possible sexual motive to his death,' the pathologist observed.

An extraordinary degree of force was used in both killings and there was no evidence to suggest that either victim had tried to defend him or herself, Dr Bradhurst said.

Moving on to the deaths of Joanne Walters and Caroline Clarke, the jury sat in stunned silence as the senior pathologist revealed the extent of their injuries. Joanne had suffered at least 14 stab wounds to the chest and neck and a gag had been placed around her mouth. An untied ligature around her neck 'suggested an attempt at strangulation or some form of restraint.'

Caroline's head had been covered with a red cloth which was peppered with bullet holes. She had been shot no fewer than ten times in the head and stabbed once in the back of the right hand side of the chest.

Dr Bradhurst said the stab wounds would have had to have been made by a 30 millimetre knife, but he did not necessarily agree that a bowie knife had been responsible.

However, he added, 'I cannot entirely exclude the knife.'

Shown Milat's bowie knife in court, he said he would have expected the blade to have caused a different sized entry wound.

Dr Bradhurst also provided further evidence about the execution-style murder of Anja Habschied who was decapitated with one blow from the back of the neck. He believed the 20 year-old German had been the victim of what he could only describe as 'a style of ceremonial execution'.

What sort of weapon could have been responsible? A machete, a sword, an axe or a large knife, thought Dr Bradhurst. Even possibly, the ceremonial sword which was found at Mrs Margaret Milat's house on the day of Ivan's arrest.

Anja's boyfriend, Gabor Neugabauer, had been shot six times in the head by .22 calibre bullets and there had also been evidence of strangulation, Dr Bradhurst told the court. A gag had been stuffed in his mouth and another tied around his head.

Most of the seven victims appeared to have been subjected to sexual assault either before or after death. And each of the bodies had been covered by forest foliage.

Police who studied the murder scenes told of the remains being elaborately covered so they would not be found. The bodies were concealed by two layers of sticks and branches.

As crime scene officer Detective Senior Constable Andrew Grosse told the court: 'Each deceased was covered by two layers—one large sticks layer and the second with smaller debris. Every scene seemed to be similar in the way that they were covered. We have a progression from the larger sticks to the small loose material. Each body was covered almost completely.'

Curiously six of the bodies were left next to a fallen tree or long piece of wood although one was found next to a large boulder. There was no reference during the trial to the possibility of a ritual element to the killings, as suggested earlier.

This was a more clinical assessment of the murder scene as described by the officers who inspected the forest shortly after the bodies were found.

Police told of bullet fragments lodged in tree trunks on the site where the German couple were lying. They also discovered bullets embedded in plastic bottles nearby, which suggested the area had been used as a shooting range.

Somewhat more sinister was the discovery of a leather leash which appeared to have been used as a restraint. The leash, plus insulating tape, cord and a plastic tie, had been wound into two loops.

Crime scene officers also reported finding a pinkish coloured cloth with both ends knotted together, forming a wrist-sized loop. It was inside a pair of pink jeans. The material might have been used as a mask or a blindfold.

For those who had never been to the Belanglo State Forest such as the jury, it was difficult to visualise the geography and in particular the specific sites where the bodies were found. Although the jurors had been handed fat files containing maps, photographs and detailed reports, there was no substitute for first hand knowledge.

That is why on the morning of Monday, April 18 the court convened in the heart of the forest for a personal inspection of the crucial areas.

Justice David Hunt said that although parts of the forest might have changed since the murders were committed he did not think the jury would have any difficulty imagining what it had been like at the time.

He emphasised that the purpose of the tour was not aimed at encouraging the jury to play detective and search for clues but to help them to better understand the evidence they had heard so far and would continue to hear over the next 15 weeks.

In order to preserve the jury's anonymity the Belanglo Forest was closed for the day. A white bus accompanied by a police escort ferried them from the court to the scene of the crime where they spent several hours before returning to Sydney.

While members of the jury were becoming extremely well-briefed about the case an important piece of the jigsaw was still missing. The amount of evidence collected at the murder sites was impressive but there was nothing to specifically link Ivan Milat to the killings. It was, as the prosecution admitted at the beginning, a largely circumstantial case.

There was, however, the blood found on two of the items in the defendant's garage which corresponded with Caroline Clarke's. Much depended on the outcome of the DNA tests which had been carried out on a white sash cord and a pillow case.

A senior forensic biologist from the Department of Health in Sydney, Mr Robert Goetz, revealed that the blood on the cord and the pillow case were the same and could have originated from a child of Ian and Jacqueline Clarke.

To reinforce his point he said, 'The blood from the rope is 118,000 times more likely to occur if the blood came from a child of the Clarkes than from anybody else in the population.

'It is extremely likely that the blood on the rope is from a child of the Clarkes and not from anyone else in the population,' he added.

He was also certain that the blood did not come from a child of Mr and Mrs Walters or the parents of the three German backpackers. He also established that it was not the blood of Ivan Milat.

However, a mix up over swabs taken from the two British backpackers meant that part of the DNA testing was flawed.

Unknown to the police investigators who handed over the swabs and a number of hairs found in the hand of Joanne Walters, the testing scientist 'had no adequate prior experience in DNA testing of forensic samples, particularly where those samples were extremely small, as in this case,' Mr Goetz explained.

Testing of the swabs was carried out several times and on each occasion there was a different result, indicating DNA material foreign to both women.

A document read to the court said some of the results were transposed onto wrong samples and suggested there had been multiple contamination from various sources including chemicals and other foreign DNA in the laboratory.

A review carried out later by two more experienced scientists confirmed that there was a very real possibility of contamination of the samples and other major errors in the testing procedures and reporting methods.

'They conclude that it would be unsafe to rely on his results,' the document revealed.

What this meant was that it would be impossible to establish whether there had ever been any foreign DNA material in the vaginal swabs.

As for the hairs there was similar confusion. On the first test the scientists found four hairs were from a female, three from a male and two were unsuccessfully tested.

When the three male hairs were tested again, two of them tested as female and the third was unsuccessful. Not unnaturally the more experienced scientists ruled that the testing was flawed and could not be relied upon,

The medical and forensic evidence over, it was time to move on to the next stage of the backpacker murder trial, which would cover Milat's arrest and the alleged involvement of another member of the family or someone closely associated with it.

The highly controversial submission by the defence that someone else was in the forest was to place a new perspective on the case.

Had Paul Onions been mistaken in his identification of Milat as the man who attacked and kidnapped him on the Hume Highway? Could he have confused him with one of Ivan's brothers? Was Onions' abductor, who according to the prosecution would also have been responsible for the seven deaths, another member of the family?

After all much of the evidence had been found at other addresses where Milat family members lived.

These were questions that both the defence and the prosecution would have to consider in great detail in the coming weeks. There would also be the testimony of Ivan Milat himself. But that was still some weeks away.

Right now it was time for the brothers to join the cast at St James's Court.

28.

RICHARD AND WALTER
DENY THEIR INVOLVEMENT

In the already well-documented description of Ivan Milat's arrest, the defendant remained astonishly calm. For a man accused of such hideous criminal behaviour it was a performance par excellence. His refusal to be intimidated by the huge police presence and his ability to brush off the allegations as though they were little more than a minor motoring offence was astonishing.

At precisely 6.50 a.m., after the somewhat surreal exchange on the telephone with Detective Sergeant Wayne Gordon, Milat and his girlfriend Chalinder Hughes finally appeared on the front doorstep.

The accused man's four letter reaction to the sight before his eyes was not altogether unexpected in the circumstances.

Senior Constable Ray Duncan, who was standing outside with a shot gun told the court, 'He turned to his right towards us and said, "shit".'

There was a small army of State Protection Group officers wearing bullet proof vests and black overalls several metres away. Each had his gun trained on the most wanted man in Australia.

In the manner of a traffic warden approaching an errant motorist another officer walked up to Milat. Except he didn't have a traffic infringement notice but a far more serious message.

Detective Sergeant Stephen Leach said he was making enquiries into an armed robbery in which an English backpacker was attacked on the Hume

Highway. The officer pointed out Milat was not obliged to say anything.

'I understand but I don't know what you're talking about,' he replied.

Leach explained he would also be asking him further questions about the deaths of seven young hitchhikers.

Again came the reply: 'I don't know what you are talking about.'

Earlier, during the 12-minute wait from the time of the first phone call to Milat's appearance on the doorstep, police said they detected a certain amount of movement coming from inside the garage.

Senior Constable Duncan told the court that he heard a door connecting the garage to the main house, opening and closing. It was in the wall cavity in the ceiling above the garage that officers were later to find parts of a Ruger 10/22 rifle wrapped in a plastic bag.

Another officer, Detective Senior Constable Peter O'Connor, explained how he had to climb a ladder in the garage to enter a manhole in the ceiling before he could access the wall cavity. It was several rafters along from the manhole and his arm was not long enough to stretch down and reach the hidden package.

O'Connor found a stick downstairs in the house and returned to the attic so he could lift the plastic bag out of the cavity. It contained a trigger assembly, a .22 calibre magazine, a spring and guide and a bolt assembly. The gun parts were not the only important find that day.

Elsewhere in the building there was a cornucopia of potentially incriminating evidence including a receiver from a Ruger 10/22 stuffed in a boot in a hall cupboard, several boxes of .22 cartridges, a camouflage-coloured mask and camping equipment.

There was also a postcard from a man named Jock in New Zealand which was addressed to Milat but began, 'Dear Bill.' It was the same Christian name Milat used in his conversation with Paul Onions.

When police told Milat that he had been identified by the English tourist as the man who attacked him four and a half years earlier, the accused man replied, 'It wasn't me.'

Asked about the gun parts found in the wall cavity and how they got there Milat insisted, 'I wouldn't have a clue. I presume youse had 'em.'

Leach pressed him about who had been in the ceiling.

'You blokes and the builders,' he responded.

There was no formal recording of the conversation that took place at 22 Cinnabar Street that day although an officer did make some notes.

However, two videos of an interview subsequently conducted at Campbelltown Police Station were shown to the court on April 23.

In one of them Milat was heard saying, 'I don't wish to talk to you in relation to any matter...I don't know anything about anything you've been talking to me about.'

In a second interview the defendant was asked to confirm he had been shown a tent and rifle parts found in his house.

'You showed me...I don't know where you got 'em from,' was his terse response.

Pressed about the murders he said,'I don't know nothing about it. I have been saying it all along...I didn't do it.'

Milat also maintained that notes of the conversation between himself and police in his home contained a 'few lies.'

The presence of a rifle and ammunition in Ivan Milat's house would not have come as much of a surprise to those who knew him. He was well known for his love of firearms, as were other members of the family.

Under Walter Milat's house at Hilltop police were to find a .303 repeating rifle, a Chinese SKS self-loading rifle, a .45 calibre single shot percussion rifle, an SKK model assault rifle, a repeating shotgun and a .357 Magnum revolver.

A thorough search of the home also uncovered two machetes, two bayonets, seven arrows and a hunting knife. There was a large quantity of ammunition including .357 magnum and .22 calibre as well.

Walter, 44, told the court the gear belonged to Ivan. About three months before his brother's arrest in May, 1994 he had helped to move the guns from Eagle Vale and stored them in an alcove beneath his Hilltop home.

'Ivan rang me up and asked me if he could store his stuff under my bathroom,' Walter said. His sister Shirley was apparently 'upset' at having it around the house and was worried it might be stolen, he explained.

Another brother, Richard, joined Walter and drove to Eagle Vale to pick up several cardboard boxes filled with ammunition and guns. Some of it had been stored in the ceiling of Ivan's house. All three brothers then helped to transport it back to Hilltop where it was stored in an alcove.

Asked by the prosecution how a blue day pack belonging to Simone Schmidl had also got there, Walter, who said he did not know it belonged to one of the dead backpackers, replied, 'We must have moved it in with the gear.'

As the courtroom grilling continued the style of Mark Tedeschi's questioning became unequivocal.

'Did you play any part in the deaths of seven backpackers whose bodies were found in the Belanglo State Forest?'

'No,' he replied emphatically.

Walter was shown an Anschutz rifle, which ballistics experts were to claim could have fired cartridges found near the bodies of Anja Habschied and Gabor Neugebauer and which was found at his home.

In court that day the Crown asked him if he had seen the gun before.

'I think so—I can't say for sure,' said Walter.

Tedeschi asked, 'Do you know who it belonged to?'

Walter Milat: 'If it's the one I'm thinking of it's Ivan's.'

Mr Milat admitted he had borrowed the gun from Ivan and it was quite possible he might have fired the weapon while out rabbit shooting in the Belanglo State Forest.

'Are you trying to help him (Ivan) by providing some explanation for how cartridges from the Anschutz were found in the forest?' Mr Tedeschi enquired

'No,' he replied.

Questioned by the defence, Walter was asked about his access to Ivan's house and his relationship with his brother, whom it emerged had had an affair with his first wife 15 years previously.

'Do you have any bitterness towards Ivan?' Mr Terry Martin asked.

'No, he's my brother,' he said.

Walter agreed he had unlimited access to his brother's home which he helped build. He also revealed that he occasionally called in to Lombardo's newsagency where Paul Onions was given a lift.

'Did you pick up a backpacker by the name of Onions?' Martin asked.

'No,' Walter replied.

Under cross-examination from Mr Tedeschi he was asked if he would ever lie to protect his brothers and sisters if it were serious enough.

'Perhaps, yes,' he conceded.

Younger brother Richard, 39, was also questioned about the existence of camping gear belonging to some of the backpackers and which was found in a cupboard in a toolshed on his property. The cupboard, he explained, had been removed from his mother's home at Guildford where both he and Ivan used to live.

He was also interrogated about a possible connection with the murders.

His response left no room for ambiguity.

'I had nothing to do with the deaths,' he told the court.

He was not in the Belanglo State Forest around the time of the killings and he had no idea who might have been responsible.

However, former workmate Desmond Butler claimed Richard once said to him, 'I know who killed the Germans.'

The disclosure was made during a late night conversation in the Boral plant at Camelia, he claimed. Richard was under the influence of marijuana.

'Normally he (Richard) would sit quiet for 15 or 20 minutes,' Mr Butler recalled.

'When he smoked that stuff he would talk repetitively for six or eight hours. You couldn't stop him,' he added.

Mr Butler thought the conversation happened before the discovery of any of the bodies in the forest but during a period of publicity about the missing Germans.

Another workmate, Mr Paul Douglas, also alleged Richard had commented about newspaper reports of the two British girls being found dead in Belanglo.

'He said, "There's more bodies out there—they haven't found them all yet".'

This happened before the remains of the other five backpackers had been discovered. It was not until some time later that the significance of the remark occurred to Mr Douglas.

The workmate also recalled a more chilling comment allegedly made by

Richard during a discussion about rapists and the light sentences they were sometimes given.

Mr Douglas said to Richard the justice system was not that good.

'And then he (Richard) said that stabbing a woman was like cutting a loaf of bread,' Mr Douglas alleged.

Richard clearly had a lot of explaining to do in court. Under questioning from the defence he was given the opportunity to put the record straight and refute the allegations made against him.

He denied making such comments and when asked about a suggestion that he killed the backpackers replied, 'I'd say that's a lie.'

He claimed he had never suggested to anyone that he had knowledge of the deaths and also denied planting certain items, including a gun, in Ivan's home.

Richard, who admitted he had occasionally been affected by cannabis and alcohol while at work, maintained the conversations with his workmates did not contain any reference about 'more bodies' being out there.

As for the alleged tasteless remark that 'stabbing a woman is like cutting a loaf of bread,' he insisted, 'I don't recall saying anything like that.'

'You know that you had those conversations don't you?' Terry Martin came back.

Richard Milat: 'No.'

Terry Martin: 'You are deliberately and dishonestly lying about that.'

Richard Milat: 'No.'

Terry Martin: 'You had knowledge about the missing backpackers, did you not?'

Richard Milat: 'No.'

He was also asked about attacking Paul Onions.

'It weren't me,' he replied.

Was he deliberately giving evasive answers to assist his brother, Mr Tedeschi enquired?

'No,' he added.

Under further cross examination he was asked about his facial appearance in January 1990 when Onions had been kidnapped by a man he said had a 'Merv Hughes'-style moustache.

Richard could not remember if he had a similar moustache at the time.

He did however concede that he spoke disparagingly about Asians and had worn a bushy moustache on occasions.

Throughout the day Richard Milat repeatedly said he could not remember or wasn't sure about certain things. But he denied he was responding in such a manner to avoid being charged with perjury.

Richard was to return to the witness box nearly a month later when he was asked about his moustache and side levers in 1990. Paul Onions had recalled seeing grey flecks in the facial hair of the man who abducted him. Richard was unable to recall any grey flecks at the time.

At one stage he was asked to stand in front of the jury so that they could inspect the moustache and the colour of his hair themselves.

The prosecution acknowledged that no grey flecks were visible.

In what was threatening to turn into a scene from a television commercial for hair dye even the judge accepted that he could see no grey in Richard Milat's hair.

29.

IVAN ENTERS THE WITNESS BOX

Ivan Milat cut a lonely figure in the witness box on the day Terry Martin decided to call him to open the case for the defence. The date was June 17, 1996, nearly three months since the trial had begun.

Mr Martin had told the court that his client would insist he had never owned a 10/22 Ruger rifle and had no knowledge of the rifle parts allegedly found in a wall cavity at his home in Cinnabar Street.

Milat would also testify that he had never visited the Belanglo State Forest and that suggestions by his former wife that they drove there on three occasions in 1983 in a Mitsubishi 4WD could be proved wrong. The particular model in question had not been manufactured until 1984.

As for the backpacker and camping gear found in his garage, he did not know how they got there.

Mr Martin said his client had been aware of police enquiries about him before his arrest in May 1994 but was not worried.

'He will tell you that he was unconcerned by the news that they were making enquiries in respect of him and his vehicle. He certainly did not know that there was a Ruger 10/22 receiver stuck in his boot in the cupboard.

'He certainly did not know that there were items belonging to deceased backpackers lying around his place...lying around his place for the police to find,' he added.

On the question of the Nissan 4WD in which Paul Onions said he had been given a lift , Mr Martin pointed out that although they were similar there were also 'significant dissimilarities.'

For example, the spare wheel which Onions claimed was on the rear of the vehicle was not fitted until a year later. At the time of the alleged attack the spare wheel had been underneath the car.

Chrome wheels, which Onions said he recalled, were not added until some time later.

Milat's deep voice echoed across the hushed courtroom after his defence barrister put his first question.

'Did you ever kill any of the persons located in the Belanglo State Forest?' asked Mr Martin, coming straight to the point.

'No,' Milat replied emphatically.

Martin: 'Were you involved in any way in respect of those deaths?

Milat: 'No way at all.'

The defendant replied without hesitation, his eyes fixed firmly on his barrister.

Martin: 'Did you have any knowledge of those offences?'

Milat: 'No.'

Martin: 'Were you involved in any way in the attack on Paul Onions?'

Milat: 'No.'

Later Mark Tedeschi asked the now clean-shaven Milat about his facial appearance in 1990.

Did he have a Merv Hughes-type moustache?

He did have a moustache but it was different from the one sported by the well-known Australian cricketer.

How was it different?

'I watch the cricket and my idea of a Merv Hughes moustache is...it sweeps back a bit,' Milat explained.

Though he did agree that he had grey flecks in his sideburns, used the name 'Bill,' worked on the roads and his family came from Yugoslavia.

'Do you agree that all of these features fit you that I have mentioned?' Mr Tedeschi put to him.

'Yes,' replied Milat.

'Do you know any other person in this world who had all of these features that I just mentioned?' he added.

'No,' came the reply.

Milat also made clear he did not have anti-Asian views or was opposed to the British in Northern Ireland, sentiments which Paul Onions' attacker had expressed in his conversation with him.

He said he was 'quite happy' about the number of Asians living in Australia and pointed out that even his girlfriend was Indian.

He said he had no view one way or the other about the British presence in Northern Ireland.

'I read the papers but I don't take much notice of things like that,' he said.

The accused man admitted he couldn't explain how camping equipment came to be in his home and insisted he had never owned a Ruger rifle. However he did concede that he had purchased the Anschutz rifle in 1988 or 1989 but only kept it for three months, explaining he had 'sold it to my brother Wally'.

Under further cross-examination by the prosecution, Milat said he had no knowledge of the sash cords found in the pillow case in his garage either, including one stained with blood.

And he denied making up a leash device which was found in the forest.

'I suggest to you that it never occurred to you that anybody would be able to trace sash cord back to you,' Mr Tedeschi remarked.

'I wouldn't know what they could do,' the accused man maintained.

Tedeschi: 'Have you got any explanation as to how these five pieces of sash cord in the pillow slip came to be in your possession?'

Milat: 'No explanation at all—I have never seen them there.'

Tedeschi: 'You have heard evidence that some of the pieces of sash cord are exactly of the same kind as the one piece of sash cord from the shelves that you don't dispute is yours...and blood on one of those pieces of sash cords in the pillow case is consistent with coming from a child of Mr and Mrs Clarke.'

Milat: 'No, I know nothing about it.'

Tedeschi: 'I suggest to you that you used sash cord to make that restraint device that was found at Area A' (where the remains of the two Germans Neugebauer and Habschied were found).

Milat: 'I never.'

Tedeschi: 'Have you got any explanation to give the jury why the same sort of black plastic ties are in your garage as the one that was found in the forest on this leash device?'

Milat: 'I wouldn't have a clue.'

Tedeschi: 'Do you agree that the black plastic cable tie (found in the garage) is of the same G series as the black plastic ties found in the forest?'

Milat: 'All I'd say is that they are black plastic ties. I wouldn't have an idea. I know where this came from-- I don't know where that one in the bush came from.'

Tedeschi: 'So you say it's just sheer awful coincidence that the same sash cord in the forest is in your garage and the same black plastic tie, as in the forest, is in your garage?'

Milat: 'All I know I got this (tie) from work. I don't know where that one in the bush came from.'

Tedeschi: 'I suggest to you that you were at the Habschied/Neugebauer death scene and were involved in those deaths.'

Milat: 'I weren't—no.'

The defendant was also asked about a tent belonging to Simone Schmidl which was found in his garage. Could he explain its presence?

'Somebody obviously put it there,' he answered.

Was he saying someone had planted it?

'Well, they must have, I never put it there,' he made clear.

Could he explain how the Compactormat strap identical to one wrapped around Ms Schmidl's head had been discovered in his garage.

'I have no explanation at all,' Milat said.

'I suggest to you that you were involved in the death of Simone Schmidl and that's how these items came to be in your garage?' the prosecution barrister came back.

'I had nothing to do with it,' Milat replied.

He also had no idea where his girlfriend Chalinder Hughes had obtained the Benetton top which was similar to the one worn by Caroline Clarke.

He said he also thought the camera which was identical to one used by Caroline Clarke and which was located in a kitchen drawer had belonged to his sister Shirley with whom he lived.

Why had he not enquired of his sister where the camera came from?

'Well I probably might have asked her, I just can't recall it. I have never made a big deal of it,' he explained.

'The reason why you never enquired of Shirley where she got that camera from, was that it was you who brought it to your house,' Mr Tedeschi claimed.

'I never did,' Milat replied.

He did agree that black plastic cable ties in the garage that were similar to those found in the forest, were his. Although he again denied making the restraining devices in which they had been used.

The cross-examination was placing Ivan Milat under intense pressure. The staccato-like interrogation was taking its toll. If the defendant was lying he would have to be extremely careful in his responses.

In the late afternoon of June 18, just a few minutes before the court was due to rise, an apparent slip of the tongue in a heated exchange between Milat and the Crown prosecutor provided a dramatic climax to the accused man's second day in the witness box.

Facing a barrage of questions Milat appeared to stumble when asked about a surgical glove found in his car by police at the time of his arrest.

Mr Tedeschi suggested that he had worn it at the scene of the crime to prevent fingerprints being left behind.

'I wore....' Milat began to say, before appearing to correct himself and adding, 'I have never seen that glove before.'

Interpreting the first two words as the beginning of an admission of guilt, Mr Tedeschi interjected: 'Were you just about to say I wore no glove in the forest?'

'No, I wore no glove in the car,' the defendant assured him.

With so much damning evidence found in his house it was always going to be difficult for Milat to explain how it got there.

That was the obvious question and his reply was typically understated: 'Well obviously somebody's trying to make me look real bad.'

Was he insinuating that he had been framed by someone else?

'You're not suggesting that the police planted any of these items like gun parts on you?' asked Mr Tedeschi.

'That's correct,' Milat replied.

Was he suggesting that someone else had deliberately planted the Ruger receiver in his boot?

'That's correct.'

And the Ruger parts in the wall cavity?'

'They must have.'

Was it 'sheer coincidence' that those gun parts had been covered in the same type of camouflage paint which he had painted on his own guns?

'I imagine so,' he agreed.

And what about the Anschutz bolt, wrapped in a piece of material from a red check shirt found in Milat's home? The weapon was hidden under Walter Milat's house and was the same gun that had been linked to cartridges located near the bodies of Gabor Neugebauer and Anja Habschied?

'I can't give any explanation,' Milat said.

So could somebody have deliberately wrapped it up in that material to implicate him?

'I don't know—I've got no idea,' he insisted once again.

There was also the question of Simone Schmidl's day pack found under Walter's house. Was it really possible for another person to access that alcove and 'plant that stuff in your property?' Mr Tedeschi wondered.

'Yes,' Milat said.

'I suggest to you that's manifestly absurd—what do you say to that?'

'I don't think so,' the defendant corrected him.

Then there was the presence of foreign currency in Milat's house including some Indonesian money. How did a man who had only ever been as far as New Zealand come to be in possession of Indonesian rupiah.

'Are you mystified by it because I am?' Milat admitted.

'I am not trying to be funny Mr Tedeschi but I have got no idea how it got there.'

Of all the evidence police uncovered on May 22, 1994 the Ruger rifle parts were the most incriminating. The prosecution knew that it was Milat's especially weak point and Tedeschi milked the cross-examination for all it was worth.

Tedeschi: 'Are you suggesting someone has come into your home and planted that item of great relevance in this case, an item that has been linked to the deaths of two of the backpackers...planted the receiver in a boot in the hall cupboard, a place where you would be likely to see it. That's right isn't it?'

Milat: 'They must have.'

Tedeschi: 'Someone, you say, has also deposited the other Ruger parts in your wall cavity, that's what you say isn't it?'

Milat: 'They must have.'

Tedeschi: 'That's a place that would be very, very hard for anyone to find.'

Milat: 'I am under the impression the police found it within 10 minutes.'

Tedeschi: 'Do you often look down your wall cavity?'

Milat: 'Never have.'

Tedeschi: 'Somebody planted all these items in your home—that's what you're asking the jury to accept isn't it?'

Milat: 'That's right.'

Tedeschi: 'I suggest to you that you placed the Ruger parts in the wall cavity.'

Milat: 'No, I didn't.'

Tedeschi: 'And I suggest to you that you got rid of the barrel of that Ruger 10/22 because you had heard or read that the police had found ballistic material in the forest.'

Milat: 'No I didn't.'

Tedeschi: 'And I suggest to you that when the police rang you on the morning of May 22 , 1994 that you hurriedly had to hide the Ruger receiver.'

Milat: 'I never hid anything.'

Tedeschi: 'Do you think someone has come into your home and used your engraver to engrave those names on your face mask?'

Milat: 'Yes.'

Tedeschi: 'Did you ever hear any suspicious engraving noises at night or something like that?'

Milat: 'When I am at home?'

Tedeschi: 'Yes.'

Milat: 'No.'

The defendant was showing signs of irritation. While surprisingly unfazed throughout most of the trial, he hated being made to look foolish. And the prosecution was certainly doing that.

Occasionally the improbability of his answers drew sniggers from the public gallery.

Milat, his eyes boiling with rage, was finding it difficult to control his anger.

This was the other side of Ivan Milat. The exact antithesis of the man who sat calmly listening from the dock. This was the only physical hint of the beast that lurked behind that 'stupid grin'.

30.

'CERTAIN MYSTERIES WILL NEVER, EVER BE RESOLVED.'

By July 3, 1996, the backpacker murder trial was drawing towards its conclusion. It was time for the prosecution to begin its closing address which centred on the backpacker who got away: Paul Thomas Onions.

The Crown argued that the attack on the English tourist was inextricably linked with the deaths of the seven young hitchhikers whose bodies were found in the forest.

If the jury accepted Milat's involvement in the attack on Mr Onions they had to accept he was also responsible for the seven murders, Mr Tedeschi told the court.

He said that such was the amount of evidence linking the 51 year-old road worker with the victims that it was almost as though he had left his finger prints at the scene of the crime.

Mr Tedeschi claimed that everything pointed to Milat being responsible for the brutal killings.

First there was the narrow escape of Mr Onions, who was abducted by a man he later identified as Milat.

All eight had been young hitchhikers who were far from home, trying to thumb a lift along the Hume Highway linking Sydney to Melbourne.

All the dead backpackers disappeared on public holidays when Milat was not at work. Mr Onions had also been attacked on a public holiday.

The surviving tourist had seen ropes in Milat's car. Ropes had also been used to subdue some of those who died.

The attacker had pulled a revolver on him. Two of the backpackers had been shot and Milat had admitted owning a handgun.

All the victims had been buried in the same manner, covered with branches and leaves.

There had been a strong sexual element in six of the seven deaths and much more force than was necessary had been used to kill them.

'These were all killings for killings sake,' said Mr Tedeschi.

Even more significantly spent cartridge cases and bullets found at the scene of the crimes showed markings consistent with being fired from a Ruger 10/22 rifle with a silencer. A silencer was found in Milat's garage and a Ruger bolt had been hidden in a wall cavity at his Sydney home.

Other items found near the bodies, including a restraining leash, sash cord and black tape, had also been linked with Mr Milat.

'It's almost as though the accused left a finger print in the forest because of the incredible coincidence of all the items being linked to him,' Mr Tedeschi told the jury.

Could Ivan Milat have secretly wanted to be caught? Certainly all the evidence pointed to that. Or did his acquittal in the past make him think he was untouchable? He had clearly enjoyed a charmed existence and this might well have contributed to what the Crown described as his 'incredible arrogance and unbelievable self confidence' in keeping gun parts connected with the backpacker killings in his home.

Turning to the jury Mr Tedeschi asserted that the accused never dreamt of the blitzkrieg that took place on May 22, 1994.

'Ladies and gentlemen this is a man who had the utter arrogance to fire a shot during an attempted abduction of Mr Onions on the Hume Highway with cars whizzing by....that was the level of his confidence, that he was prepared to do that and he got away with it. Nothing happened, nobody came knocking at his door a few days later.

'Indeed the very abduction of the backpackers, taking them in a vehicle along a road where, for all he knew, forestry officers might come along during the time that the backpackers must have been alive in the forest. There was always the possibility that someone would drive along these dirt fire trails, come upon them.

'So the incredible arrogance and the unbelievable self-confidence that the murderer had is exactly the kind of arrogance and self-confidence that led the accused to believe that no one was going to come to his house and come straight in and search it,' Mr Tedeschi went on.

And what of the likely defence argument that the backpacker killer was not Ivan Milat but one of his brothers?

Determined that the jury would not be swayed by such a theory, the prosecution warned them not to be seduced.

While the Crown conceded the very real possibility that two or more people were involved in a least some of the murders, this did not mean that Ivan Milat was innocent.

Mr Tedeschi reminded the jury that there was only one man who matched the description provided by Mr Onions, including the 'squinty eyes and stupid grin.'

'Isn't that descriptive of the accused?' he asked motioning towards the dock.

If the defence was going to suggest that the real culprit was Richard or Walter Milat, why had they not been called into the courtroom to be identified by Mr Onions?

The answer was simple, according to Mr Tedeschi.

'The reason why they didn't do that, you may think, was because they were concerned that if they gave Mr Onions the opportunity and he said "no, it's not that person", they would no longer be able to submit to you that it's reasonably possible it was not Ivan, but it was one of the other guys,' he suggested.

This was not to detract from the argument that more than one person was involved. Indeed he reminded the jury that two rifles had been used at the murder scene of Gabor Neugebauer and Anja Habschied.

He also stressed how difficult it would have been for one abductor to have carried out the kidnappings of six backpackers who were travelling as couples.

'It would have been much easier if there had been two abductors,' he agreed.

'The Crown says that none of this evidence detracts from the vast bulk of evidence implicating Ivan Milat as the central, core person responsible for all seven murders, quite possibly with another person,' Mr Mark Tedeschi concluded.

In the final analysis the Crown's case boiled down to eight points:

1. The similarities between all seven murders and the kidnapping of Mr Onions. They were all young hitchhikers who were far away from home.

2. The bodies of the seven who died were all found close to fire trails in remote sections of the Belanglo State Forest and within a few kilometres of each other.

3. All were concealed in the same manner with leaves and branches. They were also found lying near a tree or large boulder.

4. Of the seven deceased, six were attacked with a sharp cutting instrument.

5. Much more force was used to kill them than was necessary.

6. There was strong evidence of a sexual connotation at all four murder scenes and a suggestion of sexual assault in six of the seven deaths.

7. Four of the deceased had suffered stab wounds to the spine including Anja Habschied who was decapitated.

8. The cartridge cases fired at the spot where the two young British women died came from the same Ruger 10/22 as those cases found at the scene of the German couple's murder.

It was a compelling argument and one wondered how the defence would respond to such a strong case.

It did not take long to find out.

On July 5 Mr Terry Martin, summoning every ounce of his dramatic ability and raising his voice to a level that had not been heard since the trial began, took a long hard look at all 12 jury men and women and exclaimed: 'Whichever way you look at it, it is absolutely irrefutable that whoever has committed these eight offences must be either within the Milat family or so very closely associated with it, it doesn't much matter.

'Blind Freddy can see that. There can be absolutely no doubt,' he added. He paused to allow the impact of his statement to sink in.

'The question is who is it in the Milat family who committed those eight offences? The question is do you have a reasonable doubt it was Ivan Milat as opposed to someone else in the family?'

Referring to Mr Onions' kidnapping on the Hume Highway, Mr Martin cast doubt on his evidence of identification.

He said the description of his attacker given to police could also have fitted Richard Milat.

'It couldn't be, could it, that Mr Onions has noted a family resemblance in Ivan Milat and that had triggered his memory?' he asked.

'It couldn't be that Mr Richard Milat was Mr Onions' attacker?' he queried.

Mr Martin asserted that once the young Englishman had seen Ivan Milat's face on the police video in May 1994, his memory might have been contaminated by that image.

'It is all over, the damage is done, it is irretrievable because the police never put on the photo board a photo of Richard Milat or any of his family,' he added.

Mr Martin also criticised the prosecution for suggesting that the defence might have asked Mr Onions to identify Richard or Walter Milat in court.

And he reminded the jury about the spare wheel on Ivan Milat's car, which Mr Onions and Joanne Berry reported seeing at the time, but which later evidence suggested had not been fitted then.

'They didn't get it wrong,' the defence lawyer said.

'The vehicle that was used by the attacker had the back wheel on the back of it. There could not be any other explanation for two witnesses both saying the same thing,' he added.

One therefore had to conclude that this was not Ivan Milat's vehicle.

Then there were the physical features Mr Onions had used to describe his attacker. Mr Martin claimed many of the features also fitted Richard.

He also pointed out it was a 'myth' that Richard could not have been responsible for the Onions kidnapping and other offences just because his employment records proved he was working on the days in question. Mr Martin reminded the jury that some of Richard's workmates had earlier pointed out that it was possible to 'knock-off' before they were officially allowed to without being found out.

Mr Martin reiterated that Richard Milat also had access to the sash cords, firearms and ammunition used on some of the backpackers.

'If you just look at Richard Milat himself and the manner he's conducted himself in this case, do you not think it's reasonably possible he was the killer and not Mr Milat?' he asked the jury.

On the question of evidence, such as rifle parts used in the murders and found at Ivan Milat's home, the defence claimed it was perfectly reasonable to assume they had been planted there by a member of his family.

'Do you think that a person capable of this most brutal crime would give two hoots about planting gear on a brother?' he asked.

The defence barrister recalled that Ivan Milat also had an alibi for Boxing Day, 1991, when the German couple disappeared. Several members of his family said he had spent the day at his mother's home in Guildford.

If he was not responsible for the deaths of the two Germans then he could not have committed the other five murders, Mr Martin observed.

The defence lawyer said that if the jury had any doubts about the identity of the British tourist's assailant, the same doubts should apply to Ivan Milat's involvement in the seven murders.

'All that the law demands is at the end of the day, if you reasonably have a reasonable doubt about his guilt, you give him the benefit of that doubt,' he told the jury.

Mr Martin said they had the 'worst job in Australia' in trying to reach a verdict about a man facing 'the worst possible charges imaginable in Australia's history.'

'I am putting you under pressure, the Crown's putting you under pressure, the community's putting you under pressure.'

Like the prosecution, the defence case boiled down to a few key points:

1. Doubts about Paul Onions' identification of Ivan Milat.

2. Confusion over whether or not there was a spare wheel fitted to the rear of the car and if it had chrome wheels at the time of the Onions' kidnapping.

3. Mrs Karen Milat's claim that she visited the Belanglo State Forest with her ex-husband in 1983 in a Mitsubishi 4WD, evidence that was labelled 'absolute nonsense' by Mr Martin.

4. The fact that many members of the Milat family had access to property left at Mrs Margaret Milat's home in Guildford including sash cord and pull ties.

5. The discovery of a .22 calibre cartridge case which had been fired and which was found in a bedroom at 22 Cinnabar Street. Mr Martin believed 'this smells heavily of a plant.'

6. Ivan Milat's frequent visits to Lombardo's newsgency at Casula after the Onions attack. Why would he have risked going back there if he thought he might be identified as the man who kidnapped the British hitchhiker?

While the defence agreed many of the items at Milat's house had not been deliberately planted to incriminate him, they might have ended up there quite innocently when he moved from his mother's house to Eagle Vale.

Mr Martin hit the nail on the head when he looked up from his lectern and admitted: 'Members of the jury there are certain mysteries that will never, ever be resolved.'

31.

'If You Find Him Guilty, You're Dead'

After the defence wound up its case on July 11, 1996, the judge adjourned the trial until the following week to prepare his summing up. But before the court rose Justice David Hunt voiced the mood of many who had been following the trial for nearly four months when he turned to the jury and agreed they faced an arduous task.

'In 17 years as a judge and 20 years as a barrister I have never known a case such as this where the two versions put before you could be so different and the reason why they are so different is because of the enormous quantity of detail in the evidence,' he told them.

If anything his remarks were an understatement. The jury had sat through the evidence of 140 witnesses and waded through a huge quantity of documents. Now the judge had to put it all into some meaningful order without appearing to favour either side.

Seven days later the court re-assembled to listen to Justice Hunt's detailed assessment of the events of the past four months.

First he urged the jury not to be influenced by the savagery of the killings in reaching a verdict.

'You may find them to be horrible crimes and you will have sympathies for the families, but you must not let sympathy or emotion sway your judgment in this trial.'

He said theirs was a 'grave and important' public duty. And he made it clear that it was not sufficient to have a grave suspicion that Ivan Milat was the murderer of the seven backpackers or the attacker of Mr Onions. They had to be satisfied beyond reasonable doubt.

'You are 12 people drawn at random from the community to determine the guilt or otherwise of one of your fellow citizens who has been charged with very serious crimes,' he added.

Turning first to the evidence of Paul Onions, the only survivor of the backpacker killings, the judge accepted that his testimony had played a crucial role over the past four months.

'The only dispute is whether it was the accused who picked him up,' Justice Hunt told the jury.

And he cautioned against accepting all of Mr Onions' evidence of identification.

'You may well believe that Paul Onions honestly believes it was the accused that attacked him,' Justice Hunt added.

'The issue is not whether the evidence is honest - the issue here is whether the evidence is reliable.'

The judge said there were fundamental differences in Mr Onions' assessment of his attacker's height and age and those of the accused.

Equally there was no evidence that Richard Milat ever had a moustache going down the sides of his mouth, similar to the Merv Hughes version alluded to by Mr Onions. He pointed out that for Richard to have picked up the young hitchhiker in Casula on that January day in 1990 he would have had to leave work two hours earlier than his rostered finishing time.

He would also have had to get into his car, trimmed his beard—if he had one—to match the moustache Ivan had at the time and dash over to Casula all within less than half an hour.

'You might ask yourselves why he would go to all this trouble only to ensure that if something went wrong that the police would think that Ivan was the man,' the judge added.

He said the defence case rested on 'possibility upon possibility upon possibility.'

The judge also pointed out that Richard Milat had no reason to 'frame' his brother.

'This lack of logic is something that makes the explanation for the false usage of Ivan Milat's particulars just a little difficult to regard,' he added.

Turning to the possibility of more than one person being involved in the murders, Justice Hunt said the Crown was unable to establish for certain whether Ivan Milat was alone although there were strong suspicions he was not.

'The Crown case has always been one of a joint criminal enterprise because it has always conceded that there may have been more than one person involved and it has always said it is unable to establish if the accused did the act by which each person was murdered,' he explained.

It was, admittedly, a largely circumstantial case and there were 14 circumstances on which the Crown relied, the judge said.

These included the presence of camping equipment and backpackers' property at Milat's house and the homes of his mother and some of his brothers.

He had a Ruger 10/22 rifle which was used to shoot Gabor Neugebauer and Caroline Clarke.

Bullets recovered from the skull of Caroline Clarke had scratch marks consistent with a silencer being used. One was found in Milat's garage.

The defendant carried a bowie knife in his car which might have been used to stab his victims.

The ingredients of a restraint device found at the German couple's murder scene, including sash cord and ties, had been available to the defendant in his Cinnabar Street home.

Winchester brand ammunition found in Ivan's alcove underneath his brother's property had the same batch numbers as that used in Area A in the forest.

The pattern of the murders was the same.

And the attack on Paul Onions was a failed attempt to get him into the forest.

Halfway through the judge's summing up there was even more drama when the case was unexpectedly adjourned for several hours.

The reason for the interruption was kept a closely guarded secret at the time for fear of it having a prejudicial affect on Milat's trial.

When the court reconvened the next morning the public, the jury and the media were still in the dark. Though the absence of a juror indicated something serious was amiss.

Justice Hunt told the remaining seven men and four women on the panel, 'Unfortunately one of your colleagues is unable to continue as a juror and we are now obliged to proceed without him. That was a decision made with considerable regret.'

The mystery of the missing juror sent the media into a frenzy of speculation. Was he sick? Had he heard something about Milat's antecedence? Had someone tried to influence him about the verdict?

The truth was even more sinister. The juror had been stood down because someone had found out his name, which was listed in the telephone directory and made a threatening phone call to him.

The identity of the caller was never established but a transcription of what went on during a closed court session was to shed light on the quandary the judge, the prosecution and the defence faced.

In the absence of the jury, the media and the accused, Justice Hunt came quickly to the point.

Judge: 'One of the jurors was telephoned this morning just before he left to come to court. A male voice said, 'Look out, if you find (and the juror thinks the word 'my' was almost half out), 'him guilty, you're dead.'

'He says he is not worried about it. He has been told not to talk to anybody else and he said he had not told anybody before he spoke to the court officer about it.'

Mr Tedeschi: 'How many others have been approached?'

Judge: 'I do not know.'

(Later in the exchange).

Mr Martin: 'Do the other jurors know, judge?'

Judge: 'No. He said he had spoken to nobody before he told the court officer and the court officer told him not to speak to anybody.'

Mr Tedeschi: 'What I am concerned about judge, is, if any other approach has been made to any other jurors who are affected.'

Judge: 'I know. How they got hold of their telephone numbers I do not know. The only reference to their names was when they were called out in the

Banco court at the commencement of the trial. We no longer call over their names for this sort of reason, but I suppose somebody could be followed. They still have to get their name and telephone number. It is quite a mystery. The reference to 'my' of course, he obviously enough believes it would be one of the brothers.'

Mr Martin: 'Yes it puts the defence in a very awkward position.'

Judge: 'Yes it puts everybody in an awkward position because, as the Crown says, who else has been rung?'

Mr Tedeschi: 'And who has not reported it because they are worried about it?'

As the hearing proceeded in-camera the backpacker trial came extraordinarily close to being aborted.

'This is terribly serious, I am very concerned about it,' Justice Hunt admitted.

Eventually the juror himself was summoned to report what actually happened.

The man, who could not be named, said, 'Around a quarter past eight I was just leaving home and I heard the phone. I ran to the phone and answered it and a man's voice said to me if I find him guilty, look out.'

Judge: 'If you find him guilty...?

Juror: 'Look out.'

Judge: 'Look out. Is that all he said.'

Juror: 'That's all.'

Judge: 'Now what happened then?'

Juror: 'And he put the phone down.'

The juror said he was not frightened by the call and had not told any other members of the jury.

The defence was not happy. Mr Martin immediately applied for the discharge of the entire jury.

'The threat itself was very serious and immediately causes prejudice against the accused,' he told the judge.

'In this case it is compounded because the very nature of the defence argument is that a member of the accused's family has planted evidence against him. The juror would then recognise that it seems logical for the member of the family both to be planting evidence against the accused and also making threatening phone calls to have the accused discharged.'

Four hours of legal argument followed. The judge had no wish to see the trial aborted at this eleventh hour. And neither did the prosecution.

Mr Tedeschi said, 'The application to discharge the whole jury is opposed. Putting aside the juror who has come forward it is my submission that we are in the same situation in relation to the other jurors as any trial court is in relation to its jury...my submission is that it would be quite inappropriate to discharge a jury on the basis that there might have been some approach to some juror.'

After lengthy discussion Justice Hunt decided that the juror should be discharged.

He told him: 'I want to make it clear I accept entirely what you said this morning, that you feel able to put this unfortunate call out of your mind. However, I think I should point this out. There is a very old phrase used in the law which you have probably heard yourself, that justice must not only be done but it must be seen to be done, and I have acceded to the application by both parties that there is a real fear in this case that, whatever the result of the case one way or the other, there would be suspicion perhaps you may not have done your duty, even though, as I say, I accept wholeheartedly you would.

'For that reason I regret I am going to have to discharge you as a juror. The other jurors will be told that you are unable to continue with the trial, but no more than that. They will certainly not be told what has happened.

'I do not know over this period of nearly four months what sort of relationship you have built up with the other jurors, but should anybody contact you to see how you are or whatever, you should not say anything to them which would lead to them becoming aware of what has happened. I regret having to do this.

'I think that losing a juror after so long is a very unfortunate thing in any trial. You have all impressed me in this case as being a happy family, I think, applying your minds very keenly to the issues in the case. So it is a shame to see you go, but I am afraid I have to discharge you.'

32.
GUILTY

It was 2.42 p.m. on the afternoon of Wednesday July 24, 1996 when Justice David Hunt turned to the jury and said, 'Will you please now retire and consider your verdict.'

No one could forecast exactly how long their deliberations would take but few expected them to be lengthy. Outside the court the media held a sweepstake to predict the time of the jury's return. Most opted for some time the next day, although one favoured 5 p.m. Friday. In the end it took even longer.

The jury did not return until 10.56 a.m. Saturday morning, almost three days after they had retired. Did this indicate dissent among the jury? Did one of them disagree with the rest? Was it to be guilty, not guilty or even a hung jury? Under New South Wales law juries have to reach a unanimous verdict. Only one of their number had to hold out and the judge would be forced to order a re-trial.

As the court re-assembled on that Saturday morning the tension was palpable. For several minutes no one spoke as the defendant, the judge and finally the jury came back into the room.

They had deliberated for 21 hours. What was their verdict?

As each charge was read out and the foreman was asked how he found the defendant, he replied, 'Guilty.'

There was a gasp of relief from the public gallery followed by quiet sobbing among close relatives and friends.

The cold-hearted killer who showed no mercy to the victims he stabbed, shot and raped, displayed even less emotion as he listened to the words that were to put him behind bars for the rest of his natural life.

Asked by the judge if he had anything to say, Milat replied: 'I'm not guilty—that's all I can say.'

Handing down seven life sentences and a six year prison term for the kidnapping of Paul Onions, the judge said the victims had been savagely and cruelly attacked for Milat's psychological gratification.

'The case against the prisoner at the conclusion of the evidence and the address was, in my view, an overwhelming one. Although his legal representatives displayed a tactical ability of a high order and conducted his defence in a skillful and responsible manner, in my view the jury's verdicts were, in the end, inevitable. I agree entirely with those verdicts. Any other, in my view, would have flown in the face of reality,' Justice Hunt made clear.

'I commend the police and the associated Government agencies for the extensive and painstaking detection work involved in bringing this case to trial. It was a massive task and the results of it have been extraordinarily impressive. All involved in that investigation deserve the thanks of the community for their efforts.

'The maximum sentence for murder is penal servitude for life and, when imposed, that sentence is in fact served for the term of the offender's natural life. The facts of the murders in the present case may presently be said to be notorious, but it is, I believe, important that they are recorded briefly on this occasion.

'Between December 1989 and April 1992, seven backpackers disappeared shortly after they had left Sydney in order to travel south. They were Deborah Everist and James Gibson from Victoria, Simone Schmidl from Germany, Anja Habschied and Gabor Neugebauer also from Germany, and Joanne Walters and Caroline Clarke from the United Kingdom. The first of their bodies was discovered in the Belanglo State Forest in September 1992 and the last in November 1993. All of the bodies were located within a short distance of the fire trails in the forest, covered with branches and leaf litter in a way which would hide them from view but which would nevertheless assist them to decompose rapidly.

'Each of the victims was young—they were between nineteen and twenty-two years old. Each was travelling far from home, the inference being that they would not have been missed for some time if anything happened to them. I am satisfied that each set out along the Hume Highway from near Liverpool in order to hitchhike to the south. The jury's verdicts mean that the prisoner was involved, either alone or in company, in a criminal enterprise to pick them up there and then to murder them all. In my view, it is inevitable that the prisoner was not alone in that criminal enterprise, but I do not take that fact into account either in aggravation or mitigation when considering what sentences should be imposed.

'By reason of the decomposition of the bodies, the medical evidence does not disclose the actual cause of death for any of the victims. That evidence does, however, indicate the nature of some of the injuries which were inflicted and any number of those injuries would have qualified as the cause of death. The injuries which were inflicted at the time, whether or not they caused death, were nevertheless so tied up in the commission of these crimes as to be very relevant in determining their objective gravity.

'I do not propose here to list those injuries individually, or to ascribe those injuries to any of the victims. I do not wish to cause further distress to the families of the victims who have had to endure hearing the evidence itself and the description of it which I gave during the course of my summing up. Their understandable distress was evident and it is unnecessary that it should be repeated. In any event I frankly do not want to go through that ordeal again myself.

'It is sufficient here to record that each of the victims was attacked savagely and cruelly with force which was unusual and vastly more than was necessary to cause death and for some sort of psychological gratification. Each of two of the victims was shot a number of times in the head. A third was decapitated in circumstances which establish that she would have been alive at the time. The stab wounds to each of three others would have caused paralysis, two of them having had their spinal cords completely severed. The multiple stab wounds to three of the seven victims would have been likely to have penetrated their hearts. There are signs that two of them had been strangled. All but one of them appears to have been sexually interfered with either before or after death.

'These seven young persons were at the threshhold of their lives, with everything to look forward to—travel, career, happiness, love, family, and even old age. Whatever the actual causes of their death may have been in each case, it is clear that they were subjected to behaviour which, for callous indifference to suffering and complete disregard of humanity, is almost beyond belief. They would obviously have been absolutely terrified, and death is unlikely to have been swiftly applied. It is perhaps possible to imagine a worse case, but these murders must unhesitatingly be labeled as falling within the worse class of case.

'As the Crown has always conceded, it is not possible to determine whether it was the prisoner himself who inflicted the particular injuries which caused the death of any particular victim. That fact would have assumed some importance if the prisoner had to be sentenced in relation to only one murder. However, as he has been shown to have been involved in a criminal enterprise to murder all seven of them spanning four different occasions, the prisoner can hardly be heard to say that he did not know the character of the behaviour in which he was allowing himself to become involved on each occasion. I am satisfied that he is just as responsible for that behaviour as the person who did inflict the particular injuries which caused the deaths of each of the victims.

'The detention count related to Paul Onions who fitted the same pattern of victim. He too was a backpacker, young, one who would not have been missed for some time because he was from the United Kingdom and traveling, and he was picked up as a hitchhiker by the prisoner on the Hume Highway near Liverpool in order to travel south. After establishing that Onions had no friends or family in Australia and was taking his time traveling, the prisoner stopped just short of the turn-off to the Belanglo State Forest and produced a gun and a bag of ropes. When Onions ran away, the prisoner chased and caught him, holding on to his shirt. Onions was fortunately able to escape again. I am satisfied that this was a thwarted attempt to take him into the forest where he too was to be murdered, just as the others were. The detention was thus a brief one only and Onions did not receive substantial injury. The maximum sentence in those circumstances is penal servitude for fourteen years.

'There are many different purposes to be served in the sentencing process. As both the High Court and the Court of Criminal Appeal have observed, those purposes overlap, and the place to be given to each will vary in the different circumstances of different cases. So far as these murders are concerned, such was their nature that this case is not, in my opinion, one in which there is any great utility in considering the prospects of the prisoner's rehabilitation. Nor is it a case in which the subjective circumstances of the prisoner himself can play any decisive part. Nothing specific has been put before me, but I note from the evidence that the prisoner appears to have been employed continuously for some time. He has had no convictions since 1967 so that his criminal history is of little importance in the overall picture.

'In this case the need for the sentence to operate by way of a public deterrence is important, as it always is, in order to ensure that those whose character may incline them to similar behaviour in the future will be reminded powerfully that severe punishment will be imposed should they give in to temptation.

'But, above all, these truly horrible crimes of murder demand sentences which operate by way of retribution, or (as it is sometimes described) by the taking of vengeance for the injury which was done by the prisoner in committing them. Not only must the community be satisfied that the criminal is given his just deserts, it is important that those whom the victims have left behind also feel that justice has been done.

'The other sentencing principle to which I should refer is that of totality. As I propose to impose concurrent sentences, the longer of the sentences must represent the totality of the prisoner's criminality involved in all of the crimes of which he has been found guilty.

'So far as the third count is concerned, that relating to Paul Onions, the prisoner's intention was a gravely serious one but that intention was not carried into execution. The crime itself does not fall into the category of being in the worst class of case. Because the sentence is to be concurrent with the others, and will be considerably overlapped by them, I see no point in fixing minimum and additional terms. The sentence which I impose is nevertheless intended to represent the total sentence, not what would otherwise have been the minimum term.

'Ivan Robert Marko Milat, on the third count, I sentence you to a fixed term of penal servitude for six years, commencing 22 May, 1994 and concluding 21 May, 2000. On each of the remaining counts, I sentence you to penal servitude for life, commencing on 22 May, 1994 and to be served for the term of your natural life.'

If he was shocked, saddened, angered or remorseful, Milat's countenance showed no sign. Within seconds he had left the dock and a few minutes later was on his way to prison. Under the terms of the sentences just handed down he would not know freedom again.

For the parents who had sat through the trial, the verdicts were the final chapter in a desperately depressing saga of human tragedy.

Afterwards Caroline Clarke's father Ian admitted, 'We're very, very relieved and glad it's all over.'

He refused to allow Milat to destroy his life. 'We are not going to give Milat the pleasure of ruining our lives as well as Caroline's,' he went on.

'Our children were desperately unlucky. Ninety nine point nine per cent have a wonderful time, but just be careful,' he warned.

'One of the things (about backpacking) we have always felt is the need for communication between our children and ourselves. We found time and again that Caroline was ringing us and could not talk for long with just 10 cents in her hand. The message to parents is to give them a phonecard.'

Joanne's father, Ray Walters, agreed that justice had now been done.

'The only thing is it will be safer for people in Australia as it has been safer since our children have died,' he explained.

'If you lose a child in these circumstances it's there for ever. I want people to know how much Milat has destroyed lives like ours.'

Deborah's mother, Patricia Everist, made the same point.

'It has destroyed our lives. It's changed my life for ever.'

Mrs Peggy Gibson, mother of James, thanked all those who had supported them over the previous six and a half years.

'The loss of James, the gradual unfolding of how he and the other young people were killed, and being the focus of public attention, have all been very traumatic,' she said.

And she paid tribute to the police.

'We would like to thank all the police involved, but particularly the members of Task Force Air whose kindness has far exceeded that of duty.'

From Mr Clarke there was a final hint of why they felt compelled to sit through a trial which could only provide them with further torment.

'It was the last thing we could do for our children,' he explained.

'All we can say is that we were there for our children.'

At the post trial press conference he was also asked about the possibility of a second killer remaining at large.

'If that is the case we have still got the awful prospect of somebody being on the streets who shouldn't be on the streets,' he said.

'I think there's a clear message for all backpackers—it is not as safe as they think it is.'

33.

THE UNKNOWN VICTIMS

I met Noel Manning after receiving an urgent telephone call from him on December 12, 1995. It was exactly a year to the day that Ivan Milat had been committed for trial at Campbelltown magistrates court.

Clearly nervous about talking on the phone, Manning asked to see me in person. I had no idea what he had to say except that it concerned the backpacker murders.

We arranged to meet on the corner of Ridge and Miller Streets outside North Sydney Oval at 5.45 p.m. He would be wearing a pair of blue jeans and a matching denim shirt. There was no problem identifying him. He was the only person on the street corner that afternoon.

Noel Manning shared a cell with Ivan Milat in Sydney's Long Bay Gaol in the early 1974 when Manning was serving time for breaking and entering.

During their period together he claimed Milat boasted of the raping and killing he had done in the past.

'Just looking at him it was easy to believe what he said,' Manning began.

'My first thoughts were how mean and monstrous he looked. He was bigger than anybody I had ever seen, his upper arms were huge.

'He said he was on remand for the rape of two girls, openly telling me he was proud of the fact and that he was certain he was going to get off. In fact he bragged how no jury would convict him.

'Days afterwards we were talking again and he said if he was convicted, he was thinking of ways as to how he was going to break out of gaol. He said he would get a gun smuggled into prison and spoke about bullets being thrown over the wall. But he didn't dwell on it, because he was convinced he was going to beat the charges.

'Milat got whatever he wanted, there was no question of him not getting enough food and the same with his clothing. Most of the prisoners were issued with two pairs of the same clothing. But he had a different pair of pants every day, pressed and ironed. They gave him made-to-measure clothes.

'He also had contacts in the gaol. He knew who to speak to and who to ask. Most of the time he would keep to himself pretty much. There would be no way in the world anyone was going to fight with him. And because he was so convinced he would beat the rape charges he didn't want any trouble or strife. He was just in there biding his time.

'Milat was short and stocky and had terrible hands. There were sores and callouses on his hands from all the exercises he did. And he had superhuman strength. Sometimes he would summersault and rest his feet against the wall for hours at a time while his knuckles rested on the ground. He would do single and one-arm push-ups. Sly Stallone in the *Rocky* movies had nothing on him.

'He had a big chest and huge biceps which he said he developed while working with jackhammers. He told me about when he was digging the Kings Cross Tunnel and worked all through the night holding his jackhammer over his head for hours at a time. He called the Cross a gold mine because he would pick up girls and boys. He used to tell me how he raped them and it went on from there.

'Eventually he started killing people. At first I thought it was all bullshit. But he would tell you the same stories night after night and it wasn't until one night I looked into his eyes and I knew he was telling the truth.

'He said he would pick them up and then rape and kill them in the bush. He boasted how sometimes he even raped them after they were dead. He gave no names and no ages and he said he could dispose of them so no one would ever find them. He could bury them inches below the surface and no one would ever know they were there. That was his expertise he would say.

'He gave no indication of how many people he killed, male or female. I couldn't keep up with it all. It was all so horrendous. He said he had a bowie knife, crossbow and Ruger rifles. Then one day he showed me how he held them and stabbed them. He said he would put pillow cases over their heads and would stab both their front and back. Then he would blow their heads off. Apparently he liked watching the blood seep through the pillow cases.

'His descriptions were sickening. He talked about staking people by the hands and feet, cutting them so they bled, putting them near ants nests, slicing them down the back, reaching in and grabbing their ribs and caving their chests in. It might not sound real, but that's how he talked.

'The worst thing he told me was how he raped males and females after he killed them when their bodies were still warm. He used to let them know he was going to kill them so he could see the look of fear in their eyes. It used to be a great kick for him.

'I'm sure he was not making it all up. No one goes into that sort of detail if they didn't do it. He would go through it again and again in his mind, replaying it like a video in his head.

'Strangely I never feared for my own safety while I was with him. The only time I recall I was a bit concerned was one night when he showed me how he used to stab these people.

'Standing on the floor with my back to him he got me in a headlock and said, 'Imagine I have a knife in my hand.' Then he would sweep around my body and stab me.

'That's the only time I can recall being nervous because he had me in a headlock. That's the night he asked what I would do if he came 'onto' me. He just came out and said what would I do for a sexual thing. I said I'd fight him. Fortunately he changed the subject because he could have picked me up and snapped me in half like a pretzel.

'I used to fall asleep. The lights would be out, but he would still keep on talking. Sometimes he would hop up on the bunk, wake me and tell me more stories of murder and rape.'

Manning was later to tell the police about his prison conversations. He gave another statement to New South Wales police on September 26, 1994, four months after Milat's arrest. He offered to provide evidence against Milat but he killed himself on February 23, 1996, a month before the trial opened. There were no suspicious circumstances. I later read the suicide note he left.

Noel Manning never asked me for money which encouraged me to believe his story. If true it provided further evidence of Ivan Milat's wicked ways. More importantly it raised the question—how many more people fell victim to his blood lust?

34.
WELCOME TO MAITLAND

After being convicted and sentenced Milat was kept overnight under tight security in a holding cell in Sydney before being transferred to Maitland Gaol in the New South Wales' Hunter Valley. It was to be his home for the next 10 months.

The backpacker killer's arrival at Maitland did not bode well. If he thought he was going to be welcomed as a hero, the reality of his circumstances soon hit home.

As he waited in line with a group of inmates who were also being processed, another prisoner calmly walked up to him and punched him hard three times in the head including a solid sock to the jaw. It was an inauspicious start to his lifetime sentence.

If Milat was daunted by his reception he didn't show it. As a newcomer to Maitland he knew he would be picked on by other long-term gaolbirds who would be keen to test him.

In fact despite his strength and reputation as a hard man, his violent side was always kept under control behind bars. Far from being a troublemaker he would actively court the friendship of others including prison staff. It was part of his devious nature. He wanted to lull the warders into dropping their guard, to establish a level of trust with his captors so he would not attract any suspicious looks while hatching his next big plan.

Among his fellow inmates was George Savvas who was serving a 30 year sentence for drugs trafficking. He had earlier escaped from Goulburn Correctional Centre and after being recaptured was sent to Maitland where he joined Milat and several other maximum security prisoners who were regarded as high risk.

Maitland Gaol, which has since being transformed into a museum, was one of the most feared correctional institutions in New South Wales. It was built in the 1840s and until it was closed in 1998 was the longest continually-run prison in Australia.

There were 16 executions there between 1849 and 1897, many of them held in public. Sometimes condemned men were hanged at the main gates, a grim spectacle which always attracted large crowds.

Conditions inside were so bad that in 1975 inmates went on the rampage and set fire to the maintenance block in protest. Prisoners, including the bank robber Darcy Dugan, who became famous for his daring escapes, attacked wardens with home-made weapons.

Two years later another notorious criminal, Russell 'Mad Dog' Cox and half a dozen others, escaped through a ventilation shaft in the shower block, though they were recaptured after a few hours.

Escape attempts were part of the culture at Maitland so it was inevitable that Milat and Savvas would try their hand. It was an audacious plot. First they planned to overpower warders in the reception area and steal their uniforms. Then with the aid of two other inmates they intended to scale an eight metre high wall which was crowned with razor wire and monitored 24 hours a day by CCTV cameras.

From there they proposed to climb over the outside gates, which were overlooked by armed guards with Ruger rifles and make good their escape.

What they didn't know was that Corrective Services staff were already on to them. Just how the plot leaked has never been fully explained, but informers either inside or outside the prison knew enough by April 1997 to reveal the escape plan to the Independent Commission Against Corruption.

In fact according to Bob Debus, the New South Wales Correctional Services Minister at the time, Savvas and his 'underworld confederates' had been monitored for several months.

He told State Parliament that prison authorities were notified and when it was established that the planned escape was to go ahead, New South Wales police were advised.

Together they devised a sting operation codenamed Bengal. 'It was designed to not only smash the escape but also the outside ring of accomplices,' Mr Debus said.

Had Milat and Savvas embarked on their hare-brained scheme they would not have got far. They would have come face to face with a squad of heavily-armed officers from the hostage response group drawn from the police and Corrective Services.

'Hidden in the reception room, unknown to the inmates, a unit of armed men lay in wait, rather than the single guard the prisoners expected,' Mr Debus explained.

'High in the tower above was hidden a further squad of marksmen.'

The organisers of Operation Bengal had considered separating Milat and Savvas in order to undermine the escape plot but decided against this.

'It would not protect the long-term safety of staff and the community to drive Milat and Savvas underground with their internal support networks intact ready to form again and plan again in three, six or 12 months when the heat was off,' Mr Debus added.

Ultimately the operation was aborted after consideration was given to the potential danger to prison staff and the security of inmates. Instead officers moved in on Savvas and Milat before they had time to carry out their plans. The two men were placed under even tighter security and interviewed by ICAC.

Predictably both insisted they had no knowledge of an escape bid, but the warders were not taking any chances. Milat was heavily shackled and transported under armed guard to a segregation unit at Long Bay Gaol in Sydney's south.

Savvas was placed in a special segregation unit in Maitland and guarded around the clock. The cell in which he was held was effectively a steel cage, a prison within a prison.

What happened next sent shock waves through the corrective services system and its political masters. Despite the 24 hour monitoring, Savvas, who had not previously been considered a suicide risk, was found hanging from a bed sheet in the doorway to his cell the following morning.

Foiled in his final attempt at freedom, the convicted drug trafficker had become sufficiently depressed to take his own life. Or had he? When reporters arrived at Maitland to cover the story they heard some of the inmates shouting 'Murderers, murderers.' Whatever the truth, an inquest later found that Savvas had committed suicide while the balance of his mind was disturbed some time during the night.

Interestingly Milat was never charged in relation to the plot but the prison authorities were keen to send him a message that there would be no further opportunity to escape. His next stop would be Goulburn where a new maximum security wing would deprive him of any further hope of liberty.

Supermax is akin to building a gaol within a fortress. Within the high perimeter walls are inner walls and within these are sound and motion alarms which are triggered by any unusual noise or movement. Milat and other high risk prisoners are rarely allowed out of their cells to socialise with other inmates. There is a small common room where they might be allowed to meet with one other prisoner, as well as a training yard where they can exercise for up to two hours a day.

To reduce the likelihood of contraband being hidden, each occupant is rotated to another cell about once a month and the entire area and its contents X-rayed.

With telephone calls and mail always monitored, there is little in the way of privacy. And when close family friends or relatives are allowed to visit at the weekend, there is a noticeable increase in security.

People like Milat are forced to wear a padlocked orange jumpsuit and his visitors are photographed and fingerprinted as part of the procedure.

Within these seemingly impenetrable walls it would be easy to forsake all hope of freedom, of ever seeing the sun rise over the ocean or clouds scudding across distant fields. That doesn't prevent 'lifers' from having their fantasies.

In January 1999 a small hacksaw blade was found hidden inside a cellophane wrapped packet of biscuits in his cell. He denied all knowledge of it of course and even if it had remained undiscovered it is difficult to see how the tiny blade would have sawn through the heavy steel bars and barricades designed to keep him inside.

In February 2001 he swallowed three razor blades, 24 staples and a small metal chain in a protest against his solitary confinement. He was hoping to be sent for an X-ray outside the gaol but instead was treated in the prison's hospital wing.

His condition was monitored for the next 10 days but there was no untoward effect. Milat told friends in a smuggled note that it was not a suicide bid but an attempt to draw attention to his ongoing appeal.

He tried another act of self-mutilation in 2003 when he deliberately crushed his left hand in a prison door. It required 24 stitches but the injury was not considered serious enough for treatment at a public hospital. Once again Milat's escape plans were frustrated.

There were several hunger strikes too, although they rarely lasted long. The backpacker murderer apparently enjoyed his food too much to cope with an empty stomach.

Apart from court appearances, his only successful attempt to engineer a day trip outside prison came on January 26, 2009, when he cut off part of his left hand little finger with a plastic knife.

He placed it in an envelope addressed to Justice Peter McClellan of the NSW Supreme Court before giving it to a prison officer just before lock-up time at 3.30 pm. On a post-it note he'd written: 'Please—careful. Caution hazardous material.'

Clearly in pain, it had taken him 20 minutes to perform the amputation, which was designed to exert pressure on the legal system for an inquiry into his conviction.

This time, handcuffed and shackled, he succeeded in being ferried to Goulburn Base Hospital by four high risk escort officers. They packed the severed finger into an ice pack which accompanied Milat to the casualty unit but surgeons were unsuccessful in their attempt to re-attach the amputated digit.

Milat remained under heavy armed guard for about three hours before being driven back to Goulburn Gaol later that evening in an unmarked Toyota Landcruiser.

As NSW Corrective Services Commissioner Ron Woodham said at the time, 'He is very close to losing his marbles.'

Later Milat admitted in a letter to his brother Bill and published in the *Australian Women's Weekly* that it was a 'ridiculous thing to do, but in here acts like that is (sic) regarded as normal and not as severe as some.'

'I wonder if I will have enough time to prove my innocence as time flies, but it takes a long time to get a reply from the authority-courts-government,' he added.

'That was a big factor in severing the finger off, to highlight the difficulties of a prisoner who wishes to appeal his case,' he explained.

Apart from a sore finger, the immediate impact of this desperate act of self-mutilation was a withdrawal of the little luxuries Milat had won over the years for good behaviour.

As punishment, prison authorities removed his eating utensils and his toasted sandwich maker, which allowed him a degree of flexibility over the way his food was cooked.

'The prison controllers seem to think I need some punishment, so they took off my plastic plates and cup…and no means given to cut anything up and I never eat tea at 2-2.15 pm, so by the time I do feel like eating at 6-6.30-odd, it's a soggy, cold mess. And they took my Breville away. I always rely on that, use it to reheat, cook other things like bread.'

There were hints of self-pity in Ivan Milat's tone as he wrote about the possibility of becoming 'completely isolated.'

After 15 years locked up and segregated from other prisoners his mind was beginning to go. And he still didn't get it.

'Everyone around me is fairly up in arms over what I do,' he observed in the letter to Bill.

35.
LET ME OUT OF HERE

Ivan Milat had spent most of his waking hours since he was sentenced to life imprisonment on July 26, 1996, devising new ways of getting his conviction overturned. By late 2010 he appeared to have exhausted all his options.

First there had been the 1997 application to the Court of Criminal Appeal. Milat's grounds for having his conviction overturned were in essence:

1. That Paul Onions' evidence of identification was unreliable and unfair. The British witness and the woman who helped him to escape, Mrs Joanne Berry, said Milat's Nissan Patrol had a spare wheel mounted vertically on the back, when in fact it was placed underneath the vehicle.

2. That Justice David Hunt, the trial judge, did not put the defence case fairly in his summing up to the jury.

3. That inflammatory and prejudicial evidence should not have been admitted, including a reference to the 1971 rape case which had been raised at a preliminary hearing and for which Milat was acquitted.

In November 1997 the serial killer eventually got the opportunity to put his case to three appeal court judges including Chief Justice Murray Gleeson.

Milat seemed to be a little thinner than when he had last appeared in public more than a year earlier.

This time he was dressed in prison greens consisting of a sloppy joe and shorts. He carried his legal documents in a plastic carrier bag and wore headphones to monitor the proceedings.

What also set this hearing apart from his previous courtroom appearances was his lack of legal representation. Milat was on his own, after dismissing his solicitor Andrew Boe.

If he was daunted by the prospect of representing himself he didn't show it at first. There was a hint of that familiar grin as he looked across to the three judges but deep inside he must have realised that he was not up to the task.

After repeating himself several times while addressing the pre-trial publicity over the rape case, he turned to Justice Gleeson and admitted: 'I don't really know what else I can say.'

The Judge nodded in agreement.

Milat was floundering. He didn't have the intellect or the vocabulary to joust with such eminent minds as the New South Wales Chief Justice and his colleagues.

At one stage he rustled through his shopping bag and produced some handwritten notes before announcing that he no longer wished to proceed with the first ground of his appeal which concerned media intrusion.

Neither was he happy about the way his appeal had been set out and he wanted to change it.

Justice Gleeson offered him another three weeks to detail what he sought to add and reminded him that the deadline would be November 28.

During the lengthy silence that followed Milat continued to rifle through his bag of documents prompting the judge to ask him if he had a pen.

Yes he did, he assured the court, but he was becoming flustered

Justice Gleeson finally put him out of his misery at 11.40 a.m. when the hearing was adjourned and the prisoner was escorted out of the courtroom by Corrective Services officers.

Outside the court members of his family who had sat in the public gallery spoke of his physical condition as evidence of his poor treatment behind bars.

'He's very sick and weak,' his sister Dianne claimed.

'His weight is down from 87kg to 74kg and his eyes are hurting,' she told an impromptu press conference.

'I wonder if someone is putting some stuff in his tea?' she asked.

Other Milat supporters including family friend Ian McDougall called on then Labor Premier Bob Carr to take a fresh look at the case, particularly as young women were still going missing.

'He's being discriminated against,' declared McDougall who helped to form a pressure group named The Firm—or Friends of Ivan Milat.

'But he did kill seven people,' one of the reporters reminded him.

There was no answer to that.

If The Firm was correct in claiming that Ivan was being unfairly treated in prison, it might have had something to do with an article that appeared in the now defunct *Bulletin* magazine a few weeks earlier.

The Department of Corrective Services was incensed that Ivan had managed to provide the magazine with an interview in which he protested his innocence and warned that the 'real murderers' were still free and capable of further killings.

Milat agreed to answer questions put to him in written form by journalist Brett Martin in which he also alleged that he had been framed by police.

Asked if he was in any way connected to the backpacker murders he replied, 'Absolutely not.'

'Nor do I feel I have to show any feelings towards the backpacker killings because I didn't do them. I feel more for the starving children of Africa,' he added.

He also denied suggestions that he was protecting any other people or groups who might have been involved.

'I will say that people should be very concerned because I didn't do the killings which means the real monsters who did this are still out there,' he went on.

What about members of his family?

'Again I have no ideas on it. Some statements made by police and others suggest something, but I am not aware of any details,' he said.

But if he was innocent, how was it that such a huge amount of incriminating evidence was found in his house and the homes of relatives?

Milat had no answer for that either.

'During the trial a lot of evidence and statements were presented to the court that were quite different from what was described in statements by family members or friends (of the victims) when the people went missing,' he wrote.

'I saw a list of 82 items taken from our place, but only a few of those items were ever produced at court,' he claimed.

Milat denied all knowledge of the evidence found in his sister's room at Eagle Vale and in other locations. The thrust of his argument was that he was an innocent party caught up in a police plot to frame him. And one of his points appeared valid.

Referring to some property owned by Simone Schmidl which was found in his garage, he drew attention to a report that the same belongings had been handed in to police at Bright in Victoria four months after she disappeared and prior to the raid on his home.

In fact the metal framed glasses and a sleeping bag discovered in bush more than 70 kilometres south of Albury and the Hume Highway were never positively identified as Simone's. Her mother, who was shown photographs of the items, believed them to be her daughter's, but detectives weren't convinced.

'We couldn't get much information about that. Police would say when asked in court, 'No, don't know anything about that.' What can one do?'

So if he was alleging the evidence was planted who was responsible? Who else had access to his Eagle Vale home?

'A lot of family had access to our place but the police are the ones,' he alleged.

He claimed the original statements made to police by Paul Onions and Mrs Berry had gone missing 'because the description of the four-wheel drive used in the abduction didn't match my vehicle.'

Then he turned to the forensic samples taken from the bodies of the two British girls which included hairs found in the palm of Joanne Walter's hand.

These had been tested against Milat's hair and found not to match. None of the DNA samples could be linked to him.

'The prosecution came out with a report which said the tests were flawed. We asked for the tests to be done again but they said they had lost the samples,' he told *The Bulletin*.

But why would the police want to frame him? Why was he chosen and who did he think was being protected?

Milat was struggling to provide a plausible response to this.

He didn't know who else was being protected but he was certain of one thing.

'We know that the police had investigated me in late 1993 in connection with guns. They knew I never fitted the description that Onions gave in 1990 and also there wasn't enough detail of the car in 1990. Onions was the key, so they worked on him to fit in with me and after the arrest the media took over and I was sunk.'

The Bulletin's exclusive interview infuriated Bob Debus, who was still Minister for Corrective Services.

Warning of tighter restrictions on Milat's access to visitors in future, he suggested the text must have been smuggled out by a friend or relative.

'While *The Bulletin* magazine also stands condemned for publishing the 'interview' with Milat, departmental surveillances shows that no *Bulletin* journalist actually interviewed Milat,' he made clear.

'Milat is only allowed visits from his immediate family and his girlfriend and only at times that suit the department.'

However the answers were smuggled out, the prisoner had worked the interview to his advantage by casting doubts over the veracity of the police investigation and drawing attention to the frustration he was feeling about the progress of his appeal.

'I wonder at times if they will let me get to appeal. It is something they don't want me to do,' he wrote.

'A lot of obstacles are being placed in my way.'

When the New South Wales Court of Criminal Appeal handed down its judgment in February 1998, the document ran to 25 pages. The judges' response to Milat's attempt to overturn his conviction was exhaustive.

On the evidence of identification provided by Mr Onions, the court accepted there was a difference of opinion over the height of the man who attempted to abduct him. The British backpacker remembered him as six feet tall and in his mid-thirties, whereas Milat was five feet eight inches and in his mid-forties.

The judges reckoned the aggressor might have looked taller because Mr Onions was only five feet six inches.

'Not all aspects of the physical description fitted the appellant,' Justice Gleeson conceded.

'Nevertheless, taking everything into account, the jury were entitled to regard the contemporaneous description which Mr Onions gave of his attacker as strong evidence against the appellant. When to that is added the fact that a shirt, which undoubtedly belonged to Mr Onions and which had been left behind in the rucksack when he fled, was found at the appellant's mother's house with an old shirt belonging to the appellant, it is not difficult to understand how the jury could reasonably have come to the conclusion that the man who gave Mr Onions the lift was the appellant.'

As for the spare tyre on the back of the vehicle, this might have been a genuine mistake, prompted by other photographs the young Briton had been shown. Milat had proof that his Nissan Patrol did not have a spare wheel in such a position in 1990, but the court could understand how the confusion arose.

'It did not form part of the description of the vehicle when he (Onions) spoke to the police on January 25, 1990 and it appears first to have emerged in 1994. So far as his courtroom evidence was concerned, it also appears to have emerged in the context where he was shown photographs that could have suggested to him something which caused the mistake.'

Meticulously the judge addressed all six grounds for appeal including perceived irregularities by the media during the jury's deliberations. Basically Milat felt that television coverage of the case, which included shots of the victims' families waiting outside the court, placed tremendous pressure on the jurors and raised questions about the fairness of the trial.

He'd wanted a judge only trial but that was not granted.

Further Milat argued that prejudicial publicity before and during the trial made the convictions unsafe and amounted to a miscarriage of justice.

There was also the disclosure of the 1971 rape charge, which Milat was subsequently acquitted of. That slipped out in 1994 when the prosecution, giving reasons for its opposition to bail, made mention that the accused man had absconded to New Zealand after being charged with rape.

Justice Gleeson was having none of it.

'Some of the arguments advanced by the appellant are tantamount to saying that, in the events that happened, it was impossible for him to receive a fair trial in front of a jury and that if he could not have a trial without a jury he should never have been put on trial at all. I would reject this. The criminal justice system, of which trial by jury is an integral part, often has to function in circumstances of intense publicity potentially prejudicial to the accused person. Various mechanisms, including, where necessary, contempt of court, are available to protect the integrity of the system. Ultimately, however, it is the capacity of the jurors, properly instructed by trial judges, to decide cases by reference to legally admissible evidence and legally relevant arguments, and not otherwise, that is the foundation of the system.'

In dismissing the appeal the judge concluded: 'I am satisfied that the appellant had a fair trial, according to law, and that the matters complained of by the appellant produced no miscarriage of justice.'

If the New South Wales Court of Criminal Appeal thought that was the end of the matter, they didn't know Ivan Milat. He would spend much of his waking hours poring over law books and examining legal precedents which might assist him in his struggle.

In 2004 he tried to obtain leave to appeal to the High Court but that was also thrown out and a year later he made a fresh appeal to the NSW Supreme Court for an inquiry into his case, again arguing that he was wrongly convicted.

This time there was no personal appearance by the prisoner who remained in his cell while the judge read the 50 handwritten pages penned by Milat.

Once again his grounds centred on Paul Onions' evidence and the position of the spare wheel.

But Justice Graham Barr found that Milat had not raised any doubt about his guilt, accusing him of losing sight of the substantial point at issue at trial... 'namely the identity of the attacker.'

He described Milat's arguments as long winded and reminded him that the Crimes Act only provided for an inquiry into a conviction if a court established there was doubt over whether a person's guilt had been proven.

It was certainly not intended as 'yet another avenue of appeal' after the normal avenues had been exhausted.

While other prisoners might have seen this as the end of the legal road and accepted their fate, the constant rejections only seemed to fuel Milat's determination to fight on.

Soon he was seeking another order to the NSW Supreme Court, asking that his case be referred to the Court of Criminal Appeal.

On this occasion he argued that the trial judge had directed the jury to act on evidence relating to Paul Onions not established by the Crown.

Just before Christmas 2006 Justice Peter McClellan rejected the application insisting there was 'no doubt or question as to his guilt.'

'I have no unease and no sense of disquiet in allowing the convictions to stand,' he concluded.

Apart from the amputated finger and the occasional leaked remark by Milat from sources within Goulburn's Supermax Gaol, there have been no further attempts to pursue his case for a new inquiry. But that doesn't mean he has given up on the idea.

Under New South Wales law he is free to make further applications to the court but unless he reveals new evidence, they will certainly fail.

36.
HOW MANY MORE?

Such is his notoriety that Milat's name has been linked to scores of murders and missing people over the past four decades. While some of the cases have only a spurious connection, a significant number have all the hallmarks of the backpacker killer's involvement.

In the late 1970s he was working as a roadganger on the Pacific Highway near Newcastle when three young women vanished.

The first to disappear was Leanne Goodall, aged 20, who was dropped off at Muswellbrook Station on December 30, 1978 and was later spotted at the Star Hotel in Newcastle, where Milat had been staying.

Robyn Hickie, 17, went missing on April 7, 1979 after leaving her home at Belmont to wait for a bus. Milat had been working only a few kilometres away at the time. Police found one of her shoes but nothing else.

Nearly a fortnight later Amanda Robinson, aged 14, vanished in chillingly similar circumstances. On April 20, 1979 she stepped off a bus near her home at Swansea after returning from a school dance.

On October 12, 1979 Amanda Zollis, who was only 16, telephoned her father from a public call box to say she was on her way to Queensland and needed some clothes. She has not been seen since.

Police formed Strike Force Fenwick to investigate the Newcastle disappearances but were unsuccessful in their attempts to nail a killer. Detectives had several suspects in their sights but so far as we know Milat was not among them. It wasn't until his arrest over the backpacker murders that police began to form a link between his work pattern and the young women who'd gone missing in the Newcastle area.

They set up a 12-strong strike force to carry our further enquiries into these and other young people who'd disappeared in recent years.

Such was the public interest in these abductions that the authorities came under increasing pressure to take a fresh look at the deaths of Leanne Goodall, Robyn Hickie and Amanda Robinson, whose cases seemed to be so closely associated with Milat.

It led to an inquest being held by the then State Coroner, John Abernethy, in 2001 at Toronto, south of Newcastle. It also provided Ivan Milat with a rare opportunity to escape the confines of his Supermax cell and make a guest appearance as a witness.

He was one of six people of interest named by Mr Abernethy, but Milat was having none of it. Clearly savouring his day out, he denied any knowledge of the missing girls but couldn't resist making some insensitive asides to the parents who were sitting in the public gallery.

'I was mystified when I read about one person who went missing in December and they didn't report her missing 'til February,' he added.

The comment was similar to remarks he'd written in a letter to the families, via the Newcastle Legal Centre, earlier in the year and which were subsequently published in the Newcastle Herald.

Even if he were given seven life pardons and a few million dollars, he wouldn't be able to help them, he made clear.

'I feel I've done all I can to assist you...perhaps you should tell the families that due to their failures in taking more care prior to when their children went and more importantly past then (sic) that the police played in looking after their reports of the disappearances, how they responded to it and the inadequate investigations by "operation fuckwits" it is doubtful if anything will ever be known,' he explained.

While his letter wouldn't have got a pass mark for grammar—and though his sentiments seemed cold and uncaring—it did contain one admission of sympathy for the relatives.

'Frankly I don't care what you tell, your miserable attempts to frame me may satisfy them, I do feel sorry for them,' he went on.

'So good luck, I really hope you can find out whoever really did it and hope you then give me an apology.'

Milat had enjoyed his day in the public eye again but, as usual, was giving nothing away.

The coroner had done all he could to shed more light on the abductions and likely deaths of these young women but could only record that they were murdered by persons unknown.

It was of little consolation to the parents who continued to pray for closure. Even a phone call to say where the girls' bodies were left would have helped. Then at least they could have a funeral. It's not knowing what happened that gnawed away inside them.

Yet more than three decades after their cherished children disappeared without trace the likelihood of anyone coming forward with information is more remote than ever.

Much the same applies to the missing Sydney nurses, Gillian Jamieson and Deborah Balken. They were both 19 when they were last seen at the Tollgate Hotel in Parramatta on July 12, 1980. They'd been friends ever since they went to school together at Cumberland High. They also liked to party.

The pub had been a popular bikie hang-out where drugs were known to circulate freely. One of their friends later told police 'it was not unusual for Debbie or Gill to go to places with people they hardly knew on the promise of a good time.' The girls were seen in the poolroom talking to a man in dirty work clothes and wearing a broad-brimmed, black felt hat.

Later they were sighted in Parramatta in a car with two men, one of whom appeared to be dressing Gillian. The witnesses said the young women had their eyes shut and were limp and floppy.

Intriguingly one of the girls made a call to her flatmate later that evening. Deborah rang from a pay phone to say they were in Wollongong and asked the flatmate to ring their place of work on Monday to say they were ill and would not be coming in. It was the last known contact with the two young women.

But why were they in Wollongong? It's a long drive from Parramatta and was not the direction Milat would have favoured. His natural instinct was to prowl the Casula-Goulburn corridor. And as he was later to remind police, he rarely drank alcohol and didn't frequent pubs. On the face of it this disappearance didn't fit Milat.

Chillingly the man in the black felt headgear, similar to a cowboy hat, returned to the Tollgate Hotel three months later. A woman who worked in the bistro recognised his olive skin and long dark hair. Once again he was wearing his trademark hat. She remembered him from that earlier night and was unnerved by the conversation, especially when he started talking about the disappearance of the nurses.

An inquest held in May 2006 heard that he told her: 'It was a terrible thing that happened. You know they're dead. The police won't find them. It'll happen to your two sons and then you. I'm handy with a knife and I know where you live.'

Terrified, she left the pub that evening and never returned. It was a deeply unsettling experience yet she summoned the courage to talk to police and help them prepare a composite image of the man.

The inquest had been called so that the coroner could make a formal ruling on the fate of the two nurses. Yet it seemed to raise more questions than it answered. Even the Deputy Coroner Carl Milovanovich admitted there was not enough evidence to satisfy a jury that the key suspect was Milat. While he was named as one of four people of interest to the police, the coroner also raised the possibility that another serial killer could be on the loose.

Mr Milovanovich speculated whether the 'bizarre coincidence' that so many young people had gone missing at the time could be attributed to Ivan Milat.

'There may well be another serial killer out there, it could be someone else,' he suggested.

'Unfortunately his (Milat's) name comes up in every missing person's case I deal with,' the coroner added.

'None of the evidence really gets to the level that would be required of a criminal standard of proof.'

Police interviewed Milat about the young women and showed him the composite picture of the man in the felt hat. Predictably he denied all knowledge of them and insisted he didn't own such a hat at the time.

The coroner referred the case back to the police for further investigation and recommended that a reward be offered again for information.

Gillian Jamieson and Deborah Balken were formally declared dead and nothing's been heard of them since.

For whatever reason, Milat continued to take an interest in young people who went missing. From his prison cell he wrote to Regional Crime Co-ordinator Inspector Jeff Oliphant in Queensland about the disappearance of three women including British backpacker Celina Bridge.

Celina, aged 28, from Carlisle in the north of England, vanished on July 13, 1998 after staying for two nights at the Crystal Waters permaculture village near Maleny in the Sunshine Coast hinterland.

Crystal Waters is home to about 200 people, many of them alternative lifestylers.

The campsite was a natural choice for Celina, a keen environmentalist, who told manager Barry O'Connell that she was thinking of going 'woofing', the local term for working on organic farms in exchange for accommodation.

After she set off on foot the next day for Little Yabba Creek camping ground to go bird watching, several locals reported seeing her on Booloumbra Creek Road. What happened after that is not known. When she didn't turn up to meet her fiancé at Brisbane airport he reported her missing.

Two other young women disappeared from the same area the following year. Teacher's aide Sabrina Ann Glassop who lived on Booloumbra Creek Road vanished on May 28, 1999.

Three months later 16 year-old Jessica Gaudie, a schoolgirl from nearby Nambour, went missing.

Although their bodies were never, found Milat was keen to offer his input and in August 1999 sent a faxed message via his support group to Inspector Oliphant claiming knowledge of the crimes.

In one letter he noted that he was 'pretty sure what I (am) on about' and wanted to help with the investigation. More specifically he referred to a male person, whose name was not made public.

Inspector Oliphant said the fax came 'out of the blue', but the contents seemed to be wide of the mark.

In 2001 a youth who worked at a centre for troubled Aboriginals at nearby Kenilworth was found guilty of Jessica Gaudie's murder.

The same young man had helped to tend Ms Glassop's ponies on her property in Booloumba Creek Road, where Celina Bridge had last been seen alive.

The link between all three deaths was clear. Police eventually confirmed that they believed the young women were murdered by the same man, but nobody with a link to Ivan Milat.

After his 1996 trial the temptation was to blame all unsolved murders and missing persons cases on the backpacker killer. But as deputy NSW coroner Carl Milovanovich pointed out, they couldn't all be laid at Milat's feet.

Even so there were several narrow escapes reported which certainly had his mark, including the harrowing experience of John Garrihy who claimed to have been picked-up by Milat and a woman on the Hume Highway south of Melbourne in 1985.

He remembered the day because it was Ash Wednesday, 1983, when fierce bush fires swept much of south eastern Australia. John had been to see a friend in Melbourne and was hitching back to his home in Port Macquarie.

He was about 180 kms south of Goulburn when he was given a lift by 'this guy and this girl in a two door station wagon.' He put his bag in the back and they set off up the Hume Highway towards Sydney.

John was 21 and tried to strike up a conversation with the pair who kept on slipping into what sounded to him like a Yugoslavian language.

'He'd just knocked off work somewhere and was wearing stubbies and a shirt. The girl was sitting sideways on the seat and kept on looking back at me and I sensed something wasn't quite right,' he recalled.

They turned off the highway at Goulburn and parked outside an Indian takeaway where John thanked them for the lift and went to retrieve his bag from the rear of the vehicle.

'Suddenly he got a bit upset with me and wouldn't unlock the back. He told me to wait there in no uncertain terms because I was coming with them. That's when I thought "Something's not right, I'm out of here".'

When the couple disappeared into the takeaway he climbed over the back seat, grabbed his bag and ran. Even today he remembers every tiny detail.

He raced down the main street, past the post office and up to a disused service station with a toilet block behind it. Shaking and breathless, he locked the door of one of the cubicles and remained there for two hours.

'I was that scared. When I came out I looked up the street and their car was gone.'

More than a decade later he was watching the television news when he recognised the driver of that car as Ivan Milat.

'The bulletin also showed a photograph of him working on the roads when he was younger and I just froze,' John added.

Now working as a truckie and often travelling the same stretch of highway, he realises how lucky he was.

'Mate, I look back and I think I'm so glad something told me to get out of there.'

But who was the woman passenger? If this really was a genuine Milat encounter did it provide proof of a partner-in-crime? And if so, was his accomplice a woman?

37.

THE CASE FOR THE SECOND KILLER

Justice David Hunt said in 1996 that there was a strong likelihood of two people being responsible for the backpacker murders. As he reminded the jury in his summing up during the 1996 trial, the Crown case had always been one of a joint criminal enterprise.

'It has always conceded that there may have been more than one person involved and it has always said it is unable to establish if the accused did the act by which each person was murdered,' he said.

Milat's lawyer Terry Martin had tried to put the blame on another member of the family or someone very closely associated with it.

His memorable phrase, 'Blind Freddie can see that,' was not easily ignored. It had the ring of truth to it, though with much of the evidence falling into the circumstantial category, it was impossible to prove that another person was involved.

Martin told the jury that the description of a man who tried to kidnap Paul Onions could also have fitted Richard Milat. Didn't he have access to the sash cords, firearms and ammunition used on some of the backpackers, the lawyer reminded them?

It's fair to say there was a certain similarity between the two Milat brothers but there was never any evidence provided that Richard acted on his own or as Ivan's accomplice. Yet this didn't stop him being vilified by the court and public opinion. Here was a man whose reputation had been irreparably tarnished by association with his brother, yet there was never any proof that he was involved. Not even the police moved to prosecute him.

Task Force Air and its team of advisers were divided about the involvement of a second person. While one camp felt the different methods used to murder the backpackers suggested two killers, the other was convinced Ivan had the capacity to handle the situation on his own.

What no one had seriously considered until long after the trial was the possibility of a female accomplice. That extraordinary claim gained substance when Milat's former lawyer John Marsden went public shortly before his death in July 2005.

Marsden had represented Ivan and many other members of the Milat family over the years. It was Marsden's questionable tactics that got him off the 1974 rape allegation when he was accused of sexually assaulting one of two women he'd picked up on the Hume Highway three years earlier.

As the lawyer recalled in his 2005 autobiography: 'I put to her something that has haunted me to this day (and one that would never be allowed in a court room now). I suggested that her sexuality may have had something to do with what had occurred with Ivan Milat. Juries in those days were extremely prejudiced against gays and lesbians and on top of that we had put into their minds the possibility the sex may have indeed been consensual.

'I am not proud of my conduct on that day, but as a solicitor operating in a courtroom environment at that time, I had no choice but to go down that path,' he explained.

Milat couldn't have believed his luck as he walked free that day. For the next 20 years he appeared to keep his nose clean and had no reason to call on Marsden's services again until he was arrested on May 22, 1994 for kidnapping Onions.

By 2006 Marsden was seriously ill with cancer yet still giving media interviews. During one he let slip that a woman had been Milat's partner-in-crime. Maybe he'd dropped his guard while dosed up with morphine but he also mentioned a name—Shirley Soire, Ivan's sister who lived with him. Later he repeated the allegation to radio broadcaster Ray Hadley of 2GB.

'You're living in the same house at Eagle Vale. You have all the backpack stuff, you have books on serial killings etc and you think everything's normal? Now really,' he said.

But did that make her an accomplice? Where was the evidence? Marsden's allegations were made in his dying days with his brain clouded by painkillers and even he admitted to the *Sydney Morning Herald* that it was simply a 'gut' feeling.

In fact Ivan and Shirley had moved into their new home after the backpacker murders. Prior to that he'd been living with his mum in Guildford.

If Shirley had any role it was probably no more than a vague suspicion about her brother's activities. She might have seen some of his 'trophies,' clothes and other evidence belonging to the backpackers, but this did not make her a killer.

Police had charged her over the possession of an illegal firearm, a .45 calibre pistol, found at the Eagle Vale property, but the weapon was never linked to the murders. She was fined $1000 and made to pay $50 in court costs.

Shirley Soire died on February 16, 2003, after a long illness and was cremated at Rookwood Crematorium.

Clive Small agrees that there was no evidence against Shirley Soire to indicate she was an accomplice to the murders. The former head of Task Force Air remains convinced that Ivan Milat acted alone.

'My reasons for saying that are simply that Ivan was a loner. I don't believe he would have trusted anybody else,' says the retired police officer.

He points to the fact that he was fit, strong and wiry and would spend at least an hour gaining the confidence of his victims before attacking them.

'He would make an excuse to pull over to the side of the road, not far from the Belanglo turn-off, and get out to stretch his legs or whatever. At that point he'd take control and say something like, 'Look I'm not going to harm you, I'm just going to rob you so don't do anything silly.'

'Then he'd probably get one person to tie the other one up. Even if it wasn't a very secure knot it gave him long enough to control the person for a few seconds while he then tied the other person up. He'd then re-tie the first person and would have control of both of them.'

It seems a plausible theory. After all on the other occasions when his would-be victims had escaped he was always alone, including the Onions incident and another case involving two women who reported their experience to police after Milat was arrested. On that occasion the women had a lucky escape after being abducted by a man fitting Milat's description in bushland near Wombeyan Caves.

Clive Small maintains these and other examples point to a lone killer.

'He was the only member of the family who was available on all the days of the abductions—in other words the others had tight alibis for at least some of the days.

'When you look at all the property that belonged to the backpackers who were murdered it was all under the control of Ivan,' he points out.

Those members of the family who had property connected to the murder victims had been given those belongings by Ivan.

The weapons, the rope and all that was used to kill the backpackers was only in Ivan's possession.

'So everything points to him being by himself,' he concludes.

While Small makes a convincing case, others who were on the investigation take the opposite view. The most compelling evidence comes from Gerard Dutton, the ballistics expert who proved that the Ruger rifle hidden in the cavity wall of Milat's home fired the same bullets that were found in at least one of the victims.

Fifteen years after his evidence helped to convict Milat, he has no reason to change his mind about the two killer scenario.

'From my point of view, looking purely from the firearms evidence it's suggestive of a second person. It's not conclusive proof I have to say but to my way of thinking it suggests that,' he said from his new base in Tasmania.

Sergeant Dutton bases his theory on the fact that cartridge cases found near the bodies of Gabor Neugebauer and Anja Habschied were from two different brands of ammunition and were fired from different guns.

'There was no crossover of one type of cartridge being used in another gun. One brand was used in one gun and another brand in the other,' he explains.

'That to me is highly suggestive of two people with two guns and two different boxes of ammunition. Whatever they were doing, whether they were target shooting at that time or whatever, that to me suggests there were two different people. That's not definitive proof but it's what is more probable.'

Dutton, who is recognised as one of the world's most experienced ballistics experts, cannot say whether the bullets found in Neugebauer's skull came from different guns because they were too degraded by the time they were found. But they were definitely fired from a .22, the same calibre as the Ruger rifle used on Caroline Clarke.

All the bullets found in Ms Clarke's skull were from the same gun because the marks on them matched the gouges left on the bullets during test firing from the breech bolt found in Milat's cavity wall.

The ballistics expert also noted that the two British girls were slain in markedly different ways. While Caroline was shot ten times in the head Joanne Walters had been repeatedly stabbed.

To add to the mystery it appeared Caroline had been shot from three different directions. What did it all mean? Did the fact that one was subject to a frenzied stabbing and the other from a series of gunshots suggest that if there were two killers, they favoured different ways to despatch their victims?

Gerard Dutton agrees that it's possible one of the killers might not have been able to bring himself to knife his victim in cold blood and preferred the ease of pulling a trigger.

'That's a reasonable explanation, but could we say definitively? Probably not,' he admits.

But having 'two very different ways of death and no crossover of firearms evidence' forced him to conclude there were two killers rather than one.

Dr Rod Milton, the eminent forensic psychiatrist who was used as a profiler on the case, had come to the same opinion. Now in retirement, he sticks to his initial assessment of the crime scene and his view that there were two offenders.

He bases his conclusion on the 'very, very different' methods of execution of the two British women, Caroline Clarke and Joanne Walters.

Dr Milton, who visited the site where they were killed, was struck by the contrast between Caroline's death, which had been caused by repeated shots to the head and Joanne who had been subject to a frenzied stabbing.

The murders had also taken place some distance apart. Caroline had been shot in an open area whereas Joanne appeared to have been knifed in a more secluded spot beneath a rock.

Caroline had almost certainly been killed by the first bullet but the firing continued. 'There was no purpose in going on except for the satisfaction,' he points out. 'This was the action of a cold, deliberate person and contrasted with the way poor Miss Walters was stabbed to death. She was stabbed through the neck rendering her a quadriplegic and her bra was pushed up which suggested a sexual interest.'

Dr Milton continues to believe his observations reinforce the two killers theory.

'One knows the other and feels inferior to him and who's a bit embarrassed being seen by the other one. It seems to make sense,' he explains.

'When you look at Ivan he's a cold, rather distant person who might have fired shots into the head. He was much more deliberate. His personality was more formed, or, if you like, deformed. He was much more rigid whereas the other one gave the impression of being impulsive and sadistic.'

There are no hard facts to support his own view.

Yet even now, nearly two decades after he made that first visit to the forest, he cannot change his mind.

'I still have the belief there was a second person. The nature of the actions suggested two people,' Dr Milton insists.

On the other hand it is because Ivan Milat was such a complex character that it's equally possible to accept he acted on his own, according to Clive Small.

'Each time he committed one of these murders the ritual that accompanied it became more complicated. It's almost as though he went away after a murder and said, 'Now that wasn't too bad, I got a lot of satisfaction out of that but next time I can do it better.' So in his own mind he improved his killing habits as he went along.'

This could also explain why he took some time to complete the process.

'The longer he was committing the act of murder the more his satisfaction grew. We're not 100 per cent sure how the killings occurred because he hasn't told us, but there is a suggestion that he might have started by inflicting pain on one and then gone to the second person, or alternatively he's gained satisfaction from the second person hearing him murder the friend.'

If this sounds all too gruesome to contemplate it is because Milat had no moral compass once he was in control. There were no boundaries to his behaviour, nothing to stop him from fulfilling his sickening fantasies.

Clive Small remembers an incident told by Milat's ex-wife Karen, a story which typified his character.

Karen had accidentally broken a glass table while he was out.

'When he came back and found that she had broken the table he made her put all the pieces of the glass together on the floor and left them there to remind her what she'd done. Now that says a lot about his personality. He was a very controlling person.'

38.

THE UNNERVING HYPOTHESIS

Given the mountain of damning evidence against Ivan Milat and the appalling nature of his crime it is difficult to feel sorry for the man who is likely to spend the rest of his days locked up in Goulburn's Supermax prison.

Yet surprisingly there are some who sympathise with his plight, not necessarily because they believe he is innocent but because of his treatment. They argue that his isolation constitutes a breach of his human rights.

Brett Collins of the pressure group Justice Action says, 'Solitary confinement and the way he's being treated is totally unjustified. He's a little old man who should never have been put there.'

While there are many, not least the victims' relatives, who would vehemently disagree with this view, Collins believes the nature of Milat's incarceration suggests a political agenda.

He claims that his organisation was left in no doubt at a ministerial meeting that it would be ill-advised to have anything to do with Milat. 'He was going to be used as a whipping boy,' Collins recalls.

Understandably in today's political climate there are no votes for a government that shows leniency or compassion to those who have been found guilty of serious crime. Justice has to be seen to be done.

Having failed with his successive appeals and requests for a judicial inquiry, Milat has all but given up. He is still hoping that the High Court will agree to review his case and has confided to friends that that's why he cut off his finger. It had nothing to do with getting attention or trying to escape.

Instead it was a protest against the prison authorities' refusal to grant him access to law books and a computer so he could type up his application.

Milat appears to rest much of his case on the fact that none of his DNA could be linked to the victims. In fact, as mentioned earlier, poor handling of the DNA found on the bodies of the two British women rendered the testing flawed. DNA material foreign to both backpackers was found on their bodies, but the results could not be relied upon and therefore were never tendered in court.

Without his DNA there was no proof that Milat had anything to do with the killing of the backpackers in the Belanglo State Forest. Of course his assertion quietly ignored the other evidence found in his home and those of his relatives, but nevertheless he raised a relevant point.

Many of his supporters and some members of his family have always believed he was framed. They argue that because the police and the state government were so desperate to pin the blame on someone—especially in view of the damage to the tourism industry—that Ivan was fitted up. Given his antecedence and his fascination for guns, he seemed the ideal candidate to take the rap.

In a 2004 edition of the ABC's *Australian Story* Ivan's brother William and sister-in-law Carolynne both insisted he was innocent.

'I've never believed that Ivan had anything to do with this, right from the word go…the evidence is all circumstantial,' William claimed.

Carolynne went even further.

'We're not convinced that the belongings found in Ivan's home belonged to the backpacker victims. We are all convinced they were put there by the police. We believe that Ivan was framed. We believe that from the stories that Ivan has told us. He saw one of the detectives taking two bags from the boot of his car. Those bags were taken inside his house and then, all of a sudden, parts were being found in the house.'

Clive Small was incredulous, describing the comments as 'absolute nonsense.'

Long before Milat was arrested, criminal profiling of the killer suggested he would have kept souveniers of his work.

'We were quite comforted by that advice but we never expected to find the wealth of evidence that we did find,' says Small.

'One of the things we found which I felt was staggering, was a photograph of Ivan's then girlfriend wearing a shirt that belonged to one of the backpackers that he'd killed. He'd given it to his girlfriend just to remind him of his killings.'

Then there was the bloodstained rope and the Ruger rifle parts found in his house and the backpackers' belongings discovered in the homes of his relatives and friends.

'There was a whole wealth of evidence,' insists the former police superintendent.

Clive Small feels that William and Carolynne are in denial and cannot come to terms with a member of the Milat family being capable of such horror. The retired police chief has no doubt about Ivan, whom he always refers to by his Christian name, not for reasons of familiarity, but to avoid confusion with the other siblings.

Ivan declined to be interviewed when he was arrested but his silence spoke volumes.

'He was quite calm. My own belief was that in a sense he revelled in the fact that he had been arrested because I think in his own mind he still believed we didn't have enough evidence on him and that he would beat the charges,' recalls Small.

And what of the other lives Milat is believed to have taken?

Police investigators looked at 43 missing persons cases after the trial and 16 unsolved murders that fitted the style of the backpacker killings.

All things considered Small thinks Milat could have been responsible in at least three of the cases.

'We wouldn't identify those cases because it would be unfair to the victims' family and friends but there were at least three where you certainly couldn't exclude Ivan as being involved.'

If he was responsible for any of them Ivan Milat isn't saying. It's all part of the game he plays with his accusers while harbouring the glimmer of hope that one day he'll be set free.

'I think in the back of his mind Ivan still has this notion that somehow he's going to get out of gaol,' says Small.

Knowing the way his brain works, maybe one day he'll be tempted to confess.

'If someone goes to Ivan and says: 'Look you're in control here. The police know you've committed other murders but they can't prove it, so that shows you're still in control. Do you want to demonstrate to them how you are still in control by telling them about these other murders?'

'Then he might consider it,' suggests the ex-officer.

'Look he's kept his silence right throughout. He has never spoken and I doubt he ever will.'

One fact that's irrefutable is Milat was not responsible for the eighth body found in the Belanglo State Forest. The remains had been there for about 12 years or less, long after Australia's most infamous serial killer was put behind bars.

But the young woman didn't appear to have died from natural causes. Although the autopsy was inconclusive, the fact that the bones were scattered suggested foul play.

Among the items found close to the body was a small, size 10 T-shirt with the word 'Angelic' spelt out across the front in fluorescent pink. It was manufactured by Chain Reaction but did not go on sale in Australia until 2003, which indicated the body could have been there for a much shorter period.

Several teeth were in the skull and scientists managed to obtain a faint DNA profile from the bones. However, initial comparisons with DNA samples from people on the Australian missing persons data base failed to provide a match.

At the time of writing detectives were considering a worldwide search, reinforcing the theory that the skeleton was that of an overseas visitor or backpacker.

For now, whoever killed or dumped the latest Belanglo body in the forest remains a mystery. Why did they choose a site already so strongly associated with violent crime? Or did the killer or killers have such a detailed knowledge of the area that they were confident of getting away with it.

More crucially if what Justice Hunt acknowledged in his summing up in 1996 was true—that two people were almost certainly responsible for the backpacker murders—did it suggest that Milat's partner-in-crime continued to be active long after Ivan was arrested?

The retired forensic psychiatrist Dr Rod Milton who also favours the second killer theory cautions against such an assumption.

'You really can't answer it. These people wear out. They've done enough and they don't want to do any more,' he says.

'I'd be disinclined to think, if there was a second person, he would continue because the nature of the crime suggests he would have been dependent on Ivan.'

Yet why was the latest body dumped only a few kilometres from the site of the backpacker murders? Was the felon drawn to the forest because of its evil past? Or given its isolation was it just a convenient spot? Who can understand their warped logic?

So far the identity of the eighth body, the cause of death and the perpetrator of the crime remains unknown. Whatever the outcome, it does not undermine the unnerving hypothesis central to the backpacker murders. Is there a second killer still at large?

SOURCES AND REFERENCES

CHAPTER 1

Details of the latest discovery of human remains in the Belanglo State Forest drawn from the author's research, the NSW Police Media Unit, police press conferences, the *Daily Telegraph*, August 31 and September 7, 2010.

Clive Small's scepticism about Milat being linked to the body, AAP, August 30, 2010.

Speculation over the body being the remains of Anja Habschied based on author's research in *Milat–The True Horror of the Backpacker Murders*, by Roger Maynard, Margaret Gee Publishing, 1996.

Missing people details from Missing Persons Unit, Parramatta, NSW Police Media Unit and *Milat–The True Horror of the Backpacker Murders* by Roger Maynard, Margaret Gee Publishing, 1996

Milat tells prison sources he knows nothing about latest body. Sydney *Daily Telegraph*, September 1, 2010.

Details of Goulburn prison's supermax unit, Milat's cell and living conditions based on author's research and *Daily Telegraph*, February 2, 2009 and September 18, 2010.

Other backbacker murder theories and claims—http://indymedia.org.au/2010/01/10/ivan-milat-the-evidence-by-the-late-investigator-brian-raven

Judge suggests more than one person was involved: Justice David Hunt, July 18, 1995, NSW Supreme Court of NSW.

Milat's lawyer accuses brother -- Terry Martin, July 5, 1996, NSW Supreme Court of NSW.

Clive Small agrees Milat probably killed others–author's interview, November 4, 2009.

CHAPTERS 2 - 34

These chapters, completely updated where appropriate, are based on my research for *Milat–The True Horror of the Backpacker Murders*, published by Margaret Gee Publishing in 1995. The information is drawn from the many interviews I conducted and press conferences I attended from May 29, 1992, when Mrs Jean Jensen reported Caroline Clarke and Joanne Walters missing, until July 24, 1996 when Ivan Milat was found guilty and sentenced to life imprisonment.

During that period I attended Milat's pre-trial hearing at Campbelltown and his trial in the NSW Supreme Court which opened on March 25, 1996. These proceedings and the evidence of witnesses provided much of the detail and quotes I have used in explaining the extent of the police investigation, the background of the defendant and the case against him.

Some of the narrative is also drawn from stories I wrote for a number of British newspapers including *The Times, The Daily Express* and the *London Evening Standard,* as well as reports and interviews I filmed for Independent Television News.

Over those four years I also gained information from police and civilian sources who preferred to remain anonymous. Their contribution played a vital role but their identities have to necessarily remain confidential.

Biographical information about the two British victims was provided by their parents, Mr and Mrs Ray and Jill Walters and Mr and Mrs Ian and Jacqueline Clarke.

Much of the colour and reportage contained in these chapters is derived from my own work as a journalist covering the story at the time, visiting the Belanglo State Forest, attending press conferences and interviewing people associated with the case, as well as neighbours and friends of the Milat family.

New information about backpacking numbers and trends, as detailed in Chapter 4, was obtained from Tourism Research Australia, an agency of the Department of Resources, Energy and Tourism.

Reports of missing people listed in Chapter 4 are based on research conducted for *Milat–The True Horror of the Backpacker Murders,* by Roger Maynard, Margaret Gee Publishing, 1996. Information about the seven murdered backpackers is also based on that research.

CHAPTER 34

Maitland Gaol background-Maitlandjail.com.au

George Savvas and Milat escape plot–Statement by Bob Debus to NSW Parliament May 20, 1997. www.parliament.nsw.gov.au/prod/parlment/hansart.nsf/V3Key/LA19970520013

Details of Goulburn prison's supermax unit, Milat's cell and living conditions based on author's research and *Daily Telegraph,* February 2, 2009 and September 18, 2010.

Hacksaw blade found in Milat's cell–*Daily Telegraph,* January 10, 1999.

Milat swallows razor blades–*Sun-Herald,* March 4, 2001.

Milat cuts off part of finger–, Media release by NSW Department of Corrective Services, January 26, 2009, ABC News, January 26, 2009, *Daily Telegraph,* January 27, 2009

"I think he's very close to losing his marbles"–Ron Woodham, NSW Corrective Services, news.com.au/story/0,27574,24973668-1242,00.html

Letter from Ivan to Bill Milat–*Australian Women's Weekly,* June 2009.

CHAPTER 35

Background to Milat's first appeal–*Sydney Morning Herald* and *Daily Telegraph*, November 5, 1997.

Impromptu press conference with Milat supporters outside court–*Daily Telegraph*, November 5, 1997.

Milat answers questions in *The Bulletin*, October 21, 1997.

Bob Debus, Corrective Services Minister, condemns *The Bulletin*, *The Australian*, October, 1997.

Judgment by NSW Court of Criminal Appeal–*REGINA v Ivan Robert Mark Milat*, February 26, 1998–austlii.edu.au/au/cases/nsw/NSWSC/1998/795.html

Second appeal to NSW Supreme Court dismissed by Justice Graham Barr -- The Australian. November 11, 2005

Third appeal application rejected by Peter McClellan, Chief Judge in Common Law–*The Australian*, December 15, 2006

CHAPTER 36

Background on disappearances of Leanne Goodall, Robyn Hickie and Amanda Robinson–*Newcastle Herald*, April 21, 2009.

Details of missing person Amanda Zollis–Porchlight Australia.

Background to Toronto inquest into disappearances of Amanda Robinson, Robyn Hickie and Leanne Goodall. *Newcastle Herald,* April 21, 2009.

Milat's letter to the families made public–*Newcastle Herald*, April 21, 2009.

Inquest into missing Sydney nurses Gillian Jamieson and Deborah Balken–*Sydney Morning Herald* and *The Australian*, May 23, 2006.

Disappearance of Celina Bridge–author's research in 1998.

Disappearances of Sabrina Glassop and Jessica Gaudie–*Sydney Morning Herald*, September 25, 1999

Milat writes to police about Celina Bridge–AAP, October 18, 1999.

Background on youth worker found guilty of Jessica Gaudie's murder–*The Sunshine Coast Daily*, August 15, 2009.

John Garrihy's lucky escape–interview with author in September 2010.

CHAPTER 37

Judge suggests more than one person was involved–Justice David Hunt, July 18, 1995, NSW Supreme Court of NSW.

Milat's lawyer accuses a member of the family or someone closely associated with it—Terry Martin, July 5, 1996, NSW Supreme Court of NSW.

John Marsden raises possibility of a female accomplice–*Daily Telegraph*, July 16, 2005.

Marsden recalls questionable tactics in 1974 rape case–*I Am What I Am*, by John Marsden, published by Viking, July 2005.

Marsden alleges Milat's sister Shirley Soire was accomplice–Radio 2GB, July 2005, *Daily Telegraph* reveals female accomplice theory, July 17, 2005.

Marsden's "gut" feeling about female accomplice—*Sydney Morning Herald*, July 21, 2005.

Clive Small convinced Milat acted alone–interview with author November 4, 2009.

Gerard Dutton, police ballistics expert, supports two killers theory–interview with author September 2010.

Rod Milton, forensic psychiatrist, on why he believes Milat had an accomplice–interview with author September 2010.

Karen Milat and the broken glass table–story recalled in Clive Small interview with author on November 4, 2009.

CHAPTER 38

Brett Collins, Justice Action–interview with author in September 2010.

Carolynne and William Milat's comments on Ivan's innocence–*Australian Story*, ABC TV, November 8, 2004.

Clive Small's reaction to claims of innocence–*Australian Story*, ABC TV, November 8, 2004

Clive Small's comments that Ivan was guilty and acted alone -- interview with author on November 4, 2009.

Results of autopsy and investigation into the latest human remains found in the Belanglo State Forest and the search for a DNA match–NSW police media and the *Sunday Telegraph* October 3, 2010.

About the author

Roger Maynard is a former Australian correspondent for CNBC Asia, *The London Times, The Daily Express* and the *South China Morning Post*. Before moving to Australia, he worked for BBC Radio and Television in the UK.

His other books include *Where's Peter?* an exhaustive investigation into the disappearance of Peter Falconio in the Australian outback, *Fatal Flaw*, a definitive account of a Norfolk Island murder, *Life At The Top*, a portrait of some of Australia's best known business leaders and *Hell's Heroes*, the forgotten story of the worst POW camp in Japan.

Read and hear more about the author's books at rogermaynard.com.au